The NOLO *News*—

Our free magazine devoted to everyday legal & consumer issues

To thank you for sending in the postage-paid feedback card in the back of this book, you'll receive a free two-year subscription to the **NOLO** *News*—our quarterly magazine of legal, small business and consumer information. With each issue you get updates on important legal changes that affect you, helpful articles on everyday law, answers to your legal questions in Auntie Nolo's advice column, a complete Nolo catalog and, of course, our famous lawyer jokes.

Legal information online–24 hours a day

Get instant access to the legal information you need 24 hours a day.

Visit a Nolo online self-help law center and you'll find:

- hundreds of helpful articles on a wide variety of topics
- selected chapters from Nolo books
- online seminars with our lawyer authors and other experts
- downloadable demos of Nolo software
- frequently asked questons about key legal issues
- our complete catalog and online ordering info
- our ever popular lawyer jokes and more.

Here's how to find us:

America Online Just use the key word Nolo.

On the **Internet** our World Wide Web address (URL) is: http://www.nolo.com.

Prodigy/CompuServe Use the Web Browsers on CompuServe or Prodigy to access Nolo's Web site on the Internet.

1ST EDITION

Hiring Independent Contractors

THE EMPLOYERS' LEGAL GUIDE

BY ATTORNEY STEPHEN FISHMAN

NOLO PRESS **BERKELEY**

Your Responsibility When Using a Self-Help Law Book

We've done our best to give you useful and accurate information in this book. But laws and procedures change frequently and are subject to differing interpretations. If you want legal advice backed by a guarantee, see a lawyer. If you use this book, it's your responsibility to make sure that the facts and general advice contained in it are applicable to your situation.

Keeping Up-to-Date

To keep its books up-to-date, Nolo Press issues new printings and new editions periodically. New printings reflect minor legal changes and technical corrections. New editions contain major legal changes, major text additions or major reorganizations. To find out if a later printing or edition of any Nolo book is available, call Nolo Press at 510-549-1976 or check the catalog in the *Nolo News*, our quarterly publication.

To stay current, follow the "Update" service in the *Nolo News*. You can get a free two-year subscription by sending us the registration card in the back of the book. In another effort to help you use Nolo's latest materials, we offer a 25% discount off the purchase of your Nolo book when you turn in the cover of an earlier edition. (See the "Recycle Offer" in the back of this book.) This book was last revised in March1996.

Quantity Sales

For information on bulk purchases or corporate premium sales, please contact the Special Sales Department. For academic sales or textbook adoptions, ask for Academic Sales. Call 800-955-4775 or write to Nolo Press, Inc., 950 Parker Street, Berkeley, CA 94710.

First Edition	MARCH 1996
Editor	BARBARA KATE REPA
Cover Design	TONI IHARA
Illustrations	MARI STEIN
Book Design	TERRI HEARSH
Production	MICHELLE DUVAL
Proofreading	ROBERT WELLS
Index	JEAN MANN
Printing	CONSOLIDATED PRINTERS, INC.

Fishman, Stephen.
    Hiring independent contractors : the employers' legal guide / by
Stephen Fishman. — 1st National ed.
        p.   cm.
    Includes index.
    ISBN 0-87337-308-1
    1. Independent Contractors—United States. 2. Independent
contractors—United States—States. I. Title.
KF898.F57 1996
346.73'024—dc20   96-1746
[347.30624]   CIP   Printed in the USA

Acknowledgments

Many thanks to:

Barbara Kate Repa for her superb editing.

Jake Warner for his editorial contributions.

Fred Daily for many helpful comments on federal tax law.

Terri Hearsh and Michelle Duval for the outstanding book design and production.

Ely Newman for disk preparation.

Sayre Van Young for the helpful index.

Bob Wells for thorough proofreading.

Table of Contents

16 Independent Contractor Agreements

17 Help Beyond This Book

Appendix 1: Contractor's Screening Documents

Independent Contractor Questionnaire

Documentation Checklist

Appendix 2: Sample Agreements

Introduction to Sample Agreements

General Independent Contractor Agreement

Independent Contractor Agreement for Household Workers

Independent Contractor Agreement for Direct Seller

Independent Contractor Agreement for Real Estate Salesperson

Independent Contractor Agreement for Consultant

Independent Contractor Agreement for Work Made for Hire

Appendix 3: Blank IRS Forms

Form 843   Claim for Refund and Request for Abatement

Form 4669   Statement of Payments Received

Form 4670   Request for Relief from Payment of Income Tax Withholding

Form SS–8   Determination of Employee Work Status for Purposes of Federal
              Employment Taxes and Income Tax Withholding

Form W–9   Request for Taxpayer Identification Number and Certification

1

About Independent Contractors

If you run a one-person business and do all the work yourself, you don't need to worry about independent contractors. However, sooner or later, most businesses need to hire people to help them. If you're in the throes of this kind of growth, you have two alternatives.

You can:

- hire employees and take on all the financial and other burdens of being an employer—such as paying federal and state payroll taxes, providing workers' compensation insurance and fringe benefits, or
- hire independent contractors and avoid all these costs.

Independent contractors, or ICs, are people who contract to work for others without having the legal status of an employee. ICs may call themselves a variety of names—self-employed, consultants, independent business owners or entrepreneurs—it makes no difference in the eyes of the law.

There are at least five million ICs in the United States and at least 60% of all businesses use them. And these numbers are growing rapidly as U.S. businesses are forced to cut costs to the bone to compete in the world market. There is hardly any job that ICs don't perform—from construction to accounting to computer programming to nursing.

Although hiring ICs instead of employees can save a business time, money and headaches, many businesses are terrified to do so. This is because they have heard about or experienced the consequences of IRS and other government agency audits finding that workers who are really employees were misclassified as ICs. The consequences can be economically devastating for a business and its owners. (See Chapter 8.)

With some knowledge and careful planning, any business can hire ICs and keep its audit risks to a minimum. This book helps you accomplish that.

A. Who Needs to Know About ICs

This book is for business owners and top management. But they are not the only ones who need to know how to hire and deal with ICs. For a worker to qualify as an IC, he or she must be treated like one. Business managers at all levels must understand how to treat ICs, or risk inadvertently converting them into employees. Other workers who come into daily contact with ICs should have a basic understanding of the issues involved as well.

While not specifically written for ICs, many of them will find much of the information in this book useful.

B. What This Book Provides

Parts of this book might be of special interest to you as you operate your small business.

- Chapters 3 through 13 explain how to determine if a worker qualifies as an IC for purposes of federal and state payroll taxes, workers' compensation, labor and anti-discrimination laws and intellectual property ownership.
- Chapters 14 and 15 explain how you can reduce your audit exposure through careful planning and hiring procedures.
- Chapter 16 provides sample independent contractor agreements you should have ICs sign before they begin work.
- Chapter 17 introduces you to other sources containing more detailed information on the topics covered in this book.

Read this entire book before hiring ICs. In particular, don't use the independent contractor agreements in Chapter 16 without reading the previous chapters. An independent contractor agreement will not in itself make a worker an IC.

C. Using the Forms Disk

All of the forms in this book are included on a 3½" disk formatted for the PC (MS-DOS). These files can be opened and the text can be completed and printed with your word processing program.

Each form is provided in two file formats:
- the standard ASCII text file format (TXT), and
- rich text file format (RTF).

For more specific instructions on using the forms disk, see the README.TXT file included on the disk.

WHICH FILE FORMAT SHOULD YOU USE

ASCII text files (TXT) contain only text, tabs and carriage returns; all other formatting and special characters have been stripped. All word processors and text editors can read TXT files.

Rich text files (RTF) contain most of the formatting included in the sample forms found in this book and in the Appendix. Most current Windows and Macintosh word processing programs, such as Word or WordPerfect, can read RTF files.

If you are not sure which file format to use with your word processor, first try the RTF files. If you are unable to open them in your word processor, or the form or clause is missing elements that appear in the corresponding form in this book, use the TXT files.

⚠ You Will Need to Know the Basics

Each word processor uses different commands to open, format, save and print documents. Please read your word processor's manual for specific instructions on performing these tasks. Do not call Nolo Press Technical Support for instructions on how to operate your word processor.

1. System Requirements

To use the forms disk, you will need an IBM PC or compatible, PC/MS-DOS 2.0 or higher, and a 3½" floppy disk drive.

Macintosh users will need System 6 or higher, and a super disk drive and Apple File Exchange® or similar utility to read a PC disk. You will also need some type of word processing or text editing application.

2. Choosing a File

Each form and clause covered in this book is provided in a separate computer file. The chart below lists all computer files as well as the form titles and chapter and section where they are discussed. Before you open any of the files, turn to the chapter of the book that discusses that particular form or clause.

Each file is included in both TXT and RTF formats. For example, the Independent Contractor Questionnaire, discussed in Chapter 15, Section A, is on QUEST.TXT and QUEST.RTF.

Where there are alternative forms available, or alternative clauses within a form, be sure to choose the one that applies to your situation and delete those clauses that do not apply.

FILES PROVIDED ON THE FORMS DISK

Chap.	Sec.	Form or Clause	File Name
15	A6	Independent Contractor Questionnaire	QUEST
16	C	Essential Clauses of Independent Contractor Agreements	
	C	Title of Agreement	TITLE
	C	Names of IC and Hiring Firm	NAMES
	C1	Term of Agreement	TERMAGR
	C2	Services to Be Performed	SERVICES
	C3	Payment	PAYMENT
	C4	Terms of Payment	TERMPAY
	C5	Expenses	EXPENSE
	C6	Independent Contractor Status	STATUS
	C7	Business Permits, Certificates and Licenses	PERMIT
	C8	State and Federal Taxes	TAXES
	C9	Fringe Benefits	FRINGE
	C10	Workers' Compensation	WORKCOMP
	C11	Unemployment Compensation	UNEMPL
	C12	Insurance	INSURE
	C13	Terminating the Agreement	TERMIN
	C14	Exclusive Agreement	EXCLUS
	C15	Severability	SEVERAB
	C16	Applicable Law	APPLLAW
	C17	Notices	NOTICE
	C18	No Partnership	NOPART
	C19	Assignment	ASSIGNM
	C20	Signatures	SIGNS
16	D	Optional Clauses of Independent Contractor Agreements	
	D1	Attorney Fees	FEES
	D2	Modifying the Agreement	MODIFY
	D3	Work at Your Premises	PREMISE
	D4	Indemnification	INDEMN
	D5	Resolving Disputes	RESOLVE
	D6	Intellectual Property Ownership	INTPROP
	D7	Confidentiality	CONFID
	D8	Non-Solicitation	NONSOLIC
16	E	General Independent Contractor Agreement	GENAGREE
16	F1	Independent Contractor Agreement for Household Worker	HOUSEH
16	F2	Independent Contractor Agreement for Direct Seller	DIRSELL
16	F3	Independent Contractor Agreement for Real Estate Salesperson	REALEST
16	F4	Independent Contractor Agreement for Consultant	CONSULT
16	F5	Independent Contractor Agreement for Work Made for Hire	FORHIRE

3. Editing the Forms

The disk contains all forms formatted as both plain ASCII text (TXT) and rich text (RTF) files. You may open and edit the forms using most word processing programs. The files have double spacing at the end of each paragraph (two pairs of Carriage Return/Line Feed codes).

See your word processing application's documentation for instructions on how to open (load, retrieve, import) plain ASCII text (TXT) and rich text (RTF) files.

⚠ Make a Backup Copy

As with any software, it is a good idea to make a backup copy of the disk before you begin. In keeping with copyright laws, remember that copies of the disk are for your personal use only. Instructions on copying files to your hard disk are included in the file README.TXT.

You can edit the forms to suit your particular circumstances and needs. Use the regular word processing functions you would use for any text—such as cut, copy, paste, delete and insert.

When completing the forms, or selecting clauses from a file that contains only clauses, follow these rules:

- Read the corresponding chapter and follow the instructions for that form or clause. This book explains key features of all forms and guides you through the process of completing them.
- Modify and delete the language of the forms only as instructed in the book. The clauses are legally sound as designed. If, however, you change important terms, you may affect their legal validity. ■

Benefits and Risks of Hiring Independent Contractors

irms that hire ICs can obtain many benefits, but there are serious risks as well. No book can decide for you whether to use ICs in your business. But this chapter helps you make your own informed decision by summarizing the benefits and risks that may be involved.

A. Benefits of Using Independent Contractors

It can cost less to use ICs instead of employees because you don't have to pay employment taxes and various other employee expenses. In addition, you will be less vulnerable to some kinds of lawsuits. Perhaps most importantly, however, hiring ICs gives hiring firms greater flexibility in expanding and contracting the workforce.

1. Financial Savings

It usually costs more to hire employees than ICs because, in addition to their salaries or other compensation, you usually have to pay a number of employee expenses. These expenses add at least 20% to 30% to your payroll costs, often more. For example, if you pay an employee $10 per hour, you must pay an additional $2 to $3 or more per hour in employee expenses.

You incur none of these expenses when you hire an IC. Even though ICs are often paid more

per hour than employees doing the same work, you can still save money by adding them to your workforce.

In addition to the costs of payroll processing, the most common employee expenses include:

- federal payroll taxes
- unemployment compensation insurance
- workers' compensation insurance
- office space and equipment, and
- employee benefits such as vacation and health insurance.

a. Federal payroll taxes

Employers must withhold and pay federal payroll taxes for employees. They must pay a 7.65% Social Security tax and a small—usually .08%—federal unemployment tax out of their own pockets. Employees' own Social Security taxes and federal income taxes must also be withheld from their paychecks by their employers and paid to the IRS. (See Chapter 4.)

No federal payroll taxes need be withheld or paid for ICs. This not only saves hiring firms money, but accounting and bookkeeping costs as well.

b. Unemployment compensation

Employers in every state are required to contribute to a state unemployment insurance fund on behalf of most types of employees. The unemployment tax rate is usually somewhere between 2% to 5% of employee wages—up to the maximum amount of wages that are taxable under the state's unemployment compensation law. (See Chapter 9, Section A.)

c. Workers' compensation insurance

Employers must provide workers' compensation insurance coverage for most types of employees in case they become injured on the job. Workers' compensation insurance is obtained from either private insurers or state workers' comp funds.

Premiums can range from a few hundred dollars per year to thousands, depending upon the employee's occupation and a company's claims history. Workers' compensation insurance need not be provided for ICs. (See Chapter 10, Section A.)

d. Office space and equipment

Employers normally provide their employees with office space or other workplaces and whatever equipment they need to do the job. This is not necessary for ICs, who normally provide their own workplaces and equipment. Office space is usually a hiring firm's second biggest expense; only employee salaries and benefits cost more.

e. Employee benefits

Although not required by law, employers usually provide their employees with benefits such as health insurance, paid vacations, sick leave, retirement benefits and life or disability insurance. You need not and should not provide ICs with such benefits.

Health insurance costs, in particular, can be enormous. Many employers are cutting back on health insurance benefits for employees in attempts to save money. But these kinds of cutbacks can have high costs in employee discontent.

2. Reduced Exposure to Lawsuits

When you hire employees, you may be subject to some types of lawsuits for which you aren't liable when you hire ICs.

a. Labor and anti-discrimination laws

Employees have a wide array of rights under state and federal labor and anti-discrimination laws. Among other things, these laws:

- impose a minimum wage and require many employees to be paid time-and-a-half for overtime

- make it illegal for employers to discriminate against employees on the basis of race, color, religion, gender and national origin
- protect employees who wish to unionize, and
- make it unlawful for employers to knowingly hire illegal aliens.

In recent years, a growing number of employees have brought lawsuits against employers alleging violations of these laws. Some employers have had to pay hefty damages to their employees. In addition, various watchdog agencies, such as the U.S. Department of Labor and Equal Employment Opportunity Commission, have authority to take administrative or court action against employers they claim have violated these laws.

Few of these anti-discrimination and employment laws apply to ICs. So you have much less exposure to these kinds of employee claims and lawsuits when you have ICs as workers. (See Chapter 12.)

b. Wrongful termination liability

Another type of lawsuit employees can potentially file against you is for wrongful termination. In these legal actions, an employee claims that his or her firing was illegal or constitutes a breach of contract. Wrongful termination laws vary from state to state, but under some circumstances, for example, it might be a breach of contract for you to fire an employee without good cause. To guard against wrongful termination claims, hiring firms must carefully document the reasons for firing an employee.

ICs are not employees and so cannot bring wrongful termination lawsuits. However, there usually are contractual restrictions on when you can fire an IC. (See Section B5.)

c. Liability for workers' actions

When you hire an employee, you're liable for anything he or she does within the scope of employment. For example, if an employee gets into an auto accident while making a delivery, you may be liable for the damages.

Subject to several important exceptions, this is not the case with ICs. You are not liable for an IC's actions, work-related or not, unless:

- the IC you hired was not qualified to do the job and you were negligent in hiring him or her
- an injury occurs because you gave the IC bad directions
- you know the IC is violating the law in working for you—for example, you hire an unlicensed IC to perform work that requires a construction contractor license, or
- you hire an IC to do work that is inherently dangerous—for example, building demolition.

3. Flexibility in Hiring

What is most important for many hiring firms is that working with ICs provides a level of flexibility that can't be obtained with employees. An IC can be hired to accomplish a specific task and then forgotten, enabling a business to obtain specialized expertise for a short period. You need not go through the trauma and potential severance costs and lawsuits brought on by laying off or firing an employee. And an experienced IC can usually be productive immediately, eliminating the time and expense involved in training employees. By using ICs, you can expand and contract your workforce as needed, quickly and inexpensively.

B. Risks of Using Independent Contractors

After reading about the possible benefits you can get from ICs, you might be thinking: "I'll never hire an employee again, I'll just use independent contractors." But be aware that there are some substantial risks involved in classifying workers as ICs.

1. IRS Audits

The IRS wants to see as many workers as possible classified as employees, not ICs, so that it can immediately collect taxes based on payroll withholding. Being pegged as employees also makes it far more difficult for workers to under-report their income or otherwise evade taxes. In recent years, the IRS has mounted an aggressive attack on employers who, in its view, misclassify employees as ICs.

If the IRS audits your business and determines that you have misclassified employees as ICs, it may impose substantial interest and penalties. Such assessments can easily put a small company out of business. The owners of unincorporated business may be held personally liable for such assessments and penalties. But, even if your business is a corporation, you could still be held personally liable for the tax, interest and penalties. (See Chapter 8, Section C.)

2. State Audits

Audits by state agencies are even more common than IRS audits. State audits most frequently occur when workers classified as ICs apply for unemployment compensation after their services are terminated. Your state unemployment compensation agency will begin an investigation and you may be subject to fines and penalties if it is determined that workers should have been classified as employees for unemployment compensation purposes.

If workers classified as ICs are injured on the job and apply for workers' compensation benefits, you can expect an audit by your state workers' compensation agency because workers' comp benefits are for employees only. Very substantial penalties can be imposed on hiring firms that misclassify employees as ICs for workers' compensation purposes. These include fines, penalties and court orders preventing you from doing business until you obtain workers' compensation insurance. (See Chapter 10, Section E.)

3. Loss of Control

Another possible drawback to classifying workers as ICs is that you lose control over the worker. ICs cannot be treated like employees; you may not supervise their work. They must more or less be left alone to perform the agreed upon services without substantial help or interference. (See Chapter 3, Section D.)

Some business owners can't stand not being in charge of everything and everybody involved with their business. They particularly want to be able to closely supervise their workers. If you want to control how a worker performs, classify him or her as an employee.

4. Loss of Continuity

Generally, it's best to use a particular IC only as needed for short-term projects. You should spread your hiring around and not rely too much on one IC. Having workers constantly coming and going can be inconvenient and disruptive for any workplace. And the quality of work you get from various different ICs may be uneven. One reason businesses hire employees is to be able to depend on having the same workers available day after day.

5. Restrictions on Right to Fire

You do not have an unrestricted right to fire an IC as you do with most employees. Your right to terminate an IC's services is limited to where the IC breaks the terms of your agreement. If you terminate an IC who performs adequately and otherwise satisfies the terms of the agreement, you'll be liable to the IC for breaking the agreement. In other words, the IC can sue you and get an order requiring you to pay a substantial amount of money in damages. (See Chapter 5, Section B.)

6. Liability for Injuries

Employees covered by workers' compensation who are injured on the job cannot sue you for damages. They are allowed only to file workers' compensation claims and receive workers' compensation benefits. This is not the case with ICs. They can sue you for damages if they claim they were injured because of your negligence, such as your failure to provide a safe workplace. If the injuries are substantial and your negligence clear, you may end up being liable for large amounts of damages. When you hire ICs, you should have liability insurance to cover the costs of such lawsuits. This may or may not be cheaper than obtaining workers' compensation insurance. (See Chapter 10, Section A.)

7. Tax Disqualification of Retirement Plans

One of the most serious consequences of misclassifying ICs as employees is the effect it could have on a tax qualified retirement plan maintained by a hiring firm for its true employees and owners. If you're audited by the IRS, you could lose the substantial tax advantages obtained through such plans. (See Chapter 8, Section G.)

8. Possible Loss of Copyright Ownership

If you hire ICs to create works that can be copyrighted—for example, freelance writers and photographers—you can pay for the work and yet not be considered the owner unless you use written agreements transferring copyright ownership in advance. This is not the case with employees. (See Chapter 13.) ■

CHAPTER

3

Determining Worker Status

A worker is not an IC simply because you say so. Your relationship with the worker must pass the legal tests for IC status developed by courts and government agencies. This chapter provides the starting point in understanding how to apply these tests to determine whether workers qualify as independent contractors.

A. Complications in Classifying Workers

Late Supreme Court Justice Potter Stewart once said that he couldn't define what pornography was, but he knew it when he saw it. Many business owners and legal experts believe that IRS and other government auditors take this same haphazard approach in determining whether workers are independent contractors. They're at least half right. There is no single test used to determine when workers are and are not ICs. Instead, different, although often similar, legal tests are used or at least paid lip service by various government agencies and courts to determine worker status.

These government agencies include:
- the Internal Revenue Service (IRS)
- your state's unemployment compensation insurance agency
- your state's workers' compensation insurance agency
- your state's tax department, and
- the United States Labor Department and National Labor Relations Board.

Each of these agencies is concerned with classifying workers for different reasons, and has different biases and practices. Each agency normally makes its worker classification decision on its own and need not consider what other agencies have done, though they are often strongly influenced by other decisions. It's possible for one agency to find that a worker is an IC and another that he or she is an employee. It's equally possible for a worker to be deemed an IC in one state and an employee in another. These conflicts in classification are rare, but they happen.

The result is a legal morass that confuses and frightens many hiring firms. The only way to successfully wade through this legal thicket is to spend some time and effort learning how these government agencies go about classifying workers. If you fail to do so, you leave yourself vulnerable to government auditors who like nothing better than to reclassify ICs as employees and impose assessments, penalties and fines on hapless business owners. (See Chapter 8, Section D.)

B. Questions to Answer Before Hiring Any Worker

Whether a worker is an IC or employee is not one question, but many. Before you hire any worker, you should answer all the questions listed below. Rest assured that this book gives detailed explanations and guidance in answering each question for your work situation.

- **Is the worker an IC for IRS purposes?** If so, you won't need to withhold and pay federal payroll taxes for the worker, including Social Security taxes, federal disability taxes and federal income tax withholding. If the worker is an employee, you will.
- **Will your state unemployment compensation agency consider the worker an IC?** If so, you won't need to pay for state unemployment compensation coverage. Otherwise, you will.
- **If your state has income taxes, will your state tax department consider the worker an IC?** If so, you won't need to withhold state income taxes from the worker's paychecks. Otherwise, you will.
- **Would your state workers' compensation insurance agency consider the worker an IC?** If so, you won't need to provide workers' compensation coverage for the worker. Otherwise, you probably will.

- **Will the U.S. Labor Department consider the worker an IC?** If so, you won't need to pay the worker time-and-a-half for overtime. If the worker is an employee, you might have to pay it.
- **Would the worker be considered an IC under federal and state laws outlawing workplace discrimination?** If so, you're protected from many types of discrimination lawsuits.
- **Is the worker an IC for intellectual property ownership purposes?** If so, you need to take steps to obtain ownership of any intellectual property the worker creates on your behalf.

Your goal should be to ensure that a worker qualifies as an IC for all these purposes. While it is theoretically possible for a worker to have a hybrid status—that is, to be an IC for some purposes and an employee for others—in practice, this is difficult. All government agencies want workers to be employees, not ICs. If an agency discovers that you're treating a worker as an employee for any purpose, the chances go up dramatically that it will conclude that the worker is an employee for its purposes as well. Likewise, a finding by one agency that an IC is really an employee will likely lead others to reclassify the worker. Such a finding is like blood in the water to a school of circling sharks.

EXAMPLE: The Acme Widget Company hires Mike to serve as a computer consultant. Acme is sure that Mike qualifies as an IC for IRS purposes. (See Section D2.) But the company fears that Mike would be considered an employee by the state workers' compensation agency under the more expansive test that agency uses. (See Chapter 10, Section E.)

Acme decides to treat Mike as an IC for federal tax purposes and does not withhold or pay federal payroll tax for him. But Acme treats Mike as an employee for workers' compensation purposes and provides him with workers' compensation insurance coverage. This suits the workers' comp agency just fine. Acme need not worry about any workers' comp audits for Mike. However, if Acme is audited by the IRS, the auditor will view the fact that Acme provides Mike with workers' comp coverage as strong evidence that Mike is an employee for IRS purposes. This greatly increases the chances that Acme will have to reclassify Mike as an employee—and may also subject the company to fines and other penalties.

Most of the rest of this book is devoted to detailed discussions of how the various government agencies determine whether workers are ICs or employees and what they do if they find that hiring firms have misclassified workers.

- Chapters 4 through 8 cover the IRS
- Chapter 9 covers state unemployment compensation agencies and state tax departments
- Chapter 10 covers state workers' compensation insurance agencies
- Chapter 12 covers the U.S. Labor Department, National Labor Relations Board and other federal and state agencies whose job is to prevent employees from being unfairly exploited or discriminated against, and
- Chapter 13 covers the rules federal courts use to resolve intellectual property ownership disputes.

The approaches these agencies take in classifying workers often differ in many ways, but they all have certain underlying concepts in common. The rest of this chapter focuses on these basic concepts. Understanding them will make it much easier for you to understand the later chapters and answer the questions you need to ask before hiring any worker.

C. Workers Who Are ICs

An independent contractor is a person who contracts to perform services for others, but who does not have the legal status of an employee. Most people who qualify as independent contractors follow their own trade, business or profession— that is, they are in business for themselves. This is why they are called "independent" contractors. They earn their livelihoods from their own independent businesses instead of depending upon an employer to earn a living.

People who have their own businesses usually have certain working characteristics in common. They typically:

- offer their services to the general public, not just one person or company
- have their own business offices
- invest in tools, equipment and facilities
- take care of their own taxes, and
- make a profit if the business goes well, but if it goes badly they risk going broke.

Good examples of ICs are professionals with their own practices such as doctors, lawyers, dentists and accountants. You may have many choice names for your dentist, but "employee" is probably not one of them. If your dentist has his or her own practice, he or she is an independent businessperson offering dental services to the public, not your employee.

However, a worker doesn't have to be a highfalutin' doctor or lawyer to be an IC. A person you hire to paint your office or mow your lawn can also be in business for himself or herself and qualify as an IC.

1. Determining Worker Status

Sometimes it's very easy to tell if workers are or are not in business for themselves. This means it's easy to tell whether they are ICs or employees.

EXAMPLE: You start a restaurant and contract with IBM to install a computer system for your business. There is no way IBM will be viewed as your employee. You need not worry about paying employment taxes for IBM's workers. That's IBM's problem. IBM is clearly an established independent business. Not even the most hard-nosed IRS auditor would question this.

EXAMPLE: You hire several people to wait tables in your restaurant and pay them salaries, benefits and so forth. It is clear that a typical waitperson in a restaurant is not in business. He or she is an employee of the restaurant. The restaurant owner—that is, you—are the one in business.

In many other cases, however, it can be very difficult to say for certain whether a worker is or is not in business. This can be especially hard where workers perform specialized services by themselves—that is, without the help of assistants.

EXAMPLE: Instead of hiring IBM, you hire a computer consultant named Mike to install your computers. Mike has no employees, and performs all the work for you personally. He ends up spending several months working on your computers. It's difficult to say for sure that Mike was in business for himself while he worked for you. You can be sure that this is something an IRS or other government auditor would question.

It may be helpful to view every worker in America as being somewhere in a continuum. At one end are workers who are clearly employees; at the other end are those who are clearly ICs. But in between these two extremes, there is a vast middle ground where work relationships have some elements of employment and others of independence. It is where workers fall into this uncertain middle ground that problems with the IRS, state tax authorities, unemployment compensation authorities and other agencies can develop.

2. Applying Legal Tests

Government agencies and courts have developed two main tests to determine whether workers should be classified as employees or ICs:

- the common law test, which focuses on the physical control of the worker by the hiring firm, and
- the economic reality test, which focuses on whether the worker is economically dependent upon the hiring firm.

These tests, discussed in detail below, are designed to reveal how you treat the worker, and what roles the worker plays in your business and that you play in the worker's economic life.

THREE MYTHS ABOUT ICs

A few myths live on about who is and who is not an IC.

Myth #1: Saying a Worker is an IC Will Make It So

Don't get caught in the trap of thinking workers are ICs because that's what you label them. The mere fact that you call a worker an IC will not by itself convince the IRS or other government agencies that the worker really is one. Government auditors look at the substance of the relationship between the hiring firm and worker, not mere formalities. If you have the right to control a worker on the job, the worker will be considered an employee regardless of how the two of you characterize your relationship.

This is not to say that a written independent contractor agreement can't be helpful in establishing that a worker is an IC. It can be, provided that it's well-drafted and reflects reality—that is, those involved actually behave the way the agreement says they will. (See Chapter 16.)

Myth #2: People Who Work for More Than One Company Are ICs

If you have the right to control a worker on the job, the worker will be your employee even though he or she works for others at the same time. It's possible for a worker to have more than one employer at the same time.

Myth #3: Part-time and Short-term Workers Are ICs

Don't think that because you're only hiring a person for a couple of weeks, or for only a few hours a week, the worker must be an IC. To most government agencies, it doesn't make much difference whether a worker works full-time or part-time. If you have the right of control, a part-time worker will be deemed a part-time employee and a short-term worker a short-term employee.

D. Common Law Test for IC Status

The common law test is used by most government agencies to determine whether workers are employees or ICs. This is the test used by:

- the IRS
- unemployment compensation insurance agencies in many states
- workers' compensation insurance agencies in many states, and
- courts to determine copyright ownership disputes.

The common law test is based on a very simple notion: employers have the right to tell their employees what to do. The employer may not always exercise this right—for example, if an employee is experienced and well trained, the employer may not feel the need to closely supervise him or her; but the employer has the right to do so at any time.

Under the common law test, workers are employees if the people for whom they work have the right to direct and control them in the way they work—both as to the final results and as to the details of when, where and how the work is performed.

EXAMPLE: Mary takes a job as a hamburger cook at the local AcmeBurger. AcmeBurger personnel carefully train her in how to make an AcmeBurger hamburger, including the type and amount of ingredients to use, the temperature at which the hamburger should be cooked and so forth. Once Mary starts work, AcmeBurger managers closely supervise how she does her job.

Virtually every aspect of Mary's behavior on the job is under AcmeBurger control—including what time she arrives at and leaves work, when she takes her lunch break, what she wears and the sequence of the tasks she must perform. If Mary proves to be an able and conscientious worker, her supervisors may not look over her shoulder very often,

but they have the right to do so at any time. Mary is AcmeBurger's employee.

In contrast, when you hire an IC, you hire an independent businessperson. A hiring firm normally does not have the right to control the way an independent businessperson—an IC—performs agreed upon services. Its control is limited to accepting or rejecting the final results.

EXAMPLE: AcmeBurger develops a serious plumbing problem. AcmeBurger does not have any plumbers on its staff, so it hires Plumbing by Jake, an independent plumbing repair business owned by Jake. Jake looks at the problem and gives an estimate of how much to will cost to fix. The manager agrees and Jake and his assistant commence work.

In a relationship of this kind where Jake is clearly running his own business, it's virtually certain that AcmeBurger does not have the right to control the way Jake performs his plumbing services. Its control is limited to accepting or rejecting the final result. If AcmeBurger doesn't like the work Jake has done, it can refuse to pay him.

1. How to Measure Control

The difficulty in applying the common law test is deciding whether a hiring firm has the right to control its workers. The government agencies you have to deal with can't look into your mind to see whether the control exists. They must rely primarily on indirect or circumstantial evidence indicating control or lack of it—for example, whether you provide a worker with tools and equipment, pay by the hour or have the right to fire the worker. This is what government auditors will be asking you about if you're audited.

To evaluate whether a worker passes muster as an IC, you need to examine these factors. The fact they you may know in your heart that you do not control a worker is not sufficient. What matters is how your relationship with the worker appears to a government auditor who doesn't know you or the worker.

2. The IRS 20-Factor Control Test

The IRS has developed a list of 20 factors it uses to measure control under the common law test. (IRS Rev. Rul. 87-41.) This IRS test has been very influential on other government agencies and courts. Arguably, this is the single most important IC test since federal payroll taxes are a substantial financial burden on hiring firms and IRS penalties for misclassifying workers can be huge. (See Chapter 8, Section D.)

All your relationships with ICs should be structured with these 20 factors in mind. They're already incorporated into the sample IC agreements in Chapter 16 and in the advice on procedures for hiring firms in Chapter 15.

Unfortunately, it is often difficult to come up with a conclusive answer about whether a worker is an IC or employee using this unwieldy 20-factor test. This is because no one factor controls and some factors may be more important than others in some cases. Also, it's not necessary for all or even a majority of these factors to show lack of control for a worker to be considered an IC. The bottom line is that on balance, the factors showing lack of control must outweigh those that indicate control.

To make your worklife easier, this book offers a far simpler four-part test to determine worker status for IRS purposes emphasizing those factors that are most important.

You don't need to memorize the following list. It is included here primarily for reference purposes. If you ever want to know whether you're doing something wrong, go down this list of 20 factors and see how many are on the employee side of the ledger. If there are more than a handful, you're probably in trouble.

The first four factors below are the most important and are discussed in greater detail in Chapter 4, Section B.

a. Making a profit or loss

Employees. Employees are typically paid for their time and labor and have no liability for business expenses.

Independent Contractors. In addition to the gain or loss ordinarily realized by employees, ICs can earn a profit or suffer a loss as a result of the services being performed.

ICs are entrepreneurs. They make money if their businesses succeed, but risk going broke if they fail. Whether ICs make money depends on how well they use their ingenuity, initiative and judgment in conducting their business. (See Chapter 5, Section B1.)

b. Work on specific premises

Employees. Employees must work where their employers tell them, usually on the employer's premises.

Independent Contractors. ICs are usually able to choose where to perform their services.

Work at a location specified by a hiring firm implies control by the firm, especially where the work could be done elsewhere. A person working at a hiring firm's place of business is physically within the firm's direction and supervision. If the person can choose to work off the premises, the firm obviously has less control. (See Chapter 5, Section B2.)

c. Offering services to general public

Employees. Employees offer their services solely to their employers.

Independent Contractors. ICs offer services to the general public.

Since they are independent businesspeople, ICs normally make their services available to the public. (See Chapter 5, Section B3.)

d.   Right to fire

Employees. An employee typically can be discharged by the employer at any time.

Independent Contractors. An IC's relationship with a hiring firm can be terminated only according to the terms of their agreement.

If you have a right to fire a worker at any time for any reason or for no reason at all, the IRS will likely conclude that you have the right to control that worker. The ever-present threat of dismissal must inevitably cause a worker to follow your instructions and otherwise do your bidding. Even

if you never actually give the worker instructions, you have the right to do so at any time if you can fire the worker. (See Chapter 5, Section B4.)

e.   Furnishing tools and materials

Employees. Employees are typically furnished all the tools and materials necessary to do their jobs by their employers.

Independent Contractors. ICs typically furnish their own tools and materials.

The fact that a hiring firm furnishes tools and materials, such as computers and construction equipment, tends to show control because the firm can determine which tools the worker is to use and, at least to some extent, in what order and how they will be used.

Sometimes ICs have to use a hiring firm's tools or materials. For example, a computer consultant may have to perform work on the hiring firm's computers. The fact that the tools are provided in such a situation should be irrelevant.

f.   Method of payment

Employees. Employees are usually paid by unit of time.

Independent Contractors. ICs are typically paid a flat rate for a project.

Where a worker is paid by unit of time—for example, by the hour, week or month—points strongly to an employer-employee relationship. This is because the hiring firm assumes the risk that the services provided will be worth what the worker is paid. To protect its investment, the hiring firm demands the right to direct and control the worker's performance. In this way, the hiring firm makes sure it gets a day's work for a day's pay.

Payment by the job or on a straight commission generally indicates that the worker is an IC. However, in many professions and trades, payment is customarily made by unit of time. For example, lawyers, accountants and psychiatrists typically charge by the hour. Where this is the general practice, the method of payment factor will not be given great weight.

g. Working for more than one firm

Employees. Although employees can have more than one job at a time, employers can require loyalty and prevent employees from taking some alternative jobs.

Independent Contractors. ICs usually have multiple clients or customers.

Many employees have more than one job at a time. However, employees owe a duty of loyalty toward their employers—that is, employees cannot engage in activities that harm or disrupt the employer's business. This restricts employees' outside activities. For example, an employee ordinarily wouldn't be permitted to take a second job with a competitor of the first employer. An employee who did so would be subject to dismissal.

ICs are generally subject to no such restrictions. They can work for as many clients or customers as they want. Having more than one client or customer at a time is very strong evidence of IC status. People who work for several firms at the same time are generally ICs because they're usually free from control by any one of the firms.

h. Continuing relationship

Employees. Employees have a continuing relationship with their employers.

Independent Contractors. ICs generally work on one project and then move on.

Although employees can be hired for short-term projects, this type of relationship is more typical of ICs. An employee typically works for the same employer month after month, year after year,

sometimes decade after decade. Such a continuing relationship is one of the hallmarks of employment. Indeed, one of the main reasons businesses hire employees is to have workers available on a long-term basis.

i. Investment in equipment or facilities

Employees. Employees generally have no investment in equipment or facilities.

Independent Contractors. ICs have an investment in the equipment and facilities appropriate for their businesses.

This factor includes equipment and premises necessary for the work, such as office space, furniture and machinery. It does not include tools, instruments and clothing commonly provided by employees in their trade—for example, uniforms that are commonly provided by the employees themselves. Nor does it include education, experience or training.

A worker who makes a significant investment in the equipment and facilities to perform services is more likely to be considered an IC. By making such a financial investment, the worker risks losing it if the business is not profitable. Also, the worker is not dependent upon a hiring firm for the tools and facilities needed to do the work. Owning the tools and facilities also implies that the worker has the right to control their use.

On the other hand, lack of investment indicates dependence on the hiring firm for tools and facilities and is another hallmark of an employer-employee relationship.

Some types of workers typically provide their own inexpensive tools. For example, carpenters may use their own hammers and accountants their own calculators. Providing such inexpensive tools doesn't show that a worker is an IC. But a worker who provides his or her own $3,000 computer or $10,000 lathe is more likely to be an IC.

j.   Business or traveling expenses

Employees. Employees' job-related business and traveling expenses are paid by the employer.

Independent Contractors. ICs typically pay their own business and traveling expenses.

If the hiring firm pays a worker's business and traveling expenses, the worker is ordinarily an employee in the eyes of the IRS. To be able to control such expenses, the employer must retain the right to regulate and direct the worker's actions.

On the other hand, a person who is paid per project and who has to pay expenses out of pocket is generally an IC. Any worker who is accountable only to himself or herself for expenses is free to work according to individual methods and means.

Of course, some ICs typically bill their clients for certain expenses. For example, accountants normally bill clients for travel, photocopying and other incidental expenses. This does not make them employees, since their clients do not control them.

k.   Right to quit

Employees. An employee may normally quit the job at any time without incurring any liability to the employer.

Independent Contractors. An IC is legally obligated to complete the work he or she agreed to do.

Employees normally work "at will." They can quit whenever they want to without incurring liability, even if it costs the employer substantial money and inconvenience.

ICs usually agree to complete a specific job. They are legally obligated to complete the job. If they don't, they are liable to the hiring firm to make good any losses caused.

l.   Instructions

Employees. Employers have the right to give their employees oral or written instructions that the employees must obey about when, where and how they are to work.

Independent Contractors. ICs need not comply with instructions on how to perform their services; they decide on their own how to do their work.

You can have trouble evaluating this factor because there is no requirement that instructions actually be given. You must focus instead on whether you have the right to give them. Even though you have not given a worker instructions, the IRS could conclude that you have the right to do so and view this factor as indicating employment status.

If a worker is running an independent business and you are just one client or customer among many, it's likely you don't have the right to give the worker instructions about how to perform the services. Your right is usually limited to accepting or rejecting the final results.

> **EXAMPLE:** Art goes to Joe's Tailor Shop and hires Joe to make him a suit. Art chooses the fabric and style of the suit, but it's up to Joe to decide how to make the suit. When the suit is finished, Art can refuse to pay for it if he thinks it isn't made well. However, if Art had presumed to tell Joe how to go about cutting the fabric and stitching the suit together, Joe would probably have kicked him out of his shop and gone on to his next customer.

On the other hand, you probably will have the right to give instructions to workers who are not running an independent business and are largely or solely dependent upon you for their livelihood.

EXAMPLE: Joe the tailor abandons his own tailor shop when he's hired to perform full-time tailoring services for Acme Suits, a large haberdashery chain. Joe is completely dependent upon Acme for his livelihood. Acme managers undoubtedly have the right to give Joe instructions, even if they don't feel the need to do so because Joe is such a good tailor.

Note that you may give an IC detailed guidelines as to the end results to achieve. For example, a software programmer may be given highly detailed specifications describing the software programs to develop; or a building contractor may be given detailed blueprints showing precisely what the finished building should look like. Since these relate only to the end results to be achieved, not how to achieve them, they do not make the programmer or building contractor employees.

m. Sequence of work

Employees. Employees may be required to perform services in the order or sequence set for them by the employer.

Independent Contractors. ICs decide for themselves the order or sequence in which they work.

This factor is closely related to the right to give instructions. If a person must perform services in the order or sequence set by the hiring firm, it shows that the worker is not free to use discretion in working, but must follow established routines and schedules.

Often, because of the nature of the occupation, the hiring firm either does not set the order of the services or sets them infrequently. It is sufficient to show control, however, if the hiring firm retains the right to do so. For example, a salesperson who works on commission is usually permitted latitude in mapping out work activities. But one who hires such a salesperson normally has the discretion to require him or her to report to the office at specified times, follow up on leads and perform certain tasks at certain times. Such requirements interfere with and take precedence over the salesperson's own routines or plans. They indicate control by the hiring firm and employee status for the salesperson.

n. Training

Employees. Employees may receive training from their employers.

Independent Contractors. ICs ordinarily receive no training from those who purchase their services.

Training may be done by teaming a new worker with a more experienced one, by requiring attendance at meetings or seminars or even by correspondence. Training shows control because it indicates that the employer wants the services performed a particular way. This is especially true if the training is given periodically or at frequent intervals.

ICs are usually hired precisely because they don't need any training. They possess special skills or proficiencies that the hiring firm's employees do not.

o. Services performed personally

Employees. Employees are required to perform their services on their own—that is, they can't get someone else to do their jobs for them.

Independent Contractors. ICs ordinarily are not required to render services personally; for example, they can hire their own employees or even other ICs to do the work.

Ordinarily, when you hire an IC, he or she has the right to delegate all or part of the work to others without your permission. This is part and parcel of running a business. For example, if you hire an accountant to prepare your tax return, the accountant normally has the right to have assistants do all or part the work under his or her supervision.

Requiring someone you hire to perform the services personally indicates that you want to control how the work is done, not just the end results. If you were just interested in end results, you wouldn't care who did the work; you'd just make sure the work was done right when it was finished.

p. Hiring assistants

Employees. Employees hire, supervise and pay assistants only at the direction of the employer.

Independent Contractors. ICs hire, supervise and pay their own assistants.

IRS auditors will usually be very impressed by the fact that a worker hires and pays his or her own assistants. This is something employees simply do

not do and is strong evidence of IC status because it shows risk of loss it the worker's income does not match payroll expenses.

q. Set working hours

Employees. Employees ordinarily have set hours of work.

Independent Contractors. ICs are masters of their own time; they ordinarily set their own work hours.

Obviously, telling a worker when to come to work and when to leave shows that you have control over that worker.

r. Working full-time

Employees. An employee may be required to devote full-time to the employer's business.

Independent Contractors. ICs are free to work when and for whom they choose—and usually have the right to work for more than one client or customer at a time.

Requiring a worker to devote full-time to the workplace indicates that you have control over how much time he or she spends on your job and practically restricts that worker from working elsewhere.

s. Oral or written reports

Employees. Employees may be required to submit regular oral or written reports to the employer regarding the progress of their work.

Independent Contractors. ICs are generally not required to submit regular reports; they are responsible only for end results.

Submitting reports shows that the worker is compelled to account for individual actions. Reports are an important control device for an employer. They help determine whether directions are being followed, or whether new instructions should be issued.

This requirement focuses on regular reports that enable an employer to keep track of employees' day-to-day performance. It's quite common for ICs to make infrequent interim reports to hiring firms when they are working on long or complex projects. Such reports are typically tied to specific completion dates, timelines or milestones written into the contract. For example, a building contractor may be contractually required to report to the hiring firm when each phase of a complex building project is completed.

t. Integration into business

Employees. Employees typically provide services that are an integral part of the employer's day-to-day operations.

Independent Contractors. ICs services typically are not molded into the hiring firm's overall business as one integrated operation.

Integration in this context has nothing to do with race relations. It simply means that the workers are a regular part of the hiring firm's overall operations. In the IRS's view, the hiring firm would likely exercise control over such workers because they are so important to the success of the business.

> **EXAMPLE:** Fry King is a fast food outlet. It employs 15 workers per shift who prepare and sell the food. Jean is one of the workers on the night shift. Her job is to prepare all the French fries for the shift. Fry King would likely go out of business if it didn't have someone to prepare the French fries. French fry preparation is a regular or integral part of Fry King's daily business operations.

On the other had, ICs generally have special skills that the hiring firm calls upon only sporadically.

> **EXAMPLE:** Over the course of a year, Fry King hires a painter to paint its business premises, a lawyer to handle a lawsuit by a customer who suffered from food poisoning and an accountant to prepare a tax return. All of these things may be important or even essential to Fry King—otherwise it wouldn't have them done—but they are not a part of Fry King's normal overall daily operations of selling fast food.

3. Factors Used by Other Government Auditors

IRS auditors stick to the 20 factors described above when applying the common law test. But other government agencies and courts look at other factors as well. (See Section F.) The most important are discussed here.

a. Skill required to do the work

Employees. Workers whose jobs require a low level of skill and experience are more likely to be employees.

Independent Contractors. Workers with jobs requiring high skills are more likely to be ICs.

The skill required to do a job is a good indicator of whether the hiring firm has the right to control a worker. This is because you are far more likely to have control over the way low-skill workers do their jobs than you do over high-skill workers.

For example, if you hire a highly skilled repair person to maintain an expensive and complex photocopier, it's doubtful that you know enough about photocopiers to supervise the work or even tell the repair person what to do. All you are able to know is whether the results the repair person achieves meet your requirements—that is, whether the photocopier works or not.

This is not the case, however, when you hire a person to do a job that does not require high skills or training, such as answering telephones or cleaning offices. You are likely to spell out the details of how the work should be done and are certainly capable of supervising the worker. Workers in such occupations generally expect to be controlled by the person who pays them—that is, they expect to be given specific instructions as to how to work, be required to work during set hours, be provided with tools and equipment and so forth.

For these reasons, highly skilled workers are far more likely to be ICs then low-skill workers. However, not all high-skill workers are ICs. Corporate officers, doctors and lawyers, for example, can be employees just like janitors and other manual laborers if they are subject to a hiring firm's control.

EXAMPLE: Dr. Smith leaves his lucrative solo medical practice to take a salaried position teaching medicine at the local medical school. When Smith ran his own practice he was clearly an IC in business for himself. He paid all the expenses for his medical practice and collected all the fees. If the expenses exceeded the fees, he lost money.

As soon as Smith took the teaching job, he became an employee of the medical school. The school pays him a regular salary and provides him with employee benefits, so he has no risk of loss like when he was in private practice. The school also has the right to exercise control over Smith's work activities—for example, requiring him to teach certain classes. It also supplies an office and all the equipment Smith needs. He is clearly no longer in business for himself.

b. Worker benefits

Employees. Employees usually receive benefits such as health insurance, sick leave, pension benefits and paid vacation.

Independent Contractors. ICs ordinarily receive no similar workplace benefits.

If you provide a worker with employee benefits such as health insurance, sick leave, pension benefits and paid vacation, it's only logical for courts and government agencies to assume that you consider the worker to be your employee subject to your control. To keep the benefits, it's likely that the worker would obey your orders. You'll have a very hard time convincing anyone that a person you provide with employee benefits is not your employee.

On the other hand, you are not typically required to provide an IC with any benefits other than payment for completing the work.

c. Tax treatment of the worker

Employees. Employees usually have federal and state payroll taxes withheld by their employers and remitted to the government.

Independent Contractors. ICs ordinarily pay their own taxes.

Employers must ordinarily withhold and pay federal and state payroll taxes for their employees, including Social Security taxes and federal income taxes. A firm that hires an IC ordinarily need not remit or withhold any taxes for the worker. (See Chapters 4, 6 and 9.)

Treating a worker as an employee for tax purposes—that is, remitting federal and state payroll taxes for the worker—is very strong evidence that you believe the worker to be your employee and you have the right to exercise control over him or her. Indeed, one court has ruled that paying federal and state payroll taxes for a worker is a virtual admission that the worker is an employee under the common law test. (*Aymes v. Bonelli,* 980 F.2d 857 (2d Cir. 1992).)

d. Intent of the hiring firm and worker

Employees. People who hire employees normally intend to create and employer-employee relationship.

Independent Contractors. People who hire ICs normally intend to create an IC-hiring firm relationship.

Some government agencies and courts also consider the intent of the hiring firm and worker. If it appears they honestly intended to create an IC relationship, it's likely that the hiring firm would not believe it had control, nor attempt to exercise control over the worker. One way to establish intent to create an IC relationship is for the hiring firm and IC to sign an independent contractor agreement. (See Chapter 16.)

On the other hand, if it appears that you never intended to create a true IC relationship and merely classified the worker as an IC to avoid an employer's legal obligations, then you probably had the right to control the worker.

e. Custom in the trade or industry

Employees. Workers who are normally treated like employees in the trade or industry in which they work are likely to really be employees.

Independent Contractors. Workers who are normally treated like ICs in the trade or industry in which they work are likely to really be ICs.

The custom in the trade or industry involved is important as well. If the occupation is usually performed by employees, employee status is indicated. It's likely that a hiring firm would not exercise control over workers customarily treated as ICs.

> **EXAMPLE:** The longstanding custom among logging companies in the Pacific Northwest is to treat tree fellers—people who cut down trees—as ICs. They are customarily paid by the tree, receive no employee benefits and are free to work for many logging companies, not just one. None of the logging companies withhold or pay federal or state payroll taxes for tree fellers. The fellers pay their own self-employment taxes. This longstanding custom is strong evidence that the workers are ICs.

E. Economic Reality Test

Some courts and government agencies view the common law test, focusing on the hiring firm's right to physically control the worker, as too restrictive when it comes to deciding whether workers are employees or ICs for the purposes of social legislation designed to protect workers such as labor laws and workers' compensation insurance.

These courts and agencies use a different test called the economic reality test. Under this test, workers are employees if they are economically dependent upon the businesses for which they render services. Economic dependence equals an employment relationship.

1. Problems With the Test

The problem with the economic reality test is that it doesn't make any sense. All workers are economically dependent upon the people who pay them. Taken to its logical extreme, all workers would be employees under the test.

Courts and government agencies are well aware of this problem and have announced rules intended to make clear that everybody isn't an employee under the test. Unfortunately, these rules are mostly incoherent. For example, one court has held that a worker is an employee under the economic reality test only if the worker is dependent upon a particular business or organization for continued employment in that line of work. (*Donovan v. Dailamerica Marketing, Inc.*, 757 F.2d 1376 (3d Cir. 1985).) Only a worker who couldn't find another job in his or her chosen field would be an employee under this rule—in other words, only people who are unemployable are employees.

Another court has held that a worker is an employee under the test if he or she is dependent on the particular job for that income to be continued. (*Halferty v. Pulse Drug. Co.*, 821 F.2d 261 (5th Cir. 1987).) This test seems to make all workers employees, since most workers depend on their jobs for their income.

2. Factors Considered

The only thing to be said for certain about the economic reality test is that it includes all workers who would be considered employees under the common law test and other workers who government agencies and courts feel need and deserve

the special protections. These are primarily low-skill, low-paid workers—the type of workers labor and workers' compensation laws were originally intended to help.

This is borne out by the type of factors courts examine to gauge the degree of a worker's dependence on a hiring firm. They include:

- the skill required to do the work (see Section D3)
- the amount of the worker's investment in facilities and equipment (see Section D2)
- the worker's opportunities for profit or loss (see Section D2)
- whether the worker's relationship with the hiring firm is permanent or brief (see Section D2)
- the extent to which the services provided by the worker are an integral part of the hiring firm's business (see Section D2)
- whether the hiring firm has the right to control how the work is done (see Section D1), and
- the amount of initiative, judgment or foresight in open market competition with others required for the success of the worker's independent enterprise. ICs must use initiative to get business and earn a living; employees usually have guaranteed salaries.

Highly skilled, highly paid workers with substantial investments in tools and equipment are likely going to pass this test so long as they don't work full-time for just one firm. You're going to have a very hard time passing the economic reality test if you don't pay a worker very much, the worker is not highly skilled, the worker has no investment in tools or equipment and the worker doesn't have to use much individual initiative to earn a living.

A few court decisions help illustrate what may be emphasized when the economic realities test is applied.

In one case, a natural gas pipeline construction company hired pipe welders and classified them as ICs. Twenty of them sued the company, claiming they were entitled to overtime pay because they were really employees. The court concluded that the workers were ICs under the economic reality test and therefore not entitled to overtime pay. The court noted that:

- The welders' jobs were highly specialized and required great skill.
- The welders moved from company to company and from job to job, usually working no more than six weeks at a time for any one company.
- The company exercised no control over how the welders did their jobs. Instead, the company's customers specified the type of welding procedures to be used and then tested the finished results.
- The welders owned all their own welding equipment and trucks, with an average cost of $15,000.
- The welders' success depended on using their initiative to find consistent work by moving from job to job.
- Although they were paid an hourly rate, the welders' opportunity for profit or loss depended mostly on their abilities to find work and minimize welding costs.

Based upon these facts, the court concluded that the welders were in business for themselves. (*Carrell v. Sunland Constr. Inc.*, 998 F.2d 330 (5th Cir. 1993).)

In another case, the Department of Labor claimed that a nightclub operator had incorrectly classified topless dancers as ICs and was liable for overtime pay and for failing to pay the minimum wage. The court agreed. Even though the dancers' compensation was derived solely from tips they received from customers, the court found they were employees under the economic reality test. The dancers were economically dependent upon the nightclub because it set their work schedules and the minimum amounts they could charge for table dances and couch dances. Moreover, the

club played the major role in luring customers through advertising, providing customers food and beverages and other means. The only initiative the dancers provided was deciding what to wear and how provocatively to dance. *(Reich v. Circle C. Investments, Inc.*, 998 F.2d 324 (5th Cir. 1993).)

However, it's possible for even skilled workers to be considered employees under the economic realities test. For example, one federal court found that professional nurses were employees protected by the overtime pay provisions of the Fair Labor Standards Act. (See Chapter 12, Section A.) This was so even though the court admitted the nurses were highly skilled, worked for several different patients or hospitals at a time, were free to decline referrals and exercised independence and initiative in the way they did their work. (*Brock v. Superior Care, Inc.*, 840 F.2d 1054 (2d Cir. 1988).)

F. Other Tests for IC Status

About half the states use a special statutory test, also called the ABC test, to determine if workers are ICs or employees for purposes of unemployment compensation. This test focuses on just a few factors:

- whether the hiring firm controls the worker on the job
- whether the worker is operating an independent business, and
- where the work is performed—that is, where you say or where the worker wants to work.

This test is simpler than the others discussed above, but can be the hardest to satisfy. (See Chapter 9, Section B.)

The following chart lists most of the factors government auditors examine to classify workers and shows the differences among the various agencies.

FACTORS CONSIDERED IN CLASSIFYING WORKERS

	Unemployment Compensation in states using ABC Test	Unemployment Compensation in states using common law test	Workers' Compensation in states using economic reality test	Workers' Compensation in states using common law test	U.S. Labor Dept.	Copyright Ownership
No training		✔		✔		
Assistants can do work		✔		✔		✔
Worker can realize profit or loss		✔		✔	✔	
Work not done on hiring firm's premises	✔	✔		✔		
No right to fire worker		✔		✔	✔	
Worker offers services to public		✔		✔		
Worker furnishes tools and materials		✔		✔		
Payment by the project		✔		✔		✔
Worker has multiple clients or customers		✔		✔		✔
Worker and hiring firm have no continuing relationship		✔		✔	✔	✔
Worker has significant investment in equipment and facilities		✔		✔	✔	
Worker pays own business expenses		✔		✔		
Worker has no right to quit		✔		✔		
Worker sets order or sequence of work		✔		✔		
Worker provides own training		✔		✔		
Worker need not perform services personally		✔		✔		
Worker sets own hours		✔		✔		✔
Full-time work not required		✔		✔		
Reports not required		✔		✔		
Work outside hiring firm's usual business	✔	✔	✔	✔		✔
Custom in the community		✔		✔		
Worker highly skilled		✔		✔		✔
Initiative, judgment needed to succeed		✔		✔	✔	
Intent of worker and hiring firm		✔		✔		
Worker not subject to hiring firm's control		✔		✔	✔	
Worker has independent trade or business	✔	✔	✔	✔		✔
Tax treatment of worker		✔		✔		✔
No worker benefits provided		✔		✔		✔
Work typically not supervised		✔		✔		
No right to assign additional projects						✔

Federal Payroll Taxes

This chapter provides an introduction to federal payroll taxes and guides you to other chapters in the book you should read to determine if you have to pay them.

A. The Basics of Payroll Taxes

Whenever you hire a worker, one of your primary concerns should be whether you must withhold and remit federal payroll taxes. The IRS is in charge of collecting these taxes.

Federal payroll taxes include:

- Social Security and Medicare taxes—paid equally by employers and employees
- unemployment taxes—paid entirely by employers, and
- income tax withholding—deducted directly from workers' paychecks by their employers and paid to the IRS.

These taxes need be paid only by people or companies that hire employees. No federal payroll taxes need be withheld or paid for ICs. ICs pay their own Social Security and Medicare taxes in the form of self-employment taxes. They also pay income taxes directly to the IRS, usually in the form of quarterly estimated taxes. This one of the greatest advantages of hiring ICs instead of employees.

The Rules Differ for Some Workers

Rules for federal payroll taxes are different for some specialized types of workers. Skip directly to Chapter 6 if you are concerned about the status of workers in the following occupations:

- licensed real estate agents
- direct sellers
- corporate officers
- home workers
- drivers who distribute food products, beverages or laundry
- full-time life insurance salespeople, or
- traveling or city salespeople.

1. Social Security and Medicare Taxes (FICA)

Social Security and Medicare taxes are imposed on both employers and employees. The employer must collect and remit the employee's part of the taxes and also pay a matching amount. These taxes are often referred to as FICA because the legislation setting out the requirements for such taxes is called the Federal Insurance Contributions Act.

The amounts to be withheld are listed in the current edition of IRS Circular E. For 1996, for example, employers and employees were each required to pay 7.65% on the first $62,700 of employee's annual wages. The 7.65% figure is the sum of the 6.2% Social Security tax and the 1.45% Medicare tax. There is no Social Security tax on the portion of an employee's annual wages that exceed $62,700—only the Medicare tax; the employer and employee each pay the 1.45% Medicare tax on any wages over $62,700. The rates and the cut-off point for the Social Security tax change annually.

IRS *Circular E, Employer's Tax Guide,* provides detailed information on federal payroll taxes. It is an outstanding resource that you should have. You can get a free copy by calling the IRS at: 800-TAX-FORM (829-3676) or by calling or visiting your local IRS office.

2. Federal Unemployment Taxes (FUTA)

Most employers must pay both state and federal unemployment taxes. But even if an employer is exempt from the state tax, it may still have to pay the federal tax.

The federal unemployment tax is often called FUTA—an acronym derived from the name of the federal law enacting the tax, the Federal Unemployment Tax Act. The FUTA tax is imposed solely on employers. Employers may not collect or deduct it from employees' wages.

You must pay FUTA taxes if you:

- pay $1,500 or more to employees during any calendar quarter—that is, any three-month period beginning with January, or

- in each of 20 different calendar weeks during the year, there was at least a part of the day in which you had an employee to whom you paid $1,500 or more during a calendar quarter; the weeks don't have to be consecutive, nor does it have to be the same employee each week.

Technically, the FUTA tax rate is 6.2%; but, in practice, this amount is rarely paid. This is because employers are given a credit of 5.4% if they pay the applicable state unemployment tax in full and on time. This means that the actual FUTA tax rate is usually 0.8%. In 1995, the FUTA tax was assessed on the first $7,000 of an employee's annual wages. The FUTA tax, then, usually is $56 per year per employee.

3. Federal Income Tax Withholding

Employers must calculate and withhold federal income taxes from all employees' paychecks. The withheld funds are normally deposited with the employer's bank, which transmits the money to the IRS. Federal income taxes are paid entirely by employees; employers simply act as unpaid income tax collectors for the IRS.

B. Determining Worker Tax Status

Although the IRS is in charge of collecting federal payroll taxes, it's up to you to decide whether you must withhold and pay such taxes for workers. At least initially, paying federal payroll taxes is a voluntary matter for employers.

To determine whether payroll taxes must be paid for most types of workers, you have to decide whether the worker is an IC or employee, as defined by the Internal Revenue Code and IRS rules. If you decide that a worker is an IC, no payroll taxes are due. If you determine that a worker is an employee, you must file the appropriate forms with the IRS and begin to withhold and pay payroll taxes.

However, your decision about how to classify workers is subject to review by the IRS, which enforces the federal payroll tax worker classification rules. The IRS takes this enforcement task very seriously. Whenever the IRS audits any business, however small and for whatever reason, it always looks to see whether the firm has misclassified employees as ICs. If the IRS determines that you wrongly classified workers as ICs to avoid paying payroll taxes, it will impose charges and penalties that could well bankrupt you. (See Chapter 8, Section D.)

Unfortunately, making an initial decision about whether federal payroll taxes must be paid for a worker or group of similar workers can be difficult because the rules and guidelines are complex and often don't lead to easy conclusions. Your task will be easier if you take the approach described in this chapter.

Get Help If You Need It

Because IRS penalties for misclassifying employees as ICs can be substantial, it's important to classify all workers correctly. If you're not sure how to classify a worker after reading this book, seek assistance from a tax expert. (See Chapter 17, Section B.)

Except in those rare cases where special rules apply (see Section C), you should take the following two-step approach to determine workers' payroll tax status.

1. Apply the Common Law Test

You must first decide whether the workers involved are employees or ICs under the common law test.

This is what an IRS examiner will do if you're audited. Common law is judge-made law carved out through court decisions. It's the common law that is used to determine whether a worker is an employee or IC for payroll tax purposes. Workers who qualify as employees under this test are called common law employees by the IRS, and common law ICs if they don't qualify as employees.

The IRS uses a lengthy and cumbersome 20-factor test to determine if a worker is an employee or IC under the common law. (See Chapter 3, Section D.) Reading about that test may make you very discouraged. It seems needlessly complicated and highly subjective. In many cases, you just won't be sure how to classify a worker even after you wade through applying it.

To make things simpler, this book sets out a four-part test emphasizing the most important factors used by the IRS—for example, where the work is done and whether there is a right to discharge the worker. Apply this test to the workers involved to see if they are likely to qualify as common law employees or ICs. (See Chapter 5. Section B.)

2. Check the Safe Harbor Rule

Sometimes, even after diligently applying the IRS test, you won't be sure whether a worker should be classified as an employee or IC. But even if you think a worker is an IC for whom no payroll taxes are due, it's always possible that the IRS will disagree with you if you are audited. The IRS will never challenge you for classifying worker as an employee, since that means you have to pay payroll taxes.

You may get some relief from a special law, called the employer's safe harbor or Section 530, intended to help hiring firms faced with the classification dilemma. As long as you have a reasonable basis for believing that the workers involved are ICs and meet the other requirements of the safe harbor, the federal government will in essence forgive you if it turns out that the workers are actually employees under the IRS test. You won't have to pay employment taxes for these workers and the IRS cannot impose fines and penalties for your failure to pay them.

The employer's safe harbor is often your best defense against IRS claims that you owe back taxes and penalties for misclassifying workers. Take steps now to make sure you have the right to raise the safe harbor defense if you're audited. Otherwise, you could lose this valuable defense long before an audit occurs.

The employer's safe harbor is discussed in detail in Chapter 7. Read that chapter after reading Chapter 5, which covers the IRS common law test.

C. Payroll Tax Rules for Specific Occupations

Congress has enacted rules that make it much easier to determine whether you must pay federal payroll taxes for some workers in a handful of occupations. If a worker falls within any of these categories, you don't need to use the two-step approach outlined above to determine the correct payroll tax status. The IRS clearly sets out your federal payroll tax obligations based solely on the worker's occupation.

These rules apply to:

- corporate officers
- agent or commission drivers who deliver laundry, food or beverages other than milk
- certain full-time life insurance sales agents who work for only one company
- certain home workers—generally, people who make clothing, needlecraft products or other similar products at home
- certain full-time traveling or city salespeople
- licensed real estate agents, and
- certain direct sellers—for example, door-to-door salespeople.

It's usually easy to determine these workers' payroll tax status, but there is a price to pay. You may end up having to classify a worker as an employee and pay payroll taxes even if the worker would have otherwise been an IC under the common law test.

→ If a particular worker may fall within any of these categories, read Chapter 6. You may also want to read Chapter 7 concerning the safe harbor rules. You won't need to read Chapter 5 concerning the IRS 20-factor test.

D. Asking for an IRS Determination

Either you, or any of your workers, can ask the IRS for its opinion on how a worker or group of similar workers should be classified by filing IRS Form SS-8 with the IRS. An SS-8 form can be filed either before or after a worker is hired.

The vast majority of SS-8 forms are filed by workers who are classified as ICs and want to be treated as employees instead. One reason is that the hiring firm will then be required to pay one-half of the worker's Social Security tax. Many other SS-8s are filed by workers who have been classified as ICs and discover they are ineligible for unemployment compensation after being terminated by the hiring firm.

⚠ **Don't Give the IRS a Head Start**
For the reasons discussed below, it's rarely a good idea for you to file an SS-8 form. By doing so, you give the IRS a head start determining your workers' status. (See Section D3.)

1. How to File a Form SS-8

▤ A copy of IRS Form SS-8 is included in the Appendix. You may photocopy and use

this form. You don't need to obtain an original from the IRS.

To complete IRS Form SS-8, you must answer a number of detailed questions about your company and the worker's relationship with it—for example, the nature of worker's services and your business, whether the worker is given training and provided with tools, how the worker is paid, whether the worker can be discharged and many other questions.

The completed Form SS-8 is filed with the office of your local IRS district director. Call the local IRS office to find out the address.

Depending on its backlog and the length of its investigation—from three months to a year or more after receiving the completed SS-8 form—the IRS will issue a private letter ruling stating its determination. A private letter ruling is the IRS's official opinion concerning a question asked by a taxpayer.

Once the private letter ruling is issued, the IRS must follow it for that taxpayer. For example, if the ruling is that a worker or class of workers are

ICs, the IRS cannot later claim they are employees. If you receive a favorable ruling, you'll never have to worry about the IRS challenging the status of the workers involved in a subsequent audit.

A private letter ruling is simply the IRS's opinion, not a legal ruling issued by a court. It can't be relied upon by anyone other than the taxpayer who asked for it. This means that you won't be helped at all if another firm files an SS-8 and receives a ruling that workers similar to your own are ICs.

2. Adverse IRS Rulings

If the IRS decides that you've misclassified a worker as an IC, you need not immediately reclassify the worker as an employee. If you disagree with the ruling, you can continue to treat the worker as an IC. However, there will be several possible adverse consequences if you are later audited by the IRS:

First, the IRS will almost certainly conclude that the worker should have been classified as an employee. In other words, you'll lose the audit.

Second, you can't reasonably claim that you didn't know the worker was an employee after you receive the IRS ruling. This will probably mean that it won't be possible for you to claim protection under the Section 530 safe harbor rule for tax years after you received the ruling. (See Chapter 7.)

In addition, the IRS may decide that your continued misclassification of the worker after receiving the ruling was intentional and impose the maximum assessments and penalties against you for intentional worker classification. These are much higher than the assessments and penalties that may be imposed for an unintentional misclassification. (See Chapter 8, Section C.)

3. The Perils of Filing an SS-8

Nearly 90% of all IRS rulings in response to SS-8s result in a determination that the worker is an employee, not an IC. This undoubtedly reflects the IRS's strong bias in favor of classifying as many workers as possible as employees. In addition, the questions on Form SS-8 seem to be slanted in favor of finding employee status.

There is usually no reason for any hiring firm to file an SS-8. If a worker's status under the right of control test is clear, an additional determination by the IRS is pointless because it's obvious how the worker should be classified. If a worker's status is unclear, it's still pointless because the IRS will almost certainly rule that he or she is an employee. So it's rarely worth the risk to file an SS-8 and suffer the possible adverse consequences. ■

The IRS Test for Worker Status

The first step in determining whether most workers are employees or ICs for IRS federal payroll tax purposes is to apply the common law right of control test.

A. The Basics of the IRS Test

Under the common law test, you are an employer if you have the right to direct and control the workers in how they work—both as to the final results and as to the details of when, where and how the work is done. In contrast, you do not have the right to control the way ICs work. Your control is limited to accepting or rejecting the final results ICs achieve. If you're confused about this distinction, read Chapter 4, Section B, for an overview of the common law test.

1. The 20-Factor Test

The IRS has developed a list of 20 factors its auditors are supposed to use to measure how much control a hiring firm has over its workers. These include, for example, whether you have the right to give instructions, pay by the hour or by the project, provide tools and equipment and require the work to be done at your place of business. All 20 factors are discussed in detail in Chapter 3, Section D. You don't need to look at them now.

If all 20 factors show IC status, then the workers in question are unquestionably ICs and you have no problem. However, in reality, some factors are usually on the IC side of the ledger and others on the employee side. To add another complication, not all 20 factors are equally important, and their importance varies from situation to situation. Some may not apply at all to certain occupations.

According to the IRS, it's not necessary for all 20 factors, or even a majority of the factors, to show IC or employee status for a worker to be classified one way or another. Rather, taking into account the relative weight of each factor, on balance the factors must favor employee or IC status.

This means that a worker is not necessarily an IC if 11 or even 15 of the 20 factors indicate IC status. If the factors showing employee status are together more important than those indicating IC status, the worker is an employee.

2. Problems Using the IRS Test

This 20-factor test is a frequent cause of despair among hiring firms and tax experts because it often does not provide a conclusive answer about how to classify a worker. Deciding how much weight to give to each of the many factors and whether the IC factors outweigh the employee factors is a terribly subjective exercise. Reasonable people—you and the IRS auditors for example—can easily disagree about which way the scale tips. This has led to great uncertainty among hiring firms about how to classify workers.

Not even the IRS is able to apply the 20-factor test consistently. In one infamous case, the IRS found that a worker hired by one drywall company was an IC and that a worker for another drywall company was an employee. The worker in question was the same person, doing the same type of work for each company.

Since it is so often a fruitless endeavor, don't spend much time on this 20-factor weighing and balancing exercise. This chapter explains a simpler test emphasizing those factors from the list of 20 that are most important.

B. Simplified Test for IC Status

If you can answer "yes" to these four questions, you'll usually be able to convince the IRS that workers are ICs:

- Can the workers realize a profit or loss from the activity?
- Is the work performed at least in part at a place other than your business premises, or does the nature of the work require that it be performed at your premises?

- Are the workers operating their own independent businesses with multiple income sources?
- Are you prohibited from firing the workers at will?

These questions are based on the most important of the 20 factors. (See Chapter 3, Section D.) Passing this test means that these most crucial factors show IC status. These will likely outweigh any other factors in the list of 20 that may indicate employee status. All your relationships with ICs should be structured with this test in mind. (See Chapter 15.) But remember: there are no guarantees.

1. Realizing a Profit or Loss

One of the basic differences between employees and ICs is that ICs can earn profits or suffer losses far in excess of those ordinarily realized by employees.

To determine whether a worker has a risk of profit or loss, don't consider the types of risks that employees typically have. These include the risk that an employee will not get paid or may have to take a pay cut or get laid off if the employer's business does poorly. Likewise, don't consider benefits such as stock options, pay raises or bonuses that employees may obtain if the employer's business does well. These are not benefits to which ICs are usually entitled.

a. Expenses

The best way to prove opportunity to realize profit or loss by ICs is to show the IRS that they have recurring business expenses. If receipts do not match expenses, an IC loses money and may go into debt. If receipts exceed expenses, ICs earn a profit. Good examples of IC expenses include:

- hiring and paying salaries for assistants
- paying travel and other similar expenses incurred in performing the services

- having a substantial investment in equipment and materials, and
- paying for an office or workplace.

Employees do not pay for and are not liable for such expenses, so they do not bear these types of risks. Even if their employer's business fails, the employees will not be personally liable to the employer's creditors.

b. Payment by the project

The other way to prove opportunity for profit or loss by ICs is to pay them an agreed upon price for a specific project rather than by unit of time such as by the hour. If the project price is higher than the expenses, the IC will make money; if not, he or she will lose money. Employees typically are not paid on a per project basis, so they bear no such risk of loss or chance for profits.

In the IRS's view, a worker who accepts a job with a guaranteed minimum salary is assumed to have agreed that the hiring firm has the right to control the way the work is done. The same holds true when a worker—typically a salesperson on commission—is given a drawing account of a specified amount at stated intervals and is not required to repay any excess over commissions earned.

2. Work Outside Hiring Firm's Premises

If you require a worker to perform services at your place of business or another place you designate you should classify the worker as an employee unless the nature of the work requires that it be performed at your premises.

EXAMPLE: The Acme Widget Company hires Andrea, a computer programmer, to help with its computer system. Andrea is given an office at Acme and does all her work there. The nature of the work Andrea is doing does not require that she work full-time at Acme's office; the work could be done at any location. The only logical reason for Acme to want Andrea to work there is to have some control over her. This factor strongly indicates that the programmer is Acme's employee.

EXAMPLE: The Acme Widget Co. decides to paint its offices. It hires Joe, a painting contractor, to do the job. Obviously, Joe must do all the work at Acme's office. Joe is not working at Acme's office because Acme wants to control him; rather, the nature of the service Joe is providing requires him to work there. In this situation, this factor is irrelevant in determining whether Joe is an IC or Acme employee and should be given no weight.

IRS auditors place such great importance on this factor because being required to work at a location specified by a hiring firm implies control by the firm, especially where the work could be done elsewhere. A person working at a hiring firm's place of business is physically within the firm's direction and supervision. If the person can choose to work off the premises, the firm obviously has less control.

a. Employees who work off the employer's premises

The fact that a person may work off the hiring firm's premises does not necessarily mean that he or she is an IC. Many employees work outside of their employers' premises. This is often required by the nature of the job. For example, truck drivers and taxicab drivers spend most of their time on the road. The IRS is likely to find control over a worker indicating employee status where the hiring firm has the right to compel the person to travel a designated route, canvass a territory within a certain time or to work at specific places.

b. Telecommuters

Many workers telecommute—work at home and communicate with their employers by phone or fax. Although working at home is usually a mild indicator of IC status, it is often outweighed by the other factors discussed here.

EXAMPLE: Jill performs telemarketing services for the Speedy Exterminator Company. Jill works at home, using her own phone to call potential customers for Speedy. This factor indicates that Jill is an IC. However, other factors clearly show that Jill is an employee. Speedy pays Jill a salary and benefits and Jill has no risk of loss or opportunity for profit. Jill does not make her services available to the public and Speedy is the only company for which she works. Even though she works at home, Jill is Speedy's employee.

3. Economic Independence

One of the hallmarks of IC status is economic independence. ICs normally have multiple sources of income and are not completely dependent upon any one hiring firm. If a person is solely dependent upon you for his or her livelihood, classify the worker as an employee.

To prove economic independence, at the very least you must show that the workers:

- make their services available to the public, and
- have multiple clients or customers, preferably at the same time.

It will also be very helpful if the workers do not have a continuing relationship with you and do not work for you full-time.

a. Making services available to the public

There are a number of ways a person can make services available to the general public—for example, by:

- maintaining an office
- hiring assistants
- hanging out a shingle in front of a home or office advertising the services
- holding business licenses
- maintaining listings in business and telephone directories, or
- advertising in newspapers, trade journals and magazines.

b. Multiple clients

Having multiple clients shows that ICs are running independent businesses and are not dependent on any one firm for their livelihood.

It's best for an IC to work for more than one client simultaneously. The IRS will rarely question the status of an IC who works for three or four clients at the same time. It is less helpful to show that a worker served many clients over the course of a year, but only worked for one at a time. If the worker spent most of his or her time working for you, the IRS could conclude that the worker was your employee.

ANTI-COMPETITION CLAUSES INDICATE EMPLOYEE STATUS

Some hiring firms attempt to restrict outside workers' abilities to work for competitors by including anti-competition clauses in their contracts. For example, a software publisher might hire a contract programmer to work on a project and include a clause in the contract preventing the programmer from doing similar programming work for competitors for a specified time. Such clauses indicate an employee relationship. The more restrictive they are, the more likely the worker will be viewed as an employee.

---

c. No continuing relationship

ICs usually have multiple customers or clients for whom they perform specific projects or tasks. Once the project is completed, they move on and may never be heard from again. Or they may accept new projects from the same firm in the future, but only if they want to and have the time.

Lack of a continuing relationship is a strong indicator of independent contractor status. However, it's possible for some workers to have long-term relationships with their clients or customers and still qualify as ICs. For example, lawyers and accountants often perform services for the same clients for years on end. Similarly, you may use the services of a dentist, doctor, shoemaker or gardener year after year. All of these people are ICs as long as you can show they are running their own separate businesses— for example, have multiple clients or customers, risk of profit or loss, recurring business expenses and perform the work outside your business premises.

⚠ Rules for Part-Time and Seasonal Workers

Note that even a worker who works at irregular intervals, part-time, on a seasonal basis or for a short time may be deemed by the IRS to have a continuing relationship with the hiring firm. This is so whenever the work arrangement contemplates continuing or recurring work—for example, where a worker is on call, or agrees to work whenever needed by the hiring firm.

d. No full-time work

Ideally, an IC should spend no more than half of his or her time working for you and should spend the rest of the time working for others. However, it may be necessary for an IC to work full-time for you where the IC must complete a project on a short deadline. Such full-time work should be kept as short as possible.

Full-time does not necessarily mean an eight-hour day or a five-day week. Whether a worker works full-time depends on the nature of the occupation and the intent of the worker and hiring firm. For example, some companies have flextime or variable work hour arrangements enabling their employees to work on other than a five-day, 40 hour-per-week schedule. Workers in such arrangements are still full-time workers if that is the hiring firm's intent.

4. No Right to Fire at Will

If you have, or want to have, the right to fire a worker at any time for any reason or even for no reason, classify the worker as an employee. You cannot have this kind of power over a worker and at the same time prove to the IRS that the worker is an IC.

Most employees can be fired at any time and so the work relationship is called "at will." If you have a right to fire a worker at will, the IRS will likely conclude that you have the right to control that worker. The ever-present threat of dismissal

must inevitably cause a worker to follow your instructions and otherwise do your bidding. Even if you never actually give the worker instructions, you have the right to do so at any time if you can fire the worker.

EXAMPLE: Jon has an agreement with Ace Building Company to do carpentry work on houses Ace constructs. Ace can discharge Jon any time before or after he finishes a job and he has no recourse if he is fired. The IRS would likely conclude that Jon is Ace's employee. Since Ace can fire Jon, it has the inherent power to supervise Jon's work and otherwise control how he does his job. Jon has no choice but to obey Ace's orders or face being fired. Even if Ace doesn't actually supervise Jon because he's such a good worker, it still has the right to do so.

An IC's services cannot be dispensed with nearly as easily as an employee's. An IC can be terminated only according to the terms of the agreement you have with him or her. If you fire an IC who performs adequately and otherwise satisfies the terms of the agreement, you'll be liable to the IC for breaking the agreement. The IC can sue you in court and get a judgment making you liable in money damages.

The best way to prove to the IRS that you don't have the right to fire a worker is to have a signed contract with the worker saying so. (See Chapter 16, Section C.)

EXAMPLE: Anne, a painting subcontractor, signs a written contract to paint 264 houses for Ace Building Company. The agreement provides that Ace can cancel the contract only if Anne violates its terms—for example, if she does not complete the work according to the schedule set forth in the contract. Since Ace has no right to fire Anne and might be faced with an expensive lawsuit if it cancels her contract without a good reason, Ace lacks the power to control her work the way it can control its employees. Its power is limited to requiring that Anne live up to the contract terms.

However, don't assume that workers are ICs simply because they can't be fired at will. Some employees cannot be fired at will, either. A few employees negotiate oral or written agreements with their employers limiting the employers' right to fire them. Many such contracts provide that the employee can only be fired for cause—that is, a good reason such as poor job performance. Collective bargaining agreements may also limit an employer's right to fire.

C. Applying the Test

The examples below illustrate how the simplified, four-part version of the IRS test works in real-life situations.

1. IRS Examples

These three examples are taken directly from IRS publications.

EXAMPLE 1: Rose Trucking contracts to deliver material for Forest, Inc. at $140 per ton. Rose Trucking is not paid for any articles that are not delivered. At times, Jim Rose, who operates Rose Trucking, may also lease another truck and hire a driver to complete the contract. Jim pays all operating expenses, including insurance coverage. He also owns or rents all equipment and is responsible for all maintenance. None of the drivers are provided by Forest, Inc. Rose is free to contract with other companies besides Forest, and routinely does so. Jim Rose, operating as Rose Trucking, is an IC.

Analysis: This example is chock full of facts showing that Jim Rose has all kinds of opportunities for profit or loss. First, he has business expenses: he provides his own trucks, hires and pays his own drivers, pays for maintenance and insurance. Clearly, Rose can lose lots of money if his expenses exceed his earnings, and he has extra risk of loss because he won't get paid for undelivered items. Rose has multiple customers so he is not dependent upon Forest, Inc. for his livelihood. Presumably, he offers his services to the public, otherwise he wouldn't have all these customers.

These facts alone were sufficient for the IRS to conclude that Rose was an IC. If, in addition, Jim could show that he chooses his own delivery routes and cannot be fired at will, his IC status would be virtually unquestionable.

EXAMPLE 2: Connie Consultant is a systems analyst who markets her services directly to various companies to help complete short-term projects. Connie does the bulk of her work at her own office on her own computers and employs a part-time assistant. She bills her clients by the hour and is reimbursed for travel and other expenses. Connie is an IC.

Analysis: Even though Connie bills by the hour and is reimbursed for expenses, she still has a risk of loss because she has recurring business expenses: she pays for her own office and computer equipment and employs an assistant. She does most of her work at her own office. She is not economically dependent upon any one client because she does short-term work for many clients. Connie is clearly running her own independent business. It would be better if Connie charged by the project and did not bill separately for her expenses. But these two factors are clearly outweighed by all the facts showing IC status. This example shows that a person can be an IC even though some factors point to employee status.

EXAMPLE 3: Dr. White, a dentist, enters into an oral agreement with Dr. Green providing that Green will perform dental services in his own office. Green agrees to work for a salary plus a percentage of all income over a stated amount resulting from his services. He has to follow designated office hours and get White's approval for any absences. White supplies all instruments, pays all expenses and realizes all losses from unpaid accounts. He also employees the nurse who assists Green. Either Green or White can end the agreement at any time. Green is White's employee.

Analysis: All four questions in the test point clearly to employee status for Green. The fact that Green can be fired by White at any time is important since it gives White the power to control Green on the job. White clearly exercises this power by requiring Green to work designated office hours and obtain approval for any absences. Also, Green has no risk of financial loss other than that normally encountered by employees since he is paid a salary and White pays all expenses. White also supplies Green with a place to work and expensive dental equipment. The fact that White can earn a bonus if he brings in a certain amount of income does not constitute opportunity for profit to the IRS. Green

is clearly not running his own independent dental practice and is completely dependent upon White for his livelihood.

2. If You're Unsure About Classification

Even using the simplified version of the IRS test, it may not always be clear how to classify a worker. If you are not sure whether a worker qualifies as an IC for federal payroll tax purposes, or you think the worker may not qualify, take the following steps.

- See if the Section 530 safe harbor rules may apply to prevent the IRS from treating the workers as employees for employment tax purposes. (See Chapter 7.)
- Check into whether it's possible to structure your relationship with the workers involved to make them more clearly look like ICs to the IRS. (See Chapter 3, Section C and Chapter 15.)
- Carefully weigh the benefits of classifying the workers as ICs versus the potential costs if the IRS determines the workers should have been classified as employees. It might be worth taking the risk if you think a worker might qualify as an IC. Then again, it might not. (See Chapter 4, Section D.) ■

Federal Payroll Tax Rules for Specific Workers

Read this chapter only if you're concerned with the federal payroll tax status of workers in the following occupations:

- licensed real estate agents
- direct sellers
- corporate officers
- home workers
- drivers who distribute food products, beverages or laundry
- full-time life insurance salespeople, or
- traveling or city salespeople.

Specific rules govern the federal payroll tax treatment of these types of workers. Read Section C if the workers involved are real estate agents or direct sellers. Read Section B if they fall into any of the other five categories.

A. Statutory Employees

Congress has determined that workers who do the following jobs are automatically considered employees for purposes of Social Security (FICA) and federal unemployment tax (FUTA):

- corporate officers (see Section B1)
- certain home workers (see Section B2)
- certain drivers who distribute food products, beverages or laundry (see Section B3)
- certain full-time life insurance salespeople (see Section B4), and
- certain traveling or city salespeople (see Section B5).

This is so regardless of whether or not these workers would be considered employees under the common law right of control test. (See Chapter 3, Section D.) These workers are called statutory employees because their status has been predetermined by statutes passed by Congress.

You must give every statutory employee a Form W-2, Wage and Tax Statement, and check the Statutory Employee designation in box 15. The W-2 must show the Social Security and Medicare tax withheld, and the Social Security and

Medicare income. You must also file a copy with the Social Security Administration. You can obtain Form W-2 and instructions for completing it by calling the IRS at: 800-TAX-FORM (829-3676) or by calling your local IRS office.

⚠ When Withholding Isn't Required

The statutory employee classification applies only to employment taxes—FICA and sometimes FUTA—not federal income taxes. Federal income taxes must be withheld only if the worker qualifies as an employee under the common law test. (See Chapter 3, Section D.)

Employment taxes come directly out of your pocket as an employer, so you will undoubtedly prefer that a worker not be classified as a statutory employee. (See Section A2.)

EXAMPLE: Suzy is a full-time traveling salesperson for the Shady Siding Company. Suzy qualifies as a statutory employee under the rules discussed below. This means that Shady must pay FICA and FUTA taxes for Suzy, just as for any employee. Shady must also withhold Suzy's portion of the FICA tax from her paychecks.

However, Shady need not withhold federal income tax from Suzy's pay because she is an IC under the common law test. Suzy is issued a W-2 Wage and Tax Statement after the end of the year listing the amounts withheld. Box 15 is checked on the W-2 that Shady files to alert the IRS that Suzy is a statutory employee.

1. Requirements for Statutory Employees

With the exception of corporate officers, a person can be a statutory employee only if they do the work personally, make no substantial investment in the workplace and have a continuing relationship with the hiring firm.

a. Work done personally

The hiring firm and worker must agree that the worker will do almost all of the work personally. The worker cannot subcontract the work out to others.

A written agreement stating this will of course satisfy the requirement. But it is not necessary to have one. Many statutory employees are hired only on the basis of an oral agreement. If, during the course of the negotiations, you explicitly tell a worker that he or she must perform the services personally, and the worker agrees, the requirement is satisfied.

And the requirement of personally performing the work can also be implied from the circumstances. For example, telling a person: "I want you to work for me," implies that you want him or her to perform services for you personally.

b. No substantial investment

Only workers who do not have a substantial investment in the equipment and facilities used to perform the services can qualify as statutory employees. This includes equipment or workspace necessary for the work, such as office space and furniture, office equipment and machinery. It does not include tools, instruments and clothing commonly provided by employees in the trade— for example, uniforms that employees typically provide for themselves or inexpensive hand tools that carpenters typically have. Nor does it include education, experience or training. Statutory employees can also use vehicles for their transportation or for transporting goods.

c. Continuing relationship

To be a statutory employee, a worker must have a continuing relationship with the hiring firm. This includes regular part-time work and regular seasonal employment. But a single project is not enough to constitute a continuing relationship, even if the job takes a long time to complete.

2. How to Avoid Statutory Employee Status

You can avoid having a worker classified as a statutory employee by setting up the work relationship so that it does not satisfy one or more of the three threshold requirements.

- Sign a written agreement with the worker stating that he or she has the right to subcontract or delegate the work out to others. In other words, the worker doesn't have to do the work personally. But note that the agreement must reflect reality—that is, you must really intend to give the worker the right to delegate, not just say so on paper. (See Chapter 16.)
- Avoid having a continuing relationship with the worker. Use him or her for single projects, not ongoing work. Spread your hiring around by using lots of different ICs instead of a few favorite ones. Also, avoid giving ICs lengthy projects. Break down complex projects into separate tasks and hire different ICs to complete them.
- Hire workers with a substantial investment in outside facilities, such as their own offices.

If you're audited, you may be able to avoid having to pay employment taxes for statutory employees if the employer's safe harbor, also known as Section 530, applies. The safe harbor procedure allows hiring firms to avoid paying employment taxes even though workers qualify as employees.

You can claim the safe harbor for a worker who qualifies as a statutory employee. The only exception is for corporate officers. (See Section B1.) If you can show that you had a reasonable basis for treating the worker as an IC, and you meet the consistency and tax reporting requirements, you won't have to pay or withhold any employment taxes.

The reasonable basis requirement is the most difficult to meet. You have to show the IRS that you had a good reason to treat the affected workers as ICs instead of employees. One way to do this is to show that most other similar businesses in your locality treat similar workers as ICs. (See Chapter 7, Section D.)

> **EXAMPLE:** The Beckmann Tool & Dye Company treats its commissioned traveling salespeople as ICs. The IRS conducts an audit and claims that the salespeople are statutory employees. Beckmann argues that it had a reasonable basis to treat the salespeople as ICs because it is a longstanding practice of a significant segment of the tool and dye industry. Beckmann has also consistently treated all its salespeople as ICs and provided them with all the required 1099 forms. The IRS buys Beckmann's argument and holds that the company is entitled to the protection of Section 530. Beckmann won't have to pay any employment taxes for its salespeople.

B. Specific Types of Statutory Employees

Some workers are automatically pegged as statutory employees by sheer dint of the type of work they do.

1. Corporate Officers

A corporation's president, treasurer, vice president and secretary are by law automatically considered employees for both FICA and FUTA purposes. The three threshold requirements—doing the work personally, no substantial investment and a continuing relationship—do not apply. (See Section A1.)

The only exception is for an officer who performs no services for the corporation, or only minor services, and neither receives nor is entitled to receive any pay. Such an individual is not considered an employee.

> **EXAMPLE:** Murray, his sister Rose and his brother-in-law Artie start a catering business, which they set up as a corporation. Murray serves as the president, Rose as the secretary-treasurer and Artie as vice president. Murray and Rose actually run the company. Artie contributed start-up funds, but does not work for the corporation and receives no pay from it. Murray and Rose are statutory employees of the corporation; Artie is not.

2. Home Workers

This group includes people who make or sew buttons, quilts, gloves, bedspreads, clothing, needlecraft products and similar products. The work must be done away from the hiring firm's place of business—usually in the worker's own home or workshop, or in another person's home. The homeworker must satisfy the three requirements discussed above. (See Section A1.) In addition, to qualify as a statutory employee:

- the work must be done on goods or materials furnished by the hiring firm

- the work must be performed in accordance with the hiring firm's specifications; generally, such specifications are simple and consist of patterns or samples, and
- the homeworker must be required to return the processed material to the hiring firm or person designated by it.

If all these requirements are met, the hiring firm must pay the employer's share of FICA and withhold the worker's share from his or her pay. However, no FICA tax is imposed if the hiring firm pays a home worker less than $100 for a calendar year. (IRC 3121(a)(10).)

A hiring firm need not pay FUTA taxes or withhold federal income taxes for a statutory employee home worker unless the worker qualifies as an employee under the common law test. (See Chapter 3, Section D.)

EXAMPLE: Rosa sews buttons on shirts and dresses. She works at home. She does work for various companies, including Upscale Fashions, Inc. Upscale provides Rosa with all the clothing and the buttons she must sew. The only equipment Rosa provides is a needle. Upscale gives Rosa a sample of each outfit showing where the buttons are supposed to go. When Rosa finishes each batch of clothing, she returns it to Upscale.

Rosa is a statutory employee. Upscale must pay employer FICA and withhold employee FICA from Rosa's pay. But it need not pay FUTA or withhold federal income tax unless Rosa is an employee under the common law test.

3. Food, Beverage and Laundry Distributors

If the three requirements discussed above are met, drivers who distribute meat or meat products, vegetables or vegetable products, fruits or fruit products, bakery products, beverages other than milk, or laundry or dry cleaning are statutory employees.

Such workers may sell at retail or wholesale and may either be paid a salary or by commission. They may operate from their own trucks or trucks belonging to the hiring firm. Ordinarily, they service customers designated by the hiring firm as well as those they solicit. But delivery people who buy and sell merchandise on their own account or deliver to the general public as part of an independent business do not fall within this category.

EXAMPLE: Alder Laundry and Dry Cleaning enters into an agreement with Sharon to pick up and deliver clothing for its customers. Sharon has similar arrangements with several other laundries and arranges her route to serve all the laundries. None of the companies has any control over how she performs her services. She owns her own truck and is paid by commission. Sharon qualifies as an IC under the common law test.

However, she is a statutory employee because all three threshold requirements are met: her agreement with Alder acknowledges that she will do the work personally, she has no substantial investment in facilities (her truck doesn't count since it's used to deliver the product) and she has a continuing relationship with Alder. Alder must pay employment taxes for Sharon—that is, pay half of her FICA and withhold the other half from her pay, and pay all of the applicable FUTA. However, Alder need not withhold federal income tax since Sharon is an IC under the common law test.

4. Life Insurance Salespeople

This group of statutory employees includes salespeople whose full-time occupation is soliciting life insurance applications or annuity contracts, primarily for one life insurance company. The company usually provides these workers work necessities such as office space, secretarial help, forms, rate books and advertising material.

If a life insurance salesperson is a statutory employee, the hiring firm must pay FICA taxes. However, it need not pay FUTA taxes or withhold federal income taxes unless the salesperson is an employee under the common law test.

> **EXAMPLE:** Walter Neff sells life insurance full-time for the Old Reliable Life Insurance Company. He works out of Old Reliable's Omaha office where he is provided with a desk, clerical help and rate books and insurance applications. Walter is a statutory employee of Old Reliable. The company must pay employer FICA and withhold employee FICA from Walter's pay. It need not pay FUTA or withhold federal income tax unless Walter is an employee under the common law test.

5. Business-to-Business Salespeople

Some salespeople are statutory employees if they meet the three threshold requirements discussed above. (See Section A1.) In addition, they must also:

- work at least 80% of the time for one person or company, except, possibly, for sideline sales on behalf of someone else
- sell on behalf of, or turn their orders over to, the hiring firm
- sell merchandise for resale or supplies for use in the buyer's business operations, as opposed to goods purchased for personal consumption at home, and
- sell only to wholesalers, retailers, contractors or those who operate hotels, restaurants or similar establishments; this does not include manufacturers, schools, hospitals, churches, municipalities or state and federal governments.

This group does not include drivers who distribute food, beverages or laundry. (See Section B3.)

Generally, this category includes traveling salespeople who might otherwise be considered ICs. Such salespeople are ordinarily paid on a commission basis. The details of their work and the means by which they cover their territories are not typically dictated to them by others. However, they are expected to work their territories with some regularity, take purchase orders and send them to the hiring firm for delivery to the purchaser.

> **EXAMPLE:** Linda sells books to retail bookstores for the Scrivener & Sons Publishing Company. Her territory covers the entire midwest. She works only for Scrivener and is paid a commission based on the amount of each sale. She turns her orders over to Scrivener's, which ships the books to each bookstore customer. Linda is a Scrivener's statutory employee. The company must pay FICA and FUTA taxes for her. However, Scrivener need not withhold federal income taxes from her pay unless she qualifies as an employee under the common law test.

C. Statutory Independent Contractors

Direct sellers and licensed real estate agents are legally classified as ICs if:

- their pay is based on sales commissions, not on the number of hours worked, and
- there is a written contract with the hiring firm providing that they will not be treated as employees for federal tax purposes. (See Chapter 16.)

The IRS calls these workers statutory non-employees, which is bureaucratese for IC. The fortunate employers of these workers need not pay FICA or FUTA taxes or withhold federal income taxes. This is so regardless of whether they qualify as ICs or employees under the common law test. (See Chapter 3, Section D.)

⚠️ State Payroll Taxes and Workers' Compensation

These rules apply only to federal taxes—Social Security (FICA), Federal Unemployment Tax (FUTA) and federal income tax withholding. However, you may still have to pay state payroll taxes (see Chapter 9) and provide workers' compensation coverage (see Chapter 10).

1. Direct Sellers

Direct sellers are what are usually called door-to-door salespeople. They sell consumer products to people in their homes or at a place other than an established retail store—for example, at swap meets. The products they sell include tangible personal property that is used for personal, family or household purposes—for example, vacuum cleaners, cosmetics, encyclopedias, gardening equipment and other similar products.

> **EXAMPLE:** Larry is a Mavon Guy. He sells men's toiletries door-to-door. He is paid a 20% commission on all his sales. This is his only remuneration from Mavon. He has a written contract with Mavon that provides that he will not be treated as an employee for federal tax purposes. Larry is a statutory non-employee. Mavon need not pay FICA, FUTA or withhold federal income taxes for Larry. It's up to Larry to pay his own self-employment taxes. This is so whether or not Larry would qualify as an IC under the common law test.

2. Licensed Real Estate Agents

Most states require that real estate agents—called real estate salespeople in some states—be licensed and work for a licensed real estate broker who is legally responsible for their actions. Real estate agents are usually paid on a straight commission basis. Whether they pay their own expenses and how much control the broker exercises over them varies from firm to firm.

Some real estate agents would probably qualify as employees under the common law test, while others would probably be ICs. But as long as they are paid by commission and have a written agreement stating they are not employees for federal tax purposes, they are statutory non-employees. The broker need not pay FICA, FUTA or withhold federal income taxes.

> **EXAMPLE:** Mary is a licensed real estate agent who works for the Boldwell Canker real estate brokerage firm. Art, the real estate broker for whom she works, provides her with office space, pays most of her expenses and exercises a good deal of control over her actions. However, Mary's pay is based solely on commission fees from properties she lists and sells. Boldwell Canker has a written agreement with Mary providing that she will not be treated as an employee for federal tax purposes.
>
> Mary would probably qualify as Boldwell's employee under the common law test, but this doesn't matter because she is a statutory non-employee. Boldwell need not pay FICA, FUTA or withhold federal income taxes for Mary. ■

The Employment Tax Safe Harbor

This chapter provides an overview of the employer's safe harbor, a federal law that may allow you to avoid paying IRS assessments and penalties if the IRS claims you've misclassified a worker as an IC.

- Read Section A to get an overview of the law and find out whether you may be able to take advantage of its protections.
- Skip directly to Section C if your work involves technical services such as engineering and computer programming. Some specific provisions in the law may exclude you from using the safe harbor protections.
- Section B explains more of the technical requirements of complying with this law.
- Section D provides a detailed discussion of the procedures to follow to prove a safe harbor claim. Read it carefully if you represent yourself in an IRS audit.

A. Overview of Safe Harbor Protection

You may be surprised to discover that, even though you misclassify a worker as an IC, you may not have to pay federal employment taxes. This is because of the employment tax safe harbor, also known as Section 530.

Section 530 can be used when the IRS claims that workers you classified as ICs are really employees under the common law. (See Chapter 3, Section D.) If Section 530 applies, you are partly forgiven for the mistaken classification. You are not required to pay federal unemployment (FUTA) taxes or the employer's share of Social Security and Medicare (FICA) taxes for the misclassified workers, either for past or future years.

But to take advantage of Section 530, you must have consistently treated the workers involved as ICs and have had a reasonable basis—in other words, a good reason—for the IC classification. Section 530 is called a safe harbor or safe haven because it gives hiring firms a refuge from the most dire consequences of IRS worker reclassification: paying FICA and FUTA for past and future years, plus IRS assessments, interest and penalties for nonpayment in past years.

You can view Section 530 as an insurance policy. It may save you from the most drastic consequences of an unnatural disaster: an IRS claim that you have misclassified employees as ICs under the common law test.

1. Limits on Section 530 Protections

Section 530 only protects you from paying FICA and FUTA taxes, also known as employment taxes. This is a significant benefit since employment taxes are a large financial burden for employers. (See Chapter 4, Section A.) However, Section 530 does not convert a worker from an employee to an IC. Having failed the IRS common law test, the workers involved will most likely be considered employees for purposes other than payment of employment taxes.

Among other things, this means:

- you must withhold federal income taxes from the workers' wages
- federal labor and employment laws designed to protect employees will likely apply (see Chapter 12), and
- you'll have to provide the workers with all the benefits you give to other employees, such as sick leave, vacation, health insurance, pension benefits (see Chapter 2, Section A).

a. State requirements

No state has a counterpart to Section 530. The workers will likely qualify as employees under state law if they do not satisfy the IRS common law test. If so, you'll have to:

- pay state unemployment tax (see Chapter 9, Section A)
- provide workers' compensation coverage (see Chapter 10, Section A), and
- withhold state income taxes in most states (see Chapter 9, Section E).

b. Problems with the IRS

Although Section 530 is designed to help hiring firms and is supposed to be liberally applied, in practice the IRS usually puts up a battle when a hiring firm claims the safe harbor. The federal government loses payroll taxes whenever Section 530 is successfully invoked and the IRS wants this to happen as infrequently as possible.

But just because the IRS doesn't look kindly upon Section 530 doesn't mean you shouldn't use it whenever possible. It's often your best defense against the IRS. IRS officials are usually very reluctant to grant Section 530 claims outright. But, if you present a strong case, they may be willing to offer you a favorable settlement, either during the examination stage or a subsequent appeal.

If you're dissatisfied with your results with the IRS and believe you have a strong Section 530 claim, you can take the claim to federal court. (See Section D.) The federal courts have proved far more receptive to Section 530 claims by hiring firms than the IRS. Virtually every hiring firm that has taken a legitimate Section 530 claim to court in recent years has won. Fighting the IRS in federal court costs time and money, but may end up costing less than having to pay FICA and FUTA taxes and penalties for the workers involved. In one case, for example, a small mining company was able to use Section 530 to get a federal court to cancel a $60,000 IRS assessment. You'll normally need to hire a lawyer to bring this type of court action. (See Chapter 17, Section A.)

2. Section 530 Requirements

You must satisfy three requirements to obtain relief from employment taxes under Section 530:

- you must have consistently treated the workers involved, and other similar workers, as ICs
- you must file all Form 1099s reporting to the IRS your payment to the ICs, and
- you must show a reasonable basis—that is, a good reason—for treating the workers involved as ICs.

These requirements are discussed in detail in Section D. However, if you hire a lawyer, CPA or other tax professional to represent you in an audit, you don't need to become an expert on Section 530. Concentrate on taking the steps necessary to preserve your right to raise a Section 530 claim in an IRS audit. (See Section B.)

Do Some Legal Research

Although not mandatory, it can be very helpful to research IRS and court rulings before classifying a worker as an IC. If you can find a decision or ruling holding that workers in similar circumstances qualified as ICs, it can provide you with a reasonable basis for classifying your worker as an IC. (See Section D.) The reasonable basis requirement is usually the most difficult hurdle to overcome in using the safe harbor.

You may wish to hire a lawyer or CPA to do such research for you, or you can do it yourself. (See Chapter 17, Section B.)

B. Preserving Your Section 530 Claim

You'll lose your right to raise Section 530 in an audit long before it occurs unless you take the following steps.

1. Treat Similar Workers as ICs

If you treat a worker as an employee, from that day forward you're barred from using Section 530 not only for that worker, but for all other workers holding similar positions, even if you've always treated them as ICs.

a. Treating workers as ICs

You will be seen to treat a worker as an employee if you:

- withhold federal income tax or FICA tax from the worker's wages whether or not the tax is paid over to the IRS

- file a federal employment tax return for the worker: IRS Forms 940 through 943, or
- file a W-2 Wage and Tax Statement for an individual, whether or not tax is actually withheld. (Rev. Proc. 85-18.)

EXAMPLE: A roofing company hired 57 people to work as roofing applicators. The company consistently treated 56 of the applicators as ICs. It didn't withhold payroll taxes, file employment tax returns or provide them with W-2 statements. However, the company filed IRS Form 941, the Employer's Quarterly Federal Tax Return, for one applicator and paid his FICA taxes. The IRS ruled that the company could not use Section 530 for any of the applicators because they were not all treated as ICs. (Technical Advice Memo 8127010.)

Make absolutely sure that whoever does your payroll taxes does not withhold payroll taxes or file W-2 forms for any workers you classify as ICs. Such workers should only be given a Form 1099-MISC reporting how much you've paid them. (See Chapter 15, Section C.)

b. ICs in similar positions

Workers are in substantially similar positions if their job duties are similar. The IRS is likely to construe "substantially similar" as broadly as possible to deny Section 530 relief to as many hiring firms as possible. For example, if you're an employee who owns an incorporated business, it's quite possible that you would be denied Section 530 relief if you hire ICs to perform duties similar to those that you perform.

To preserve your right to claim Section 530, you must keep the work your employees and ICs do separate—that is, they can't perform similar functions. For example, a trucking company can't classify some drivers as ICs and some as employees and use Section 530. All the drivers would have to be classified as ICs to satisfy the consistency requirement. Before you hire an employee, make sure you haven't used ICs to perform similar services. Before you hire an IC, make sure you haven't used employees to perform similar services. If you have in either case, you'll sacrifice Section 530 by hiring the worker.

2. File All Required 1099s

To use Section 530, you must have filed the appropriate federal tax forms for the workers involved. For ICs other than corporations, this means filing IRS Form 1099-MISC for any IC who is paid $600 or more in any year after 1977. The 1099s must be filed with the IRS by February 28 of the year after the year in which the work was performed. (See Chapter 15, Section C.)

Filing Form 1099s for all ICs will not only help you use Section 530, but greatly reduce the assessments the IRS can impose if it claims you misclassified workers as ICs. (See Chapter 8, Section C.)

C. Restrictions on Technical Service Firms

Many hiring firms obtain the services of temporary or highly specialized workers through brokers. This is particularly common in technical fields such as computer programming and engineering. In these situations, three people are involved in the relationship: the client contracts with the broker who in turn contracts with the worker to provide services for the client. The broker is in effect a middleman. The client pays the broker who pays the worker after taking its own cut.

> **EXAMPLE:** Acme Technical Services is a broker that provides computer programmers to others. Acme contracts with Burt, a freelance programmer, to perform programming services for the Old Reliable Insurance Company. Reliable pays Acme who in turn pays Burt after deducting a broker's fee.

A special provision in Section 530, sometimes referred to as Section 1706, prevents brokers who provide certain types of technical service workers to others from using Section 530. The safe harbor may not be used by brokers, also called technical services firms or consulting firms, that contract to provide third party clients with:

- engineers
- designers
- drafters
- computer programmers
- systems analysts, or
- other similarly skilled workers.

This does not mean that such workers are automatically considered employees. It just means that the broker or consulting firm that served as the middleman between them and their clients can't use Section 530. The workers may still be ICs under the IRS common law test. (See Chapter 3, Section D.)

The prohibition on using Section 530 applies only to the broker in the middle of the relationship, not to the client. The client could use the safe harbor if it was audited by the IRS and the examiner claimed the worker was the client's employee under the common law test.

> **EXAMPLE:** Old Reliable Insurance Company contracts with Acme Technical Services to obtain the services of Burt, a freelance programmer. Reliable is then audited by the IRS. The examiner claims that Reliable has the right to exert sufficient control over Burt for him to be Reliable's employee under the common law test. Reliable can use Section 530 if it meets the requirements discussed above—reasonable basis, consistency, filing 1099s.

Section 530 can always be used where a firm contracts directly with a technical service worker, rather than going through a broker or consulting firm.

> **EXAMPLE:** Old Reliable Insurance Company contracts with Burt directly to provide it with programming services—that is, it does not go through a broker. If Reliable is audited, it can claim the Section 530 safe harbor, provided that it satisfies the requirements.

D. Proving a Section 530 Claim

Read this section if you are representing yourself in an IRS audit. If your case is a small one—for example, you've only classified a handful of workers as ICs and there are no other problems that could result in large IRS assessments and penalties—it may not be worth the expense of hiring an attorney, CPA or other tax professional to handle the audit. But it's still worthwhile for you to raise Section 530. Business owners have successfully used Section 530 to avoid paying employment taxes on their own, without legal assistance. After reading this chapter, you'll know as much about Section 530 as most IRS personnel.

The IRS examiner is supposed to provide you with a letter informing you about Section 530 before an examination begins. You can raise the Section 530 defense at any time, even after the examiner has completed the audit. You can also raise it for the first time on appeal. However, you lose nothing by raising Section 530 during the audit. The examiner will first determine whether the workers in question should have been classified as employees under the common law test. If so, the examiner will then consider your claim that Section 530 applies. It's unlikely that the examiner will agree that Section 530 applies. But, if you sound like you know what you're talking about and present a strong case, you may be able to get a favorable settlement of your case, either from the examiner or on appeal. (See Chapter 8, Section B.)

Help With the IRS From the IRS
The IRS has developed the chart below for its examiners to determine if Section 530 relief should be granted to a hiring firm. It may help you determine if you can use Section 530.

1. Consistent Worker Treatment

The first requirement to use Section 530 is that you must have consistently treated all workers performing similar services as ICs. You must not withhold or pay federal payroll taxes, provide the

SECTION 530 FLOWCHART

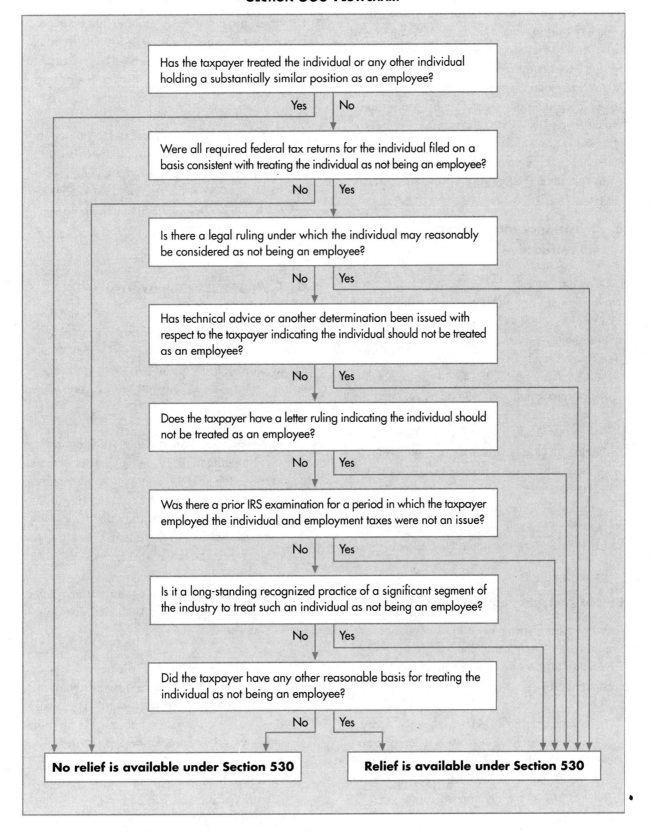

worker with a W-2 Wage and Tax Statement or file employment tax returns for the worker. If your work arrangement is set up this way, the IRS will concede that you have not treated that worker as an employee.

An IRS auditor can easily discover whether you've consistently treated workers performing similar services as ICs by examining your payroll tax returns and similar records. If you fail the consistency requirement, there's nothing you can do to backtrack. Forget about using Section 530.

a. Consistency requirement not retroactive

Luckily, the consistency requirement is not retro-active. You are not prevented from using Section 530 for any period before you treated a worker in a substantially similar position as an employee.

> **EXAMPLE:** Quickie Roofing treats all its applicators as ICs in 1994 and 1995—that is, it does not withhold federal taxes, file employ-ment tax returns or give the workers W-2s. In 1996, Quickie begins treating some applica-tors as employees—that is, it does withhold federal tax from their paychecks and files employment tax returns for the workers. Quickie may still claim Section 530 relief for 1994 and 1995, but not 1996 or after.

b. No switching employees to ICs

One intended consequence of the consistency requirement is that it prevents you from taking advantage of the safe harbor rule if you have converted employees into ICs.

> **EXAMPLE:** From 1978 through 1994, Acme Trucking treated all its drivers as employees. It then switched them all to IC status in 1995. Acme cannot claim the Section 530 safe harbor for its drivers for 1995 or any future year.

c. You can switch ICs to employees

However, the consistency requirement does not prevent you from using Section 530 where you switch ICs to employees. The safe harbor can be used as long as all the workers were ICs during the time before the switch was made.

> **EXAMPLE:** Acme Trucking treated all its driv-ers as ICs from 1978 through 1994. In 1995, it began treating all its drivers as employees. Acme may claim the Section 530 safe harbor for the years before 1995, assuming it meets the other requirements.

d. Changes in company ownership

If you've purchased your company from somebody else, the prior owner's classification practices could prevent you from using Section 530. This is because the consistency requirement applies to both a current hiring firm and prior owners. (Rev. Proc. 78-35.)

> **EXAMPLE:** Joe started Acme Trucking in 1978, treating all of his truckers as employees. In 1990, Joe sold the company to Eve. She treats all the truckers as ICs. If the IRS audits Acme for the years after the sale, Eve cannot claim the Section 530 safe harbor because Joe did not treat the same workers as ICs.

This rule also prevents hiring firms from evading the consistency requirement by reincorporating their businesses.

> **EXAMPLE:** Ace Trucking Inc. treats all its drivers as employees. Ace's owners want to convert all the drivers to IC status. The owners dissolve the corporation and transfer all the assets to a new corporation, Joker Trucking Inc. Joker hires all of Ace's old drivers and classifies them as ICs. Joker Trucking cannot use the Section 530 safe harbor.

A TRAP TO AVOID WHEN BEING AUDITED

If you're audited, watch out for the following trap: An IRS examiner suggests that you file current employment tax returns for workers you've classified as ICs. The examiner tells you you'll save on possible penalties and interest because filing the returns during the audit allows you to avoid a subsequent delinquent filing of employment tax returns if the workers involved are determined to be employees.

Don't do it. If you file the current employment tax return, the IRS will conclude that you treat your ICs as employees. This means you cannot later claim the Section 530 safe harbor. If you have to file a delinquent or amended employment tax return because of an audit, you can still claim Section 530 because such a filing isn't considered treating a worker as an employee.

2. Form 1099s Must Be Timely Filed

You can only raise a Section 530 claim if all 1099s reporting the payments made to the ICs were timely filed. (See Chapter 15, Section C.) Fortunately, there is no consistency requirement for 1099s. You are prevented from claiming Section 530 only for those payments to workers not timely reported on Form 1099. For example, if you filed 1099s for some workers, but not others, you can use the safe harbor for the workers for whom 1099s were filed.

3. Proving a Reasonable Basis for Classification

By far your most difficult task in presenting a strong Section 530 claim is showing that you had a reasonable basis for treating the workers involved as ICs. Reasonable basis is just a fancy way of saying that you must have a good reason for classifying a worker as an IC.

There are several ways to show a reasonable basis:

- a longstanding practice in the industry
- reliance on past court decisions or IRS rulings
- reliance on a past IRS audit, or
- some other reasonable basis for the IC classification.

a. Industry practice

The most common means hiring firms use to establish a reasonable basis for treating a worker as an IC under Section 530 is showing that such treatment is a longstanding recognized practice of a significant segment of the workers' industry. In other words, in this instance, the plea "everybody else does it" may be a valid excuse.

If the IRS questions your categorization of workers, it's up to you to show that a significant segment of the industry treats them as ICs.

However, you don't have to prove that everybody in the country in the same business as you treats workers similar to yours as ICs. You only need to look at the geographic area in which you do business.

> **EXAMPLE:** A gold mine operator in Gila County, Arizona, who treated mine laborers as ICs only had to show that other mine operators in the same county also treated their laborers as ICs to establish that the a significant segment of the industry classified such workers as ICs. As a result, a federal employment tax assessment of over $60,000 was canceled. (*General Investment Corp. v. U.S.*, 823 F.2d 337 (9th Cir. 1987).)

IRS officials have indicated that 80% of an industry constitutes a significant segment—in other words, you would have to prove that eight out of ten businesses in your geographic area treat similar workers as ICs. However, some tax experts claim that as little as 25% might constitute a significant segment. It's doubtful the IRS would agree to such a small number, but a federal court might.

PROVING A RECOGNIZED INDUSTRY PRACTICE

It can be difficult to prove that treating a worker as an IC is a recognized practice of a significant segment of your industry. You can't just testify as to your own experiences. Hard evidence must be presented. This might include:

- results of a survey of similar businesses conducted by the hiring firms, or
- affidavits, or sworn statements, from the other business owners in your industry that they treat the type of workers involved as ICs.

Industry or trade associations can also be very helpful here. They may already have conducted surveys or know of others who have done so. Or they may help you conduct your own survey or find other firms to provide you with affidavits.

Unfortunately, there is a good chance you'll discover that your competitors are unwilling to help you prove your Section 530 claim. The reason is fear. Companies are afraid that if they cooperate, the IRS will target them and they will be audited, too.

The IRS requires that your industry must have been in existence in 1978 when Section 530 was enacted. And the industry practice in treating the workers involved as ICs had to exist in 1978, as well as the years at issue in the IRS audit. (Technical Advice Memo 8749001.) So if you're in a business or industry that didn't exist in 1978—biotechnology could be one example—you won't be able to use the longstanding practice safe harbor.

However, your particular business didn't have to exist in 1978—only the industry. This means that you can rely on the fact that other older firms classified the type of workers involved as ICs in 1978 and later.

> **EXAMPLE:** Acme Trucking began doing business in 1994. Acme treats its drivers as ICs. The IRS audits Acme for the years 1994 and 1995 and claims the drivers should have been classified as employees under the common law test. Acme can use the Section 530 safe harbor if it can show that treating drivers as ICs was a recognized practice of a significant segment of the trucking industry in 1978 and 1994 and 1995. The fact that Acme Trucking itself was not in business in 1978 doesn't matter.

To show the same or similar industries existed since 1978, you must provide the IRS with a statement showing:

- the number of entities that you know work in the industry in the locality involved; the locality must be specified—for example, a city of 500,000 population; and you must also include the source of the information
- the names of entities currently in business in the industry with whom you compete which treat the same class of workers as ICs and the approximate period these entities have done so, and
- the date you began treating the workers involved as ICs.

You must also provide photocopies of any information you obtained from an industry or trade association if you relied upon such an association's direction in treating the workers as ICs.

b. Court decisions or IRS rulings

Another way to establish a reasonable basis for classifying workers as ICs is to show that you relied on past federal court decisions. These are decisions by any federal tax court, federal district court, federal court of appeals or the U.S. Supreme Court holding that workers in similar situations were not employees for federal tax purposes.

You may also use published IRS rulings to show a reasonable basis. These include IRS letter rulings and revenue rulings. You may rely on technical advice given to you by the IRS. This includes a specific letter ruling or determination letter from the IRS. You may not, however, rely on IRS technical advice given to other taxpayers. IRS officials will be most impressed by federal tax court rulings, published IRS rulings and decisions of the federal appeals or circuit courts. Federal district court decisions will not be given as much weight.

The facts involved in such court decisions or IRS rulings do not have to be absolutely identical to your situation. Nor do they necessarily have to involve the particular industry or business in which you're engaged. They just have to be similar enough for you to rely upon them in good faith. You must provide the IRS auditor with a copy of the court decision or ruling you relied upon and explain why it was reasonable for you to do so.

EXAMPLE: A company hired several telephone solicitors to sell periodicals under the company's name, either from the company's office or from their homes. The company made a long distance telephone line available to the solicitors and encouraged them to cover specific territories. The company furnished customer leads, but the solicitors were not required to contact them. On audit, the company claimed that it was entitled to Section 530 relief because it relied upon a published IRS Revenue Ruling.

The ruling provided that a telephone solicitor who called numbers from the telephone directory was an IC for employment tax purposes. The facts involved in the ruling were not identical to the company's situation. In both cases, the solicitors were paid on a commission basis with no minimum guarantee. But the phone solicitor in the ruling worked part-time only from her own home and paid all expenses. She was not furnished with office space or a long distance telephone line. Nevertheless, the IRS concluded the ruling was close enough for the company to have reasonably relied upon it in good faith and Section 530 applied. This meant the company didn't have to pay FICA or FUTA taxes for the ICs for past or any future years. (Technical Advice Memo 8216003.)

Most of the time, you probably won't be able to find a court decision or IRS ruling to rely upon. There are thousands of published IRS rulings, but the vast majority hold that the workers involved were employees. There are not as many federal court rulings on this issue, and the chances of finding a favorable one that you may reasonably rely upon are fairly slim in most cases. However, there are favorable court rulings for some industries—for example, cases involving drywall installers, construction workers and truckers who own their own trucks.

c. Past IRS audits

If your business has been audited by the IRS anytime after 1977, you could be in luck. If, after the audit, you were not assessed back taxes for workers you classified as ICs, the IRS cannot later claim that any of your workers holding similar positions are employees. If it does, you should be able to use the Section 530 safe harbor to avoid having to pay employment tax assessments and penalties for those workers.

The audit need not have focused on worker classification or employment taxes. It is sufficient that the IRS conducted an audit for any purpose. But the audit must have been for your business. An audit of your own personal tax returns doesn't count. And you can't rely upon audits by state and local tax authorities.

> **EXAMPLE:** The AAA Funeral Home was audited by the IRS in 1989. Afterward, AAA was assessed $5,000 for improperly deducting certain expenses. However, during the audit, the IRS examiner did not question the status of AAA's grave diggers who were classified as ICs. AAA paid the $5,000 and the IRS closed the audit. AAA was audited again in 1995. The new examiner claimed that the grave diggers are employees under the IRS common law test.
>
> However, AAA can successfully use the Section 530 safe harbor because their status was not questioned in the 1989 audit. This means AAA cannot be made to pay employment taxes for the grave diggers, even if they're employees under the common law test.

You may rely on a prior audit only if the workers whose status is in question in the current audit hold substantially similar positions as the workers whose IC status was not challenged by the IRS during the previous audit. The term substantially similar is not defined in Section 530. (See Section B1.)

TAX COMPLIANCE CHECKS ARE NOT AUDITS

To avoid giving hiring firms a possible ground for claiming the Section 530 safe harbor, the IRS does not treat some employment tax inquiries as tax audits. Instead, it calls them employment tax compliance checks. The compliance check is similar to an audit in that the IRS examiner interviews the taxpayer, reviews quarterly payroll tax returns, wage and payment statements, payment records, withholding allowance certificates and related documents. Yet the IRS claims that such a check is not an audit, just a compliance check.

A hiring firm cannot use such a check to invoke the Section 530 prior audit safe harbor. You'll receive a letter from the IRS saying as much if it conducts a compliance check of your business. If this happens to you, this is an issue you might have a lawyer raise in a federal cour appeal.

---

d. Other reasonable basis

If you're unable to meet any of the three safe havens discussed above, you're still entitled to Section 530 relief if you can demonstrate, in some other way, a reasonable basis for treating the workers as ICs. Such a reasonable basis might include, for example, proof of reliance upon information from an industry or trade association or similar group that the workers may be classified as ICs.

Most significantly, courts have held that a reasonable basis can include a hiring firm's reasonable, good faith—though possibly mistaken—belief that the workers qualified as ICs under the IRS common law test.

EXAMPLE: A firm that provided specialized temporary registered nurses to hospitals classified the nurses as ICs. The firm thought the classification was correct under the common law right of control test. The IRS disagreed, and claimed that the firm should have classified the nurses as employees. The firm appealed to federal court and the court held that it could use the Section 530 safe harbor because it had reasonably concluded that the nurses qualified as ICs under the IRS common law test. This was enough to provide a reasonable basis for the classification. As a result, the firm didn't have to pay employment taxes for the nurses. (*Critical Care Registered Nursing, Inc. v. U.S.*, 776 F.Supp. 1025 (DC Pa. 1991).)

The common law test is complex and subjective. Many workers fall into a gray area where it is not entirely clear how they should be classified. Review the 20 factors the IRS uses to determine if a worker is a common law employee. (See Chapter 3, Section D.) If a number of these factors point to IC status for the affected workers, you can make a strong case that you reasonably believed they were ICs under the common law test.

As you might expect, the IRS will likely fight tooth and nail against any hiring firm that tries to claim that it had a reasonable basis for treating workers as ICs because it thought they satisfied the common law test. However, it may provide a basis for you to claim the Section 530 safe harbor if no other grounds exist.

If Section 530 Applies

You must notify any affected workers if you obtain Section 530 relief. The workers will then have to pay the employee's share of the FICA tax which you must withhold from their wages.

As mentioned above, the workers must be treated as employees for all federal tax purposes other than payment of employment taxes. The workers will also likely qualify as employees for most other purposes as well. For example, they will be entitled to workers' compensation coverage, unemployment insurance, employee benefits and so forth. ■

IRS Audits

This chapter provides an overview of IRS audits —including the considerable assessments and penalties the IRS can impose on companies that misclassify workers. If a number of workers are misclassified, these assessments can easily put a small company out of business.

Dealing with IRS audits is a very complex subject. This chapter does not cover the entire audit process in detail. For detailed information on handling IRS audits, see *Tax Savvy for Small Business* by Frederick W. Daily (Nolo Press).

A. Why Audits Occur

Whenever you classify a worker as an IC, you become an IRS target. The IRS would prefer all workers to be classified as employees, not ICs. That way, it could collect workers' income and Social Security taxes directly from their employers through payroll withholding.

Because employers must withhold taxes from employees' paychecks, it is far more difficult for them to under-report their income or otherwise evade taxes than it is for ICs who are not subject to withholding. The IRS estimated that, in one recent year, it lost over $17 billion in taxes because workers classified as ICs failed to report and pay taxes on all their income, took excessive business deductions or failed to file tax returns at all. The IRS also claims that about $2 billion of this tax loss came from workers who should have been classified as employees.

To close this tax gap, the IRS has mounted an aggressive nationwide attack on hiring firms that, in its view, incorrectly classify employees as ICs. Whenever the IRS audits any business, one of its top priorities is to determine whether the business has misclassified workers.

If you stay in business long enough, it's likely you'll be audited at least once by the IRS. Some businesses are audited far more often. Repeat audits are especially likely if past audits turned up serious problems. You should always be prepared to defend your worker classification practices to the IRS. At the very least, you want to put yourself in a position where the IRS can impose only the minimum assessments and penalties allowed by law if it determines you have misclassified employees as ICs.

B. Audit Basics

An audit is an examination by the IRS of your business, its tax returns and the records used to create the returns. The worker classification issue can and almost always will be brought up during such scrutiny. In addition, the IRS has assigned hundreds of revenue officers to run special audits with the sole purpose of uncovering worker misclassification by businesses with assets of less than $3 million. In one recent year, the IRS audited 16,000 such businesses and issued fines of $94 million against employers for worker misclassification.

1. Who Gets Audited

There are a number of ways you can be chosen by the IRS for an employment tax audit.

- You may be chosen for a general tax audit by the IRS computer; a small business has about one chance in 35 of being chosen in any year.
- The IRS may receive complaints from disgruntled workers or even business competitors that you are misclassifying workers.
- You may be in an industry that has worker classification practices the IRS is targeting. In past years, the IRS has targeted hair salons, trucking firms, couriers, securities dealers, high technology firms, roofers, temporary employment agencies, nurses' registries, building contractors and manufacturers'

representatives. If you're in a business or industry where classifying workers as ICs is common, the IRS is sure to target it sooner or later.

- The IRS may be notified by a state agency that you have misclassified workers under state law. This most commonly occurs when terminated ICs apply for unemployment compensation and agency officials there determine they should have been classified as employees under state law. (See Chapter 9, Section A.)
- The IRS may conduct a snap inspection of your payroll tax records in which you're given seven days to make your records available for on-site review.
- The IRS may compare the earnings reported on the 1099 Form you gave an IC with the earnings reported on the worker's tax return. If this shows that the worker received all of his or her income from you, the IRS will likely conclude the worker is an employee.
- You may come to the IRS's attention through an audit of an IC who hasn't been paying income or self-employment taxes.

2. Audit Time Limits

As a general rule, the IRS has up to 36 months to audit a tax return after it's filed. Employee payroll taxes are reported on employment tax returns, IRS Form 941. The date of filing these returns determines when the time limit for audits concerning your worker classification practices can begin. Employment tax returns must be filed every three months, but for the purposes of this time limit, such returns are all deemed filed on April 15 of the following year.

EXAMPLE: Acme Sandblasting Corporation files quarterly employment tax returns for its employees in 1995. Acme also has workers it classifies as ICs who were not included in the employment tax returns. Acme's four 1995 employment tax returns are all deemed filed on April 15, 1996. This is the day the 36-month audit time limit starts to run. The IRS will lose the right to audit Acme's employment tax returns for 1995 on April 16, 1999. After that date, the IRS may not question Acme's worker classification practices for 1995.

If you have some workers you classify as employees and you file employment tax returns, the IRS will only be able to conduct audits for the previous three years. These are also known as open years. The IRS usually audits only one or two of these open years.

⚠ Longer Time Limits If You Fail to File

The audit time limit period—called a statute of limitations—starts to run only if you actually file an employment tax return. In other words, years in which you don't file an employment tax return are theoretically open to IRS scrutiny forever. If you've never hired employees, but have hired ICs, there is no time limit on a worker classification audit because you have never filed an employment tax return.

In addition, there is no time limit on IRS audits where you filed a false or fraudulent return with the intent of evading taxes. This won't apply where a worker misclassification was due to an innocent or negligent mistake. But the IRS might invoke the fraud rule if it believes you knew the workers involved were employees and deliberately classified them as ICs to evade payroll taxes. In this event, the IRS may impose extremely harsh penalties. (See Section C2.)

Fortunately, the IRS has a general policy of not going back more than six years in conducting audits, even in cases of fraud or failure to file.

3. What the Auditor Does

As a first step, the IRS auditor will interview you. If your business is very small—a sole proprietorship grossing less than $100,000 per year—the auditor will probably request that you come to the local IRS office.

But if your business is a corporation, partnership or sole proprietorship grossing more than $100,000 per year, the IRS will usually seek to conduct the audit at your place of business. This is also known as a field audit. You're entitled to request that the audit be conducted elsewhere—for example, the IRS office or the office of your attorney or accountant. Explain that your business will be disrupted if the auditor comes there. It is usually a good idea to ward off on-site audits because you don't want an IRS auditor snooping around your business premises.

The auditor will also try to talk to any workers he or she thinks might be misclassified. You can't prevent the auditor from doing this.

The Independent Contractor Questionnaire shows the type of information the auditor will try to obtain. (See Section H.)

IRS auditors have broad powers to inspect your records. To identify workers who may have been misclassified as ICs, IRS auditors often ask to see the following documents for the years being audited:

- copies of all IRS Form 1099s you've issued reporting payments of $600 or more to a worker in a year
- your payroll records and cash disbursement journals
- accounts payable records, and
- copies of all written contracts requiring outside workers to perform services on your behalf.

Among other things, IRS auditors will look for large payments to workers classified as ICs, and try to trace whether payments have been made regularly over a number of years. Both may indicate employee status. (See Chapter 3, Section C.)

4. What You Need to Prove in an Audit

When the IRS audits a business, all people who work there are presumed to be employees. If questions arise, it's up to the business to prove to the IRS that workers classified as ICs really are ICs.

First, you want to convince the auditor that workers you've classified as ICs qualify as ICs under the common law test. (See Chapter 3, Section D.) To do this, you need to show the auditor that the ICs are in business for themselves. Examples of the information and documentation you should provide the auditor include:

- your signed IC agreements with the workers (see Chapter 16)
- documentation provided by the ICs showing that they're in business, such as proof of insurance, business cards and stationery, copies of advertisements, professional licenses and copies of articles of incorporation
- a list of any IC's employees
- a list of the equipment and facilities owned by the workers
- the invoices the ICs submitted for billing purposes
- the names and addresses of other firms the ICs have worked for, preferably at the same time they worked for you, and
- copies of the 1099 forms you filed reporting the payments made to unincorporated ICs to the IRS.

You should already have all this documentation and information in your IC files. (See Chapter 15, Section A.) If you don't have it at hand, obtain it as quickly as possible.

If an auditor claims that workers you've classified as ICs are really employees under the common law test, your next line of defense is Section 530, also known as the employer's safe harbor. If you satisfy the requirements for the safe harbor, you will not be required to pay employment taxes for misclassified workers. (The safe harbor rules are discussed in detail in Chapter 7.)

Basically, to qualify for its protection, you must have:

- filed all required 1099s reporting to the IRS payments made to the workers
- consistently treated all workers holding substantially similar positions as ICs, and
- had a good reason for treating the workers as ICs instead of employees.

For detailed guidance on dealing with IRS auditors, see *Tax Savvy for Small Business* by Frederick W. Daily (Nolo Press).

5. Appealing an Audit

After the audit ends, you will be mailed an IRS examination report. This signals that the IRS considers the audit to be completed. Read the report carefully. If assessments and penalties have been imposed, check to see that they've been calculated correctly. (See Section D.)

a. Informal negotiations

Examination reports are not etched in stone. You can attempt to negotiate with the auditor to have the results changed. However, it's not helpful to simply ask—or beg—the auditor to lower the amount of the assessments. Instead, you need to show the auditor that he or she was mistaken on the legal issues involved. You must show either that:

- the auditor was mistaken in finding that workers failed to qualify as ICs under the common law test, or
- even if the workers didn't qualify as ICs, you're entitled to use the employer's safe harbor.

If you can't get satisfaction from the auditor, you may have more success speaking with the auditor's manager. IRS managers are often more reasonable than field auditors.

b. Administrative appeals

If informal negotiations don't work, you can appeal the examination report. The first level of appeal is usually within the IRS itself to the IRS Appeals Office, a department separate from the audit division. However, the IRS has discretion to deny you the right to an administrative appeal. If this happens, you'll have to go straight to federal court if you wish to appeal.

An IRS appeals officer will handle your administrative appeal. You may be given the opportunity to have a face-to-face meeting, or the entire matter may be handled by phone or mail.

If all your arguments on the legal issues fail, you can try to compromise by making an offer of future compliance. Offer to sign an agreement to treat the affected workers as employees in the future if the IRS will forgo imposing assessments and penalties for past years. Such a proposal has a good chance of being accepted, especially if the IRS fears you might win if you go to court.

If it appears you have a good case, the appeals officer might offer you a compromise. If you have a good chance of winning on appeal, consider carefully before accepting such a compromise. It will save you from having to pay assessments and penalties for past years and save the costs of appealing, but you'll have to treat the affected workers as employees for all future years. This could cost far more than appealing.

c. Federal court appeals

You also have the right to appeal in federal court. You can do this if you are dissatisfied with the outcome in the IRS administrative appeal, or you can forgo the administrative appeal and go straight to court. But before you can appeal in court, you must pay the tax and penalties due and file a claim for refund with the IRS. After the IRS rejects the claim, you can sue for a refund in federal district court or the U.S. Claims Court.

For detailed guidance on IRS appeals, see *Stand Up to the IRS* by Frederick W. Daily (Nolo Press).

You have the right to be represented by a lawyer or CPA in an audit and during the administrative and court appeals process. If you are facing the possibility of having to pay substantial assessments and penalties—over $5,000—it's probably sensible to hire professional help. (See Chapter 17.) An accountant, general business attorney or other small business people in your community may be able to refer you to a good local tax professional.

C. IRS Assessments for Worker Misclassification

The assessments the IRS can impose for worker misclassification vary enormously, depending upon whether the IRS views your misclassification as intentional or unintentional. The most strict penalties, of course, are imposed for intentional misclassification—where you knew the workers were your employees but classified them as ICs anyway to avoid paying payroll taxes. The IRS will likely conclude your misclassification was intentional if you admit you knew the workers were employees or if it should have been clear to any reasonable person that the workers were employees under the common law test. (See Chapter 3, Section D.)

EXAMPLE: Bolo Press, a publisher of sports books, has a six-person production department. Bolo reclassifies its production employees as ICs so it can stop paying payroll taxes for them. After the reclassification, Bolo's owners treat the production workers just the same as when they were classified as employees— they tell the workers what time to come in and leave, closely supervise their work and give them fringe benefits such as health insurance and pension benefits. The production workers work solely for Bolo and make no attempt to market their services elsewhere.

In an audit, the IRS concludes that the workers are employees. IRS auditors would likely conclude that the misclassification was intentional. Bolo clearly knew the production workers were really employees and reclassified them as ICs in disregard of the law simply to avoid paying payroll taxes.

On the other hand, worker misclassification is unintentional if you believed in good faith, though mistakenly in the view of the IRS, that the workers were ICs. This can involve tricky semantics. The common law test for worker classification used by the IRS is complex and difficult to apply and often does not provide a conclusive answer about how to classify a worker. (See Chapter 3, Section D.)

Many workers fall into a gray area where it is unclear how to classify them. If you can show that some of the common law factors indicate IC status, your misclassification should be regarded as unintentional. You should be able to do this in all but the most blatant misclassification cases.

1. Penalties for Unintentional Misclassification

When you hire an IC that is not a corporation, you are normally required to report the payments made to the worker on Form 1099-MISC. (See Chapter 15, Section C.) There are two ranges of assessments the IRS may impose for unintentional worker misclassification: one is imposed where you filed all required 1099s for the workers the IRS claims you misclassified, and the other is imposed where 1099s weren't filed. (IRC 3509.)

a. 1099s filed

If 1099s were filed, you will be required to pay a sum equal to:

- 20% of the FICA taxes (Social Security and Medicare) the employees should have had withheld from their pay—that is, 1.24% of the of the misclassified workers' wages up to the FICA Social Security tax ceiling plus 0.29% of all the workers' wages, plus
- 100% of the FICA taxes you should have paid on the workers' behalf as their employer —that is, 6.2% of the employees' wages up to the Social Security tax ceiling plus 1.45% of all the employees' wages, plus
- 1.5% of all the wages that were paid to the misclassified workers—a penalty for your failure to withhold federal income taxes from the workers' paychecks, plus
- all FUTA taxes (federal unemployment taxes) that should have been paid—the FUTA tax rate is 6.2% of the first $7,000 in employee wages, or .08% of the first $7,000 if the applicable state unemployment tax

was timely paid; if a worker was paid $7,000 or more for a year, this amounts to either $434 or $56.

FICA SOCIAL SECURITY TAX CEILING

FICA taxes actually consist of two separate taxes: a 6.2% Social Security tax and a 1.45% Medicare tax on both the employer and employee. There is a ceiling on the Social Security tax—that is, a salary level beyond which the tax need not be paid. The ceiling increases every year. In 1995, for example, the ceiling was $61,200. In 1996, the tax ceiling is $62,700. However, the Medicare tax must be paid on all the compensation paid to an employee.

You must pay the assessments for your failure to withhold employee FICA and income taxes from misclassified workers' compensation even if the workers paid all these taxes themselves. And these assessments will not be reduced where you can prove the workers paid the taxes. This means that the IRS could end up collecting more tax than would have been due had you classified the workers as employees and paid payroll taxes.

Together, these assessments amount to 16.88% of the compensation you paid each misclassified worker up to the $7,000 FUTA tax ceiling and then 10.68% of compensation up to the FICA Social Security tax ceiling. Any payments to a worker in excess of the Social Security tax ceiling are assessed at a 3.24% rate.

EXAMPLE: The IRS decides that Acme Sand-blasting Corporation unintentionally misclassified five workers as ICs during 1995. Acme paid each worker $20,000 during that year and reported the payments on Form 1099. Based on this $100,000 in payments, the IRS assessment would be $12,850. This is calculated as follows:

20% of employee FICA tax	=	$1,300
100% of employer FICA tax	=	$7,650
1.5% of all employee wages	=	$1,500
6.2% FUTA tax for five workers each paid $20,000	=	$2,170

b. 1099s not filed

If you failed to file Form 1099s, the employee FICA and income tax assessments are doubled. You must pay a sum equal to:

- 40% of the FICA (Social Security and Medicare) taxes the employee should have had withheld—that is, 2.48% of the misclassified workers' wages up to the FICA Social Security tax ceiling plus 0.58% of all the workers' wages, plus
- 100% of the FICA taxes you should have paid on the misclassified workers' behalf as

their employer—that is, 6.2% of the employees' wages up to the Social Security tax ceiling plus 1.45% of all the employees' wages, plus

- 3% of all the wages that were paid to each misclassified worker as a penalty for your failure to withhold federal income taxes from the workers' paychecks, plus
- all FUTA taxes that should have been paid—6.2% or .08% of the first $7,000 in compensation.

EXAMPLE: Recall the example above, in which $12,850 was assessed on $100,000 in payments to five misclassified workers. If, however, you did not file Form 1099 for those workers, you'd have to pay $15,880. This would break down as follows:

40% of employee FICA tax	=	$3,060
100% of employer FICA tax	=	$7,650
3% of all employee wages	=	$3,000
6.2% FUTA tax for five workers each paid $20,000	=	$2,170

2. Penalties for Intentional Misclassification

IRS assessments are far higher if the IRS concludes that you intentionally misclassified as ICs workers you knew to be employees. You will be required to pay out of your own pocket all the FICA tax that you should have withheld from the employees' paychecks. You must pay:

- 100% of the FICA (Social Security and Medicare) taxes the misclassified workers should have had withheld—that is. 7.65% of the employee's wages subject to FICA, plus
- 100% of the FICA taxes you should have paid on the workers' behalf as their employer—that is, 7.65% of the employee's wages subject to FICA, plus
- 20% of all the wages that were paid to the workers to make up for your failure to

withhold federal income taxes from their paychecks, plus

- all FUTA taxes that should have been paid— 6.2% of the first $7,000 in worker compensation or .08% if state unemployment taxes were paid.

Together, these assessments amount to a whopping 41.50% of worker compensation up to the $7,000 FUTA tax ceiling and then 35.3% of payments up to the Social Security tax ceiling.

Comparing these assessments with those that can be imposed for unintentional misclassification is a sobering exercise. As illustrated above, if you paid $100,000 to five workers the IRS claimed you unintentionally misclassified as employees during 1995, the assessments would total $12,850 if you filed 1099s, or $15,880 if you failed to file 1099s. But if the IRS claims you intentionally misclassified the workers, the assessments would total $37,470. This breaks down as follows:

100% of employee FICA tax	=	$7,650
100% of employer FICA tax	=	$7,650
20% of all employee wages	=	$20,000
6.2% FUTA tax for five workers who were each paid $20,000	=	$2,170

a. Offsets for worker income tax payments

The only good thing about the intentional misclassification assessment is that the income tax portion can be reduced if you can prove that the misclassified worker paid his or her income taxes for the years in question. Such a reduction is called an offset or abatement.

The IRS will not help you prove income taxes were paid. IRS examiners will not request that workers provide copies of their income tax returns nor will the IRS give these returns to you. Instead, you need to file IRS Form 4669, Employee Wage Statement. This form states how much tax the worker paid tax on the wages. The

worker must sign the form under penalty of perjury. You must file a Form 4669 for each worker involved along with Form 4670, Request for Relief From Payment of Income Tax Withholding, which is used to summarize and transmit the Form 4669.

 See the Appendix for copies of both Form 4669 and Form 4670.

The IRS examiner has the discretion to accept Forms 4669 and 4670 before the examination is closed and reduce the assessment. Otherwise, you must file them with your IRS service center.

> **EXAMPLE:** The IRS determines that Acme Sandblasting Corporation intentionally misclassified a computer consultant as an IC in 1994. Acme paid the worker $100,000. The IRS assessment is $30,848.40. However, the consultant paid all income taxes due on her compensation. Acme has the consultant sign IRS form 4669 and submits it to the examiner along with Form 4670 before the IRS examination is closed. The examiner wipes out the entire 20% income tax penalty. The assessment is reduced by $20,000.

b. Offsets for worker FICA tax payments

Theoretically, if the misclassified workers paid their FICA taxes, you may also be entitled to an offset of the employee FICA portion of the assessment. However, in practice, this offset is difficult or impossible to obtain because a misclassified worker has a right to claim a refund for all the self-employment taxes he or she paid for the years covered by the audit. If the worker claims the refund, you can't get the offset. Because of this right, the IRS will not give you an employee FICA offset unless the misclassified worker fails to file a claim for a refund of these taxes within the statutory time limit, either two or three years.

INTENTIONAL MISCLASSIFICATION ASSESSMENTS MAY BE LOWER

Oddly, if you are able to get an offset for the income tax portion of an intentional misclassification assessment, the final assessment may be less than that which could be imposed for an unintentional misclassification. (See Section 2a above.) However, you are not allowed to choose which assessment rules will be used. If your misclassification was unintentional, the assessment rules will apply and you will not be entitled to any offsets. Some hiring firms have actually attempted to convince the IRS that a misclassification was intentional so that they could obtain assessment offsets.

D. Penalties for Worker Misclassification

In addition to the assessments discussed above, the IRS has the option of imposing an array of other penalties on hiring firms that misclassify workers.

1. Trust Fund Recovery Penalty

As far as the IRS is concerned, an employer's most important duty is to withhold FICA and income taxes from its employees' paychecks and pay the money to the IRS. Employee FICA and federal income taxes are also known as trust fund taxes because the employer is deemed to hold the withheld funds in trust for the U.S. government. The IRS considers failure to pay trust fund taxes to be a very serious transgression.

The IRS may impose a penalty known as the trust fund recovery penalty, formerly the 100% penalty, against individual employers or other people associated with the business. These are people the IRS deems responsible for failing to withhold employee FICA and federal income taxes and pay the withheld sums to the IRS. Failure to pay payroll taxes is willful if you knew the taxes were due and didn't pay them. The IRS will conclude you have acted willfully if you should have known the workers involved were employees, not ICs. (Internal Revenue Code Sec. 6672.)

The trust fund recovery penalty is also known at the 100% penalty because the amount of the penalty is equal to 100% of the total amount of employee FICA and federal income taxes the employer failed to withhold and pay to the IRS. This can be a staggering sum.

EXAMPLE: The IRS determines that Acme Sandblasting Corporation intentionally misclassified a computer consultant as an IC in 1994. Acme paid the consultant $100,000. The IRS decides to impose the trust fund recovery penalty against Acme. Acme should have withheld and paid to the IRS $7,650 in employee FICA taxes and withheld $25,000 in federal income taxes, for a total of $32,650 in trust fund taxes. The 100% penalty is $32,650.

a. Liability for 100% penalty

If you're a business owner, you'll be personally liable for the 100% penalty—in other words, you will have to pay it out of your own pocket. Business owners include sole proprietors, general partners and corporate officers such as the president, vice president, secretary and treasurer, whether or not they own any stock.

However, the scariest thing about the trust fund recovery penalty is that non-owner employees such as office managers, accountants, bookkeepers and even some clerks may also be held personally liable for it. They may be on the hook if the IRS concludes they willfully prevented the IRS from collecting the unpaid payroll taxes—in other words, they knew the taxes were due and didn't do anything about it. Most vulnerable are those who:

- made the business's financial decisions
- had authority to sign checks
- had the power to decide which bills to pay, and
- signed the business's payroll tax returns, such as the quarterly IRS Form 941.

b. Appealing a penalty

If you are found to be a responsible person by an IRS Revenue Officer, you will be sent a notice and tax bill. You are entitled to appeal the penalty and have a hearing before an IRS Appeals Officer. One basis for an appeal is that you aren't a responsible person. You must file an appeal within 30 days.

 For a detailed discussion of IRS appeals, see *Stand Up to the IRS* by Fred Daily (Nolo Press).

2. Other Penalties

The IRS has the option of imposing many other penalties on hiring firms that misclassify workers. These include:

- A $50 penalty for each W-2 that you failed to file for misclassified workers. The penalty is larger if the failure to file was intentional. (IRC 6721, 6724(d)(1)(A)(iv).)
- A $50 penalty for each W-2 you failed to send a misclassified employee. The penalty is larger if the failure to file was intentional. (IRC 6722, 6724(d)(2)(C).)
- A $50 penalty for each 1099-MISC you failed to file. (IRC 6721.)
- If the IRS determines you intentionally disregarded the rules requiring 1099s to be filed, a penalty equal to the greater of $100 or 10% of the compensation paid the worker can be imposed. (IRC 6721(e)(1).)
- If employment tax returns were not filed, a delinquency penalty of up to 25% of the tax determined to be due. (IRC 6651(a)(1).)

- A penalty for failure to pay taxes of ½% per month on the unpaid taxes for up to 50 months. (IRC 6651(a)(2).)
- For failing to deposit the taxes found to be due, a penalty of up to 15% of the additional tax. (IRC 6656.)
- A penalty for negligently or intentionally disregarding IRS rules and regulations of up to 20% of the underpayment that is due to the negligence. (IRC 6662.)
- A fraud penalty of 75% of the underpayment if the IRS determines that the underpayment is due to fraud; no negligence penalty is imposed in this event. (IRC 6663.)

Generally, the more severe penalties are imposed only where you intentionally misclassified workers.

E. Interest Assessments

The IRS can impose interest on employment tax assessments and penalties. The interest rate is adjusted every three months and compounded daily. It is currently around 8%.

THE BOTTOM LINE: ALL YOU COULD OWE

Factoring in all these assessments, penalties and interest, you can make a rough estimate of what you'll have to pay.

If the IRS determines you unintentionally misclassified a worker for whom you filed all required 1099s, you'll have to pay about 20 cents for every dollar you paid the worker, and 25 cents for every dollar if you didn't file 1099s. But if the IRS finds you misclassification intentional, you'll have to pay about 50 cents for each dollar you paid the worker.

F. Criminal Sanctions

In rare cases where a hiring firm has intentionally misclassified as ICs workers it knew to be employees, the IRS may conduct a criminal investigation and have the U.S. Justice Department prosecute. Criminal fines and even jail time can be imposed if you're convicted of tax fraud.

G. Retirement Plan Audits

If your company has a retirement plan, you should be concerned about IRS retirement plan audits. Retirement plans are not audited as part of an ordinary business or employment tax audit. Instead, the IRS has specially trained revenue agents in every district just for retirement plan audits. This type of audit may derive from a prior business audit or from a review of annual IRS tax reporting Form 5500, which is required for most retirement plans.

Hiring firms with tax qualified retirement plans may have special problems with retirement plan audits where they classify workers as ICs.

1. Tax Qualified Retirement Plans

A tax qualified retirement plan is a retirement plan that covers business owners and employees and that satisfies the requirements of the federal Employee Retirement Income Security Act, or ERISA. That law is enforced by the U.S. Department of Labor, the IRS and the Pension Benefit Guarantee Corporation.

Contributions to a tax qualified retirement plan are tax deductible by the business, as are contributions by participating employees. In addition, income from retirement plan investments is tax free until it is withdrawn by the plan participants.

2. Anti-Discrimination Rules

You must satisfy complex ERISA rules to obtain these tax benefits. The most important are anti-discrimination requirements providing that the principal owners of a business cannot provide benefits only to themselves, corporate officers or only highly paid employees. If there are other employees, many, but not all, must be included in the plan as well. In general, employees don't have to be covered the moment they're hired—but if they're employed long enough and are old enough, you have to bring them into the plan.

ERISA has even more complex rules concerning which workers must be counted under the anti-discrimination rules and how many need to be covered. The anti-discrimination rules are satisfied, for example, if 70% of employees are covered. There are other ways to satisfy the rules that may require that fewer employees be included in the plan.

3. Losing Tax Qualified Status

If the IRS determines that workers you classify as ICs are really employees for ERISA purposes, it's possible that not enough employees will be covered to satisfy the anti-discrimination rules. This can mean that your pension plan will lose its tax qualified status. In this event, all previous tax deductions for benefits or contributions to the plan can be thrown out. Your business can lose the deductions, and the benefit recipients will have to pay taxes on the benefits.

> **EXAMPLE:** Acme Sandblasting Corporation has a tax-qualified retirement plan. Acme has 100 employees and another 100 workers classified as ICs. Seventy of the 100 employees are covered by the pension plan, apparently satisfying the anti-discrimination rules because 70% of workers Acme classifies as employees are covered. However, the IRS determines that the 100 ICs should be classified as employees for ERISA purposes. Acme really has 200 employees and 140 had to be covered. As a result, Acme's retirement plan loses its tax qualified status.

The IRS uses the common law right of control test to determine if workers are employees or ICs for ERISA purposes. If a worker qualifies as an employee for federal payroll tax purposes, he or she is an employee for ERISA purposes as well. (See Chapter 6.)

Get Help

This is an extraordinarily complex area of the law, beyond the competence of most attorneys, let alone lay people. You should discuss this issue with your retirement plan administrator, or seek advice from a retirement plan consultant or an attorney or CPA specializing in this field.

H. IRS Initial Interview Questionnaire

IRS auditors use the following questionnaire for initial interviews of hiring firms. It gives you a good idea what IRS auditors are going to ask you about when they come to your workplace or you go to their office.

Most of the questions concern the 20 common law factors the IRS uses to determine how much control a hiring firm has over a worker. (See Chapter 3.) However, not all of these factors are equally important. (See Chapter 5.) If these factors don't point to IC status, you're going to have big trouble convincing an auditor that a worker is not an employee.

INITIAL INTERVIEW QUESTIONNAIRE

Name of taxpayer: _____

Type of entity: _____

Employer Identification Number (EIN): _____

Names of owners/partners/corporate officers:

_____

_____

_____

_____

_____

Social Security Number (if sole proprietorship): _____

What is product or service? _____

_____

Business history: _____

_____

_____

_____

_____

Filing history: Information returns

Form	Years filed or N/A	Form	Years filed or N/A	Form	Years filed or N/A
941	_____	1040 (Sole Prop.)	_____	W-2	_____
940	_____	1065 (Partnership)	_____	1096/1099	_____
942	_____	1120 (Corporation)	_____	W-9	_____
943	_____	2290	_____	Other	_____

Worker classified: ☐ as employee   ☐ as independent contractor

If independent contractors are employed:

A. What is the worker's job function? _____

_____

B. Why does the firm consider the worker to be an independent contractor? _____

_____

C. Is there a signed work agreement?   ☐ Yes   ☐ No

D. How were the worker's services obtained?   ☐ Want ad   ☐ Bid   ☐ Union   ☐ Other _____

_____

COMMON LAW FACTORS

1. Instructions

   Is the worker required to comply with instructions about: ☐ When to work   ☐ Where to work   ☐ How to work

   Are lunches and breaks controlled? .... Yes ☐   No ☐

   Is the type and use of equipment controlled? .... Yes ☐   No ☐

2. Training

   Given by experienced people? .... Yes ☐   No ☐

   Regular attendance of meetings? .... Yes ☐   No ☐

3. Integration

   Worker's job merged into operation? .... Yes ☐   No ☐

   Worker's job incidental to operation? .... Yes ☐   No ☐

4. Must services be rendered personally or can they be delegated? .... Yes ☐   No ☐

5. Does the worker hire, supervise, and pay assistants? .... Yes ☐   No ☐

6. Is the work relationship: ☐ continuous   ☐ indefinite   ☐ specific period

7. Does the employer set the hours of work? .... Yes ☐   No ☐

   Require the worker to work at certain times? .... Yes ☐   No ☐

8. Is full time required? .... Yes ☐   No ☐

9. Does the employer provide a place to work? .... Yes ☐   No ☐

   If outside salesperson, is a route or territory designated? .... Yes ☐   No ☐

10. Does the employer require certain things be done in a particular order? .... Yes ☐   No ☐

11. Are regular reports, oral or written, required? .... Yes ☐   No ☐

12. Is the method of payment by time worked—by the hour, week or month? .... Yes ☐   No ☐

13. Are business or travel expenses paid? .... Yes ☐   No ☐

14. Who furnishes tools? .... ☐ worker   ☐ employer

    Who furnishes materials? .... ☐ worker   ☐ employer

    Who furnishes supplies? .... ☐ worker   ☐ employer

15. Does the worker have any capital investment or premises other than tools or vehicle? .... Yes ☐   No ☐

16. Does worker take any risk for out of pocket loss? .... Yes ☐   No ☐

17. Does worker work for more than one firm at a time? .... Yes ☐   No ☐

18. Does worker make services available to the public by:

    ☐ Listing in directories?   ☐ Maintaining an office?

    ☐ Advertising?   ☐ Does worker require a license?

    ☐ Using a business name?   ☐ Does employer require worker to have a license?

19. Can the employer discharge the worker even if the terms of the contract are being met? .... Yes ☐   No ☐

20. Can worker terminate before specific job is complete without liability? .... Yes ☐   No ☐

State Payroll Taxes

Employers in all states are required to pay and withhold state payroll taxes for employees. These taxes include:

- state unemployment compensation taxes in all states
- state income tax withholding in most states, and
- state disability taxes in a few states.

State payroll taxes need not be withheld or paid for ICs. Whenever you hire a worker, you must decide whether the worker is an employee or IC under your state's payroll tax laws. This is not a decision to be taken lightly because state payroll tax audits are the most common type of audits hiring firms have to fear.

A. State Unemployment Compensation

Federal law requires that all states provide most types of employees with unemployment compensation, or UC, called unemployment insurance in some states. Employers are required to contribute to a state unemployment insurance fund. Employees make no contributions, except in Alaska, New Jersey, Pennsylvania and Rhode Island where small employee contributions are withheld from

employees' paychecks by their employers. An employee who is laid off or fired for reasons other than serious misconduct is entitled to receive unemployment benefits from the state fund.

Unemployment compensation is only for employees; ICs cannot collect it. Firms that hire ICs don't have to pay unemployment compensation taxes for them. This is one of the significant benefits of classifying workers as ICs, since unemployment compensation taxes typically amount to hundreds of dollars per year for each employee.

THE COST OF UNEMPLOYMENT COMPENSATION INSURANCE

The unemployment tax rate varies from state to state, and depends partly on the age of the hiring firm, the type of industry and how many claims have been filed by a firm's employees. Employers who maintain a stable payroll and file and pay their unemployment taxes on time will generally have a lower unemployment tax rate than employers with high turnovers or large fluctuations in their payroll and those who do not file or pay their taxes on time.

As a general rule, however, the unemployment tax rate is usually somewhere between 2% to 5% of wages—up to the maximum amount of wages that are taxable under the state's unemployment compensation law. The taxable limit in a majority of states ranges from $7,000 to $10,000, but in some states is much higher.

1. Unemployment Compensation Audits

You're more likely to be audited by a state UC auditor than by any other type of government auditor, including the IRS. There are two main reasons for this. First, most states have become very aggressive in auditing hiring firms for UC purposes. The more workers that are classified as ICs for UC purposes, the less money there is for the state's UC fund—and states are increasingly more aggressive about guarding these funds. In addition, state unemployment auditors are often the first to become aware of a firm's worker classification practices because ICs often apply for unemployment compensation when their work for a hiring firm ends.

When a worker classified as an IC files an unemployment compensation application, state unemployment auditors will investigate the hiring firm to determine if the worker was in fact an employee under the state's unemployment compensation law and may be entitled to unemployment benefits. If the state auditors determine the worker should have been classified as an employee, the hiring firm will be required to pay all the unemployment taxes that should have been paid for the worker going back several years—three years is common—plus interest.

In addition, penalties will usually be imposed for the misclassification. Penalties vary from state to state. A 10% penalty is common, but penalties are much higher in some states. For example, if a California employer willfully misclassifies a worker as an IC—that is, classifies the worker as an IC even though the firm knows he or she is an employee—a penalty equal to about 50% of the total compensation paid the worker for the prior three years may be imposed.

Unfortunately for hiring firms, unemployment compensation agencies in a great many states share information with other state agencies and the IRS. For example, they inform other agencies that a worker was misclassified for UC purposes. The IRS and other agencies will likely assume that the worker has been misclassified for their purposes as well and conduct an audit. An unemployment compensation audit may only be the first of many audits: workers' compensation, state income tax

and IRS audits may well follow. Clearly, deciding how to classify a worker for unemployment compensation purposes is a very important decision for any hiring firm.

2. Threshold Requirements for UC Taxes

Before going to the time and trouble of trying to decide whether workers are employees or ICs under your state UC law, first see whether you're required to pay for UC coverage for your employees. In most states, if your payroll is very small, you won't have to pay UC taxes. It will make no difference to you whether a worker is an IC or employee; either way, no UC taxes will be due.

In most states, you must pay state UC taxes for employees if you're paying federal UC taxes, also called FUTA taxes. This means you must pay state UC taxes if:

- you pay $1,500 or more to employees during any calendar quarter—that is, any three-month period beginning with January, or
- in each of 20 different calendar weeks during the year, there was at least a part of the day in which you had an employee to whom you paid $1,500 or more during a calendar quarter; the weeks don't have to be consecutive, nor does it have to be the same employee each week.

But a large number of states have more strict requirements.

Eight states provide the broadest possible UC coverage by requiring employers to pay UC taxes for any employee. These states are Alaska, Colorado, Hawaii, Maryland, Pennsylvania, Rhode Island and Washington.

Nine states have payroll or service requirements that are less than the FUTA requirements. For example, a California employer must pay UC taxes if it pays one or more employees $100 or more per quarter. Other states in this category include Massachusetts, Montana, Nevada, New

Jersey, New York, Oregon, Utah and Wyoming. Contact your state unemployment agency for the exact service and payroll amounts.

B. State UC Classification Tests

Each state has its own unemployment compensation law administered by a state agency, often called the department of labor. Each state's law defines who is and who is not an employee for unemployment compensation purposes. Almost all states fall into one of three categories:

- the common law test
- a three-part ABC test, and
- a modified ABC test.

Find the category for your state on the list below and then read the appropriate discussion in Section B1, B2 or B3. This should give you a general idea of whether a particular worker is an employee or IC for UC purposes. For more detailed information, contact the unemployment compensation agency in your state. Most of these agencies have free information pamphlets. (See Section E for contact details.)

1. The Common Law Test

Many of the most populous states—including California, New York, Texas, Florida and Massachusetts—use the common law test to determine whether a worker is an employee or IC for UC purposes. Under this test, a worker is an employee if the person for whom he or she works has the right to direct and control how the work is performed, both as to the final results, and as to the details of when, where and how the work is to be done.

This is the same test that the IRS uses to determine if a worker is an employee or IC for federal unemployment tax (FUTA) purposes, although not all states use exactly the same 20 factors to measure control as does the IRS. (See Chapter 3, Section D.)

EXAMPLE: Milton, a tilesetter, orally agrees to work full-time at construction sites for ABC Construction, Inc. He performs his tile setting services in the order designated by ABC and according to its specifications. ABC supplies all materials, makes frequent inspections of his work, pays him on an hourly basis and carries workers' compensation insurance for him. Milton can quit at any time and ABC can fire him at any time. Milton is ABC's employee. ABC must pay the applicable state unemployment compensation payroll tax for Milton.

EXAMPLE: Art contracts with ABC Construction to complete the roofing on an ABC housing complex. Art is paid a flat amount for the work. Art is a licensed roofer and provides his own tools, materials and workers to finish the job. He treats his workers as his employees—that is, he withholds and pays federal and state employment taxes for them, provides them with workers' compensation coverage and employee benefits and controls them on the job. Art is required to do the roofing work according to the specifications contained in the contract with ABC. If there is a problem with the roofing work, Art is responsible for doing any repairs. But ABC has no authority over Art or his workers while doing the job. Art is an IC. ABC need not pay unemployment compensation payroll tax for Art.

A written agreement stating that you have no right to control the worker will be helpful, but only if it's true. Written IC agreements should be used as a matter of course. (See Chapter 16.)

2. The ABC Test

About half the states use a statutory test written by their legislatures to determine if a worker is an IC or employee for unemployment compensation purposes. This test is called the ABC test because it contains three parts.

State Tests for Unemployment Compensation

State	Test
Alabama	Common Law
Alaska	ABC
Arizona	Common Law
Arkansas	ABC
California	Common Law
Colorado	Modified ABC (A C)
Connecticut	ABC
Delaware	Common Law
District of Columbia	Common Law
Florida	Common Law
Georgia	ABC
Hawaii	ABC
Idaho	Modified ABC (A C)
Illinois	ABC
Indiana	ABC
Iowa	Common Law
Kansas	Modified ABC (A B)
Kentucky	Common Law
Louisiana	ABC
Maine	ABC
Maryland	ABC
Massachusetts	ABC
Michigan	Other (Economic Reality)
Minnesota	Common Law
Mississippi	Common Law
Missouri	Common Law

State	Test
Montana	Modified ABC (A C)
Nebraska	ABC
Nevada	ABC
New Hampshire	ABC
New Jersey	ABC
New Mexico	ABC
New York	Common Law
North Carolina	Common Law
North Dakota	Common Law
Ohio	ABC
Oklahoma	Modified ABC (A B or A C)
Oregon	Other (8 factors)
Pennsylvania	Modified ABC (A C)
Rhode Island	ABC
South Carolina	Common Law
South Dakota	Modified ABC (A C)
Tennessee	ABC
Texas	Common Law
Utah	Common Law
Vermont	ABC
Virginia	Modified ABC (A B or A C)
Washington	ABC
West Virginia	ABC
Wisconsin	Modified ABC (A C)
Wyoming	ABC

THE STRICTEST TEST AROUND

The full-blown ABC test is the most strict worker classification test. It is possible for a worker to qualify as an IC for IRS and other purposes under the less strict common law test and be an employee under the ABC test for state unemployment compensation purposes. This means that you could classify as worker as an IC for IRS purposes and as an employee for state UC purposes. You wouldn't withhold or pay federal payroll taxes, but would pay state UC taxes.

But this poses practical problems. Paying UC taxes for a worker makes the worker look like your employee. You could attempt to explain to an IRS auditor that your state has an extremely strict ABC test, but the auditor will still likely view payment of state IC taxes for a worker as a strong indicator of employee status. The safest course is to classify a worker who fails the ABC test as an employee for all purposes.

To qualify as an IC for state unemployment compensation purposes, a worker must satisfy all three prongs of the ABC test. You must show that:

- The worker is free from your control or direction in performing the services, both in any oral or written contract of service and in reality. (See Section 2a.)
- The worker's services are either outside your firm's usual course of business, or performed outside of all of your places of business. (See Section 2b.)
- The worker is carrying on an independently established trade, occupation, profession or business. (See Section 2c.)

If any one of the three prongs of the ABC test is not satisfied, the worker will be classified as an employee for unemployment compensation purposes—and you must pay state unemployment compensation taxes for that individual.

a. Control or direction of the work

The first part of the ABC test, prong A, requires that you must not have the right to exercise control or direction over the worker's services. Your control must be limited to accepting or rejecting the results the worker achieves, not how he or she achieves them. This is simply a restatement of the common law right of control test—the test used to determine worker status for IRS and many other purposes. (See Chapter 3, Section D.)

The factors state UC auditors examine to determine if you have the right to control a worker differ somewhat from state to state and are determined by state UC laws, regulations and court rulings. For example, Maryland regulations provide that a worker is considered to be free from a hiring firm's direction or control if the firm does not:

- require the worker to comply with detailed instructions about when, where and how the person is to work
- train the worker
- establish set hours of work
- establish a schedule or routine for the worker, or
- have the power to fire the worker for failing to obey specific instructions. (Md. Regs. Code title 24, Sec. 24.02.01.18(B)(3)(a).)

In Oklahoma, unemployment compensation auditors focus on a slightly different set of factors, including whether the hiring firm:

- provides the worker with tools and equipment
- pays the worker's business expenses
- assumes all financial risks involved with the work
- hires the worker's assistants, and
- obtains and maintains all business, tax and occupational licenses. (Oklahoma Employment Security Commission Rules.)

All of these factors, and most others that state UC auditors use to measure control, are covered in Chapter 3.

b. Outside service

The second, or B prong, of the ABC test focuses on whether the worker's services are outside your normal business. The B prong is satisfied if either:

- the worker's service is outside the usual course of your business operations, or
- the work is performed completely outside your usual places of business.

Part of business operations. State auditors seek to determine whether the worker's services are an integral part of—that is, closely related to—your normal daily business operations. You're likely to exercise control over such workers because they are so important to your business's success or continuation.

EXAMPLE: Jeremy works part-time on the assembly line at the General Widget Corp. Jeremy helps assemble widgets, which is what General Widget is in the business of producing. Jeremy's services are clearly essential to the nature of General Widget's business because it can't produce widgets without people working on the assembly line. Jeremy therefore can't satisfy the part of the B prong requiring work outside the hiring firm's normal course of business.

EXAMPLE: General Widget Corp. hires Jessica, an attorney with her own practice, to defend it in a products liability lawsuit. General Widget is in the business of producing widgets, not defending lawsuits, so Jessica's services are clearly outside General's normal business, satisfying one part of the ABC test.

Work performed outside the business. Even if a worker's services are an integral part of your business operations, you can still satisfy this part of the test if the worker's services are performed outside of all your places of business. In other words, the worker must not work on any of your firm's business premises.

EXAMPLE: General Widget Corp. contracts with Arnie to provide important component parts for its widgets. Arnie builds the components in his own workshop and delivers them to General. Arnie's services are an integral part of General's business operations, but this part of the test is still satisfied because Arnie performs the services at his own business premises.

Some states that use the ABC test take the position that if a hiring firm has no fixed place of business—for example, a sales firm—a worker cannot satisfy the off-premises test if the services are performed at a temporary work site or where customers or prospective customers are located. This can make it impossible for workers for many types of hiring firms to qualify as ICs for unemployment compensation purposes.

EXAMPLE: Sam is a home widget installer. He works for a number of different widget sales companies, including Best Buy Widgets. When Best Buy obtains an order, it tells Sam and he goes to the customer's house to install the widget. He does no widget installing at Best Buy's sales office. Sam cannot meet the off-premises test in most states that use the ABC test because he works at temporary work sites where Best Buy's customers are located—their homes. He would be deemed an employee of Best Buy for unemployment compensation purposes.

c. Independent business or trade

The final, or C prong, of the ABC test requires that the worker be engaged in an independently established trade, occupation, profession or business. This means that the worker's business activity must exist independently of, and apart from, the service relationship with the hiring firm. It must be a stable, lasting enterprise which will survive termination of the relationship with the hiring firm.

Some of the ways you can show that a worker is in an independent business or trade include proof that the worker:

- has a separate office or business location
- maintains a business listing in the telephone directory
- has his or her own equipment needed to perform the services
- employs assistants
- has a financial investment in the business and the ability to incur a loss
- has his or her or liability or workers' compensation insurance
- performs services for more than one unrelated hiring firm at the same time
- is paid by the job rather than by the hour

- possesses all applicable business licenses, and
- files business (Schedule C) federal income tax returns.

3. Modified ABC Tests

Nine states use a modified version of the ABC test. These states do not require that all three prongs of the standard ABC test discussed above be satisfied; they drop one of the three requirements. The following list shows which prongs of the ABC test these states use.

STATES USING A MODIFIED ABC TEST

State	Prongs Used
Colorado	A C
Idaho	A C
Kansas	A B
Montana	A C
Oklahoma	A B or A C
Pennsylvania	A C
South Dakota	A C
Virginia	A B or A C
Wisconsin	A C

Colorado, Idaho, Montana, Pennsylvania, South Dakota and Wisconsin drop the B outside-service prong. In these states, a worker will be considered an IC for unemployment compensation purposes if he or she is not under the direction and control of the hiring firm and is engaged in an independent business and trade.

Kansas drops the C independent-business prong. In Kansas, a worker will be an IC for unemployment purposes if he or she is not under the hiring firm's direction and control and the work is either outside the hiring firm's usual business or is performed outside the firm's business premises.

In Oklahoma and Virginia, a worker qualifies as an IC if either the A B or A C prongs are satisfied—that is, lack of control plus outside service; or lack of control plus independent business.

Obviously, it is somewhat easier to establish that a worker is an IC in these states than in those that require that all three prongs of the ABC test be met.

4. Other Tests—Michigan and Oregon

Two states, Michigan and Oregon, don't use any of the three tests discussed above.

a. Michigan

Michigan uses an "economic reality" test to determine if a worker is an employee or IC. This test focuses on the economic reality of the relationship between worker and hiring firm, rather than exclusively upon the right to control the worker. A worker who is economically dependent upon the hiring firm is the firm's employee. The factors considered are:

- who controls the worker's duties; control by the hiring firm indicates employee status
- how the worker is paid; hourly payment indicates employee status, payment by the project indicates IC status
- whether the hiring firm has the right to fire and discipline the worker; if so, employee status is strongly indicated, and
- whether the performance of the worker's duties are an integral part of the hiring firm's business toward the accomplishment of a common goal. (*Williams v. Cleveland Cliffs Iron Co.*, 476 N.W.2d 414 (1991).)

(See Chapter 3, Section E for more detail on the economic reality test.)

b. Oregon

Oregon has a single test that is used to determine the employment status of Oregon workers for unemployment compensation, workers' compensation and state income tax purposes. Under this test, a worker is an IC only if all the following eight factors are met:

- the worker is free from the hiring firm's direction and control in performing the services, although the firm can specify the desired results
- the worker is responsible for obtaining all applicable business licenses and registrations
- the worker furnishes the tools and equipment needed to perform the services
- the worker has the authority to hire and fire assistants
- payment is made on completion of specific portions of the project or is made on the basis of an annual or periodic retainer and not hourly
- the worker is registered with the state if required by Oregon law
- federal and state income tax returns in the name of the worker or the worker's business (Schedule C) were filed for the previous year if the person worked as an IC the previous year, and
- the worker is engaged in an independently established trade or business. (Oregon Revised Statutes 670.600.)

5. Statutory Employees

Certain types or workers are automatically covered by the unemployment insurance laws of most states. You must pay UC taxes for these workers whether or not they qualify as employees under your state UC law.

Such statutory employees typically include:

- corporate officers
- drivers who distribute food products, beverages or laundry, and
- traveling or city salespeople.

These rules track federal law. Corporate officers, drivers and salespeople are statutory employees for federal unemployment compensation (FUTA) purposes as well. (See Chapter 6, Section A.)

California contractors must pay careful attention to some especially strict unemployment compensation rules. If you hire an unlicensed worker or unlicensed subcontractor to perform work requiring a contractor's license, you're automatically deemed the worker's or subcontractor's employer for all state payroll tax purposes, including unemployment compensation and state income tax. (Cal. Unemployment Ins. Code 621.5, Cal. Labor Code 2750.5.)

EXAMPLE: Tom, a licensed contractor, agrees to do a room addition. Lacking the time to do the job himself, he subcontracts the work out to Bill, who does not have a construction contractor license. Although Bill would easily qualify as an IC under the normal rules, he is considered Tom's employee because he is unlicensed. Tom must pay all applicable California payroll taxes for Bill.

Neither the IRS nor virtually any other state has a rule similar to California's. Bill, in the example above, would be an IC for IRS purposes, and would be an IC in most other states as well.

In addition, California law provides that the author of a work commissioned by another is deemed the employee of the commissioning party for state payroll tax purposes if the work is done under a written agreement specifying that the work is made for hire. (See Chapter 16.)

6. Exemptions From Coverage

Most states exempt certain services from unemployment compensation coverage. This includes services performed by:

- your spouse, minor children or parents (but services by a parent are not exempt in New York)
- licensed real estate brokers who work on commission, and
- real estate salespeople who work on commission.

But the most important exemption from unemployment compensation coverage is for casual labor. Casual labor is a term used by hiring firms to describe temporary or part-time workers. Under the laws of most states, workers performing casual labor are not covered by unemployment compensation if the services are not performed within the hiring firm's course of trade or business.

EXAMPLE: The Leopold and Loeb law firm hires John to paint one of its offices. Painting does not fall within the law firm's trade or business, so John may qualify for the casual labor exemption.

FIGHTING UNEMPLOYMENT COMPENSATION CLAIMS

If a worker you classified as an IC files a claim for unemployment compensation, you don't have to simply accept the worker's assertion that he or she should have been classified as an employee. You have the right to fight the worker's claim, both in administrative proceedings before the state unemployment agency and, if this fails, in state court.

Procedures differ from state to state, but are generally handled in the following way.

First, the worker will file a claim with the state UC agency. You'll be notified in writing of the claim and can file a written objection, usually within seven to 10 days. Be sure to review your state's worker classification test and timely file an objection and explaining why the worker is an IC. Include copies of documentation showing that the worker is in business for himself or herself. You should already have this material in your files. (See Chapter 15, Section A.)

Next, the UC agency will determine if the worker is eligible to receive UC benefits. There's usually no hearing at this stage.

If either you or the worker don't like the UC agency's ruling, you can demand a hearing. This is usually held at the UC agency's office before a hearing officer on the agency's staff, called a referee in many states. You should present your written documentation showing that the worker was an IC, not your employee. You can testify yourself and also present oral testimony from witnesses—for example, supervisors or other people who dealt with the worker. The more relevant persuasive evidence you have, the better off you'll be.

Before the hearing, ask to see the UC agency's complete file on the claim, since it may contain inaccurate statements you'll need to refute.

You're entitled to have an attorney represent you at the hearing. If you can afford it, this is not a bad idea because an adverse ruling may result in audits of other workers you've classified as ICs by the UC agency and other government agencies, including the IRS.

Either side can then appeal the UC hearing officer's ruling to a state administrative agency such as a board of review. You should usually hire a lawyer to do this. Such appeals are usually not successful.

Finally, you can appeal to your state courts. Again, you will probably need the help of a lawyer to do this. Your appeal will likely fail unless you can show the prior rulings were contrary to law or not supported by substantial evidence.

However, the casual labor exemption is lost if the worker performs services for more than 24 days during a calendar quarter—that is, any three-month period beginning with January—or during the previous calendar quarter.

EXAMPLE: John, the painter, works for Leopold and Loeb for 25 days in March and 15 days in April. He doesn't qualify for the casual labor exemption for either the first or second calendar quarter. He worked more than 24 days during the January-February-March calendar quarter, so the exemption is lost for that quarter. In addition, the exemption is lost for the April-May-June calendar quarter because he worked more than 24 days during the previous quarter.

The following states do not have a casual labor exemption: Delaware, Idaho, Illinois, Iowa, Kansas, Maine, Michigan, Missouri, Nevada, New Jersey, New Mexico, New York, Oklahoma, South Dakota, Tennessee, Texas, West Virginia, Wisconsin and Wyoming.

C. State Unemployment Tax Agencies

Below is a list state unemployment tax agencies. If the telephone number listed for your state is a long distance call from your area, check your telephone book under the name of your state's agency to find a local number.

STATE UNEMPLOYMENT TAX AGENCIES

Alabama
Department of Industrial Relations
649 Monroe Street
Montgomery, AL 36131
334-242-8371

Alaska
Employment Security Division
P.O. Box 25509
Juneau, AK 99802-5509
907-465-5937

Arizona
Department of Economic Security
2801 North 33rd Avenue
Phoenix, AZ 85009
602-255-4755

Arkansas
Employment Security Division
P.O. Box 2981
Little Rock, AR 72203
501-682-3253

California
Employment Development
Department, MIC-90
P.O. Box 942880
Sacramento, CA 94280-0001
916-653-1528

Colorado
Department of Labor and
Employment
1515 Arapahoe, Tower 3,
Suite 400
Denver, CO 80202-2117
303-620-4793

Connecticut
Employment Security Division
Labor Department
200 Folley Brook Blvd.
Wethersfield, CT 06109
203-566-2128

Delaware
Department of Labor
Division of Unemployment Insurance
P.O. Box 9029
Newark, DE 19714
302-368-6731

District of Columbia
Department of Employment Services
500 C Street, NW, Room 501,
Washington, DC 20001
202-724-7462

Florida
Department of Labor and
Employment Security
102 Caldwell Building
Tallahassee, FL 32399-0211
904-921-3108

Georgia
Department of Labor
148 International Blvd.
Atlanta, GA 30303
404-656-6225

Hawaii
Department of Labor and Industrial
Relations
800 Punchbowl Street
Honolulu, HI 96813
808-586-8927

Idaho
Department of Employment
317 Main Street
Boise, ID 83735
208-334-6240

Illinois
Bureau of Employment Security
401 South State Street
Chicago, IL 60605
312-793-1916

Indiana
Division of Workforce Development
10 North Senate Avenue
Indianapolis, IN 46204
317-232-7698

Iowa
Department of Job Services
1000 East Grand Avenue
Des Moines, IA 50319
515-281-8200

Kansas
Department of Human Resources
401 Topeka Avenue
Topeka, KS 66603
913-296-5026

Kentucky
Division of Unemployment Insurance
P.O. Box 948
Frankfort, KY 40602
502-564-6838

Louisiana
Office of Employment Security
P.O. Box 98146
Baton Rouge, LA 70804
504-342-2992

Maine
Maine Department of Labor
P.O. Box 309
Augusta, ME 04332-0309
207-287-1239

Maryland
Office of Unemployment Insurance
1100 North Eutaw Street
Baltimore, MD 21201
410-767-2488

Massachusetts
Department of Employment and
Training
19 Staniford Street
Boston, MA 02114
617-727-5054

Michigan
Employment Security Division
7310 Woodward Avenue
Detroit, MI 48202
313-876-5131

Minnesota
Department of Economic Security
390 North Robert Street
St. Paul, MN 55101
612-296-3736

Mississippi
Employment Security Commission
P.O. Box 22781
Jackson, MS 39225-2781
601-961-7755

STATE UNEMPLOYMENT TAX AGENCIES (CONTINUED)

Missouri
Division of Employment Security
Box 59
Jefferson City, MO 65104
314-751-3328

Montana
Unemployment Insurance Division
P.O. Box 1728
Helena, MT 59604
406-444-3686

Nebraska
Division of Employment
Box 94600 State House Station
Lincoln, NE 68509
402-471-9839

Nevada
Department of Employment,
Training, and Rehabilitation
500 East Third Street
Carson City, NV 89713
702-687-4599

New Hampshire
Department of Employment Security
32 South Main Street
Concord, NH 03301
603-224-3311 (Ext. 270)

New Jersey
New Jersey Department of Labor
CN 947
Trenton, NJ 08625-0947
609-292-2810

New Mexico
Employment Security Department
P.O. Box 2281
Albuquerque, NM 87103
505-841-8568

New York
State Department of Labor
State Campus, Building 12
Albany, NY 12240
518-457-4120

North Carolina
Employment Security Commission
P.O. Box 26504
Raleigh, NC 27611
919-733-7395

North Dakota
Job Service of North Dakota
P.O. Box 5507
Bismarck, ND 58502
701-328-2814

Ohio
Bureau of Employment Services
P.O. Box 923
Columbus, OH 43216
614-466-2578

Oklahoma
Employment Security Commission
Will Rogers Memorial Office Building
Oklahoma City, OK 73105
405-557-7135

Oregon
Employment Department
875 Union Street, NE
Salem, OR 97311
503-378-3257

Pennsylvania
Department of Labor and Industry
Labor and Industry Building
7th and Forster Street
Harrisburg, PA 17121
717-787-2097

Rhode Island
Department of Employment & Training
1 01 Friendship Street
Providence, RI 02903
401-277-3688

South Carolina
Employment Security Commission
P.O. Box 995
Columbia, SC 29202
803-737-3070

South Dakota
Department of Employment Security
P.O. Box 4730
Aberdeen, SD 57401
605-626-2312

Tennessee
Department of Employment Security
500 James Robertson Parkway
8th Floor, Volunteer Plaza Building
Nashville, TN 37245-3500
615-741-2346

Texas
Employment Commission
TEC Building
Austin, TX 78778
512-463-2712

Utah
Department of Employment Security
P.O. Box 45288
Salt Lake City, UT 84145
801-536-7755

Vermont
Department of Employment Security
P.O. Box 488
Montpelier, VT 05602
802-828-4242

Virginia
Employment Commission
P.O. Box 1358
Richmond, VA 23211
804-786-1256

Washington
Employment Security Department
P.O. Box 9046
Olympia, WA 98507-9046
206-753-3822

West Virginia
Unemployment Compensation
Division
112 California Avenue
Charleston, WV 25305-0112
304-558-2675

Wisconsin
Department of Industry, Labor, and
Human Relations
P.O. Box 7942–GEF 1
Madison, WI 53702
608-266-3177

Wyoming
Employment Resources Division
P.O. Box 2760
Casper, WY 82606
307-235-3201

D. State Disability Insurance

Employers in all states must provide their employees with workers' compensation insurance to cover work-related injuries. (See Chapter 10.)

Five states also have state disability insurance that provides employees with coverage for injuries or illnesses that are not related to work. These states include: California, Hawaii, New Jersey, New York and Rhode Island. Puerto Rico also has a disability insurance program.

In these states, employees make disability insurance contributions, which are withheld from their paychecks by their employers. Employers must also make contributions in Hawaii, New Jersey and New York.

Except in New York, the disability insurance coverage requirements are the same as for UC insurance. If you pay UC for a worker, you must withhold and pay disability insurance premiums

as well. Disability need not be provided for ICs. The determination whether a worker is an employee or IC is made under the same rules as for state UC insurance. (See Section B.)

In California, New Jersey and Rhode Island, disability insurance is handled by the state unemployment compensation agency. The same employee records are used for UC and disability—and employers submit contribution reports for both taxes at the same time. New York's disability program is administered by the Workers' Compensation Board. In Hawaii, the Temporary Disability Insurance Division of the Department of Labor and Industrial Relations handles disability insurance.

E. State Income Taxes

All states except Alaska, Florida, Nevada, South Dakota, Texas, Washington and Wyoming have income taxation. If you do business in a state that imposes state income taxes, you must withhold the applicable tax from your employees' paychecks and pay it over to the state taxing authority. No state income tax withholding is required for workers who qualify as ICs.

It's very easy to determine whether you need to withhold state income taxes for a worker: if you are withholding federal income taxes, then you must withhold state income taxes as well. Contact your state tax department for the appropriate forms.

But if a worker qualifies as an IC for IRS purposes and no federal income taxes need be withheld, you won't need to withhold state income taxes, either.

A list of state income tax offices follows.

STATE TAX OFFICES

Alabama
Dept. of Revenue
4112 Gordon Persons Bldg.
50 N. Ripley St.
Montgomery, AL 36132
205-242-1175

Alaska
Dept. of Revenue
P.O. Box S
Juneau, AK 99811
907-465-2300

Arizona
Dept. of Revenue
1600 W. Monroe St.
Phoenix, AZ 85007
602-542-3572

Arkansas
Dept. of Revenue
P.O. Box 3278
Little Rock, AR 72203
501-682-2242

California
Employment Development Dept.
10969 Trade Center Drive, Suite 200
Rancho Cordova, CA 95670
916-464-1056

Colorado
Dept. of Revenue
State Capitol Annex
1375 Sherman St.
Denver, CO 80261
303-866-3091

Connecticut
Dept. of Revenue
92 Farmington Ave.
Hartford, CT 06105
203-297-5650 or 203-566-8520

Delaware
Division of Revenue
Carvel State Building
820 N. French St.
Wilmington, DE 19801
302-577-3315

District of Columbia
Dept. of Finance & Revenue
300 Indiana Ave., N.W.
Washington, D.C. 20001
202-727-6460

Florida
Dept. of Revenue
104 Carlton Bldg.
501 Calhoun St.
Tallahassee, FL 32399-0100
904-488-5050

Georgia
Dept. of Revenue
Room 434
Trinity-Washington Bldg.
Atlanta, GA 30334
404-656-4071

Hawaii
Dept. of Taxation
P.O. Box 259
Honolulu, HI 96809
808-548-7650

Idaho
State Tax Commission
700 W. State
Boise, ID 83722
208-334-3660

Illinois
Dept. of Revenue
101 W. Jefferson
Springfield, IL 62794
217-785-2602

Indiana
Dept. of Revenue
100 North Senate,
202 State Office Bldg.
Indianapolis, IN 46204
317-232-2101

Iowa
Dept. of Revenue & Finance
Hoover State Office Bldg.,
E. 13th & Walnut
Des Moines, IA 50319
515-281-3204

Kansas
Dept. of Revenue
State Office Bldg.
Topeka, KS 66612
913-296-3041

Kentucky
Revenue Cabinet
430 Capitol Annex Bldg.
Frankfort, KY 40601
502-564-3226

Louisiana
Dept. of Revenue & Tax
Box 201
330 N. Ardenwood Drive
Baton Rouge, LA 70821
504-925-7680

Maine
Bureau of Taxation
State Office Bldg.
Augusta, ME 04333
207-289-2076

Maryland
State Comptroller
Treasury Bldg.
P.O. Box 466
Annapolis, MD 21404
301-974-3801

Massachusetts
Dept. of Revenue
Saltonstall Bldg.
100 Cambridge St.
Boston, MA 02204
617-727-4201

Michigan
Division of Revenue
Treasury Bldg.
Lansing, MI 48922
517-373-3196

Minnesota
Dept. of Revenue
10 River Park Plaza
St. Paul, MN 55146
612-296-3401 or 612-297-4160

State Tax Offices (continued)

Mississippi
State Tax Commission
P.O. Box 1033
Jackson, MS 39215
601-359-1098

Missouri
Dept. of Revenue
P.O. Box 311
Jefferson City, MO 65105
314-751-4450

Montana
Dept. of Revenue
Mitchell Bldg.
Helena, MT 59620
406-444-2460

Nebraska
Dept. of Revenue
301 Centennial Mall South
P.O. Box 94818
Lincoln, NE 68509
402-471-2971

Nevada
Dept. of Taxation
Capitol Complex
1340 S. Curry St.
Carson City, NV 89710
702-885-4892

New Hampshire
Dept. of Revenue
61 S. Spring St.
P.O. Box 457
Concord, NH 03302
603-271-3400

New Jersey
Div. of Taxation
50 Barrback St., CN 269
Trenton, NJ 08646-0269
609-292-5185

New Mexico
Dept. of Taxation & Revenue
P.O. Box 630
Santa Fe, NM 87509
505-827-0341

New York
Dept. of Taxation & Finance
State Office Bldg. Campus
Albany, NY 12227
518-457-2244

New York City
Commission of Finance
500 Municipal Bldg.
Centre St., Room 500
New York, NY 10007
212-669-4855

North Carolina
Dept. of Revenue
P.O. Box 25000
Raleigh, NC 27640
919-733-7211

North Dakota
Tax Dept.
8th Floor, Capitol Bldg.
Bismarck, ND 58505
701-224-2770

Ohio
Dept. of Taxation
State Office Tower
P.O. Box 530
Columbus, OH 43216
614-466-2166

Oklahoma
State Tax Commission
2501 Lincoln Blvd.
Oklahoma City, OK 73194
405-521-3115

Oregon
Dept. of Revenue
Revenue Bldg.
955 Center St., N.E.
Salem, OR 97310
503-378-3363

Pennsylvania
Dept. of Revenue
1133 Strawberry Square
Harrisburg, PA 17128-1100
717-783-3680

Rhode Island
Div. of Taxation
289 Promenade St.
Providence, RI 02908
401-277-3050

South Carolina
State Tax Commission
Calhoun Office Bldg.
P.O. Box 125
Columbia, SC 29214
803-737-9820

South Dakota
Dept. of Revenue
700 Governor's Dr.
Pierre, SD 57501
605-773-3311

Tennessee
Dept. of Revenue
Andrew Jackson State Office Bldg.
500 Deaderick St.
Nashville, TN 37242
615-741-2461

Texas
Comptroller of Public Accounts
LBJ State Office Bldg., Room 104
111 E. 17th St.
Austin, TX 78774
512-463-4000

Utah
State Tax Commission
Heber M. Wells Office Bldg.
160 East 300 South
Salt Lake City, UT 84134
801-530-4848

Vermont
Dept. of Taxes
Pavilion Office Bldg.
109 State St.
Montpelier, VT 05602
802-828-2505

Virginia
Dept. of Taxation
P.O. Box 6-L
Richmond, VA 23282
804-367-8005

STATE TAX OFFICES (CONTINUED)

Washington
Dept. of Revenue
415 General Administration Bldg.
Washington St. E.
Olympia, WA 98504-0090
206-753-5574

West Virginia
Tax Dept.
Room 300-WV, State Capitol Bldg.
Washington St. East
Charleston, WV 25305
304-558-2501

Wisconsin
Dept. of Revenue
P.O. Box 8933
125 S. Webster St.
Madison, WI 53708
608-266-6466

Wyoming
Dept. of Revenue
Herschler Bldg.
122 W. 25th St.
Cheyenne, WY 82002-0110
307-777-5287

■

Workers' Compensation

This chapter provides an overview of the workers' compensation system. It also explains when you need to provide workers' compensation insurance for workers and what happens if you don't.

A. Basics of the Workers' Compensation System

Each state has its own workers' compensation system that is designed to provide replacement income and medical expenses for employees who suffer work-related injuries or illnesses. Benefits may also extend to the survivors of workers who are killed on the job. To pay for this, employers in all but three states—New Jersey, South Carolina and Texas, where workers' comp is optional—are required to pay for workers' compensation insurance for their employees, either though a state fund or a private insurance company. Employees do not pay for workers' compensation insurance.

Before the first workers' compensation laws were adopted about 80 years ago, an employee injured on the job had only one recourse: sue the employer in court for negligence—a difficult, time-consuming and expensive process. The workers' compensation laws changed this by establishing a no-fault system. Injured employees give up their rights to sue in court. In return, employees are entitled to receive compensation without having to prove that the employer caused the injury. In exchange for paying for workers' compensation insurance, employers are spared from having to defend lawsuits by injured employees and paying out damages.

1. ICs Are Excluded

You generally need not provide workers' compensation for a worker who qualifies as an IC under your state workers' compensation law. (See Section C.) This can result in substantial savings. However, unlike employees who are covered by workers'

comp, ICs can sue you for work-related injuries. (See Section B.)

2. Cost of Coverage

The cost of workers' compensation varies from state to state and depends upon a number of factors including:

- the size of the employer's payroll
- the nature of the industry involved, and
- how many claims have been filed in the past by the employer's employees.

As you might expect, it costs far more to insure employees in hazardous occupations such as construction, than it does to provide coverage for those in relatively safe jobs such as clerical work. It might cost $200 to $300 a year to insure a clerical worker and perhaps ten times as much to insure a roofer or lumberjack.

Depending on the state in which you live, you can obtain workers' comp insurance from a state fund, a private insurer or both. (See Section F.)

B. Injured ICs' Rights to Sue You

An employee who is injured on the job can file a workers' compensation claim and collect benefits from your workers' compensation insurer, but cannot sue you in court except in rare cases where you intended to cause the injury—for example, where you beat up an employee. Workers' comp benefits are set by state law and are usually modest. Employees can obtain reimbursement for medical and rehabilitation expenses and lost income, but can't collect benefits for pain and suffering or mental anguish caused by an injury.

EXAMPLE: Sam, a construction worker for the Acme Building Company, accidentally severs a muscle in his arm while using a power saw on an Acme construction site. Since Sam is an Acme employee, he is covered by Acme's workers' compensation insurance policy.

Sam may file a workers' compensation claim and receive benefits from Acme's workers' comp insurer. Under the law of Sam's state—California—Sam is entitled to receive a maximum of $2,520 to make up for lost income plus medical and rehabilitation expenses. All of this is paid by Acme's workers' comp insurer, not by Acme itself. This is all Sam is entitled to collect. He cannot sue Acme in court for damages arising from his injuries.

Your workers' comp premiums will likely go up if many employees file workers' comp claims, but the premiums will almost certainly be cheaper than defending employee lawsuits.

But an IC who is not covered by workers' comp can sue you for damages for personal injuries if your negligence—that is, carelessness or failure to take proper safety precautions—caused or contributed to the injury. You will also be held responsible for the negligence of your employees.

EXAMPLE: Trish, a self-employed trucker, contracts to haul produce for the Acme Produce Company. Trish is an IC and Acme does not provide her with workers' comp insurance. Trish loses her little finger when an Acme employee negligently drops a load of asparagus on her hand. Since Trish is an IC, she can't collect workers' comp benefits from Acme's insurer, but she can sue Acme in court for negligence. If she can prove Acme' was negligent, Trish can collect damages not only for her lost wages and medical expenses, but for her pain and suffering as well.

These damages could far exceed the modest sums that workers' comp benefits would have provided. Had Trish been Acme's employee, it might have cost Acme several hundred dollars a year to provide workers' comp coverage for her. But since she was an IC, it could cost Acme thousands to defend her lawsuit and pay out damages.

Of course, an IC must actually prove that your negligence or that of your employees caused or contributed to the work-related accident to recover any damages at all. So if you were not negligent, the IC may end up losing a lawsuit or decide not to file one in the first place. In this event, the injured worker might decide to file a workers' comp claim against you claiming that he or she is your employee. A worker who is determined to be your employee will be entitled to workers' comp benefits without having to prove that the work-related injury was due to your negligence.

1. The Need for Liability Insurance

No matter how small your business, if you hire ICs, it is vital that you obtain general liability insurance to protect yourself against personal injury claims by people who are not your employees. A general liability insurer will defend you in court if an IC, customer or any other nonemployee claims you caused or helped cause an injury. The insurer will also pay out damages or settlements up to the policy limits. Such insurance can be cheaper and easier to obtain than workers' comp coverage for employees, so you can still save on insurance premiums by hiring ICs rather than employees.

If you don't have general liability insurance already, contact an insurance broker or agent to obtain a policy.

2. Requiring ICs to Obtain Their Own Coverage

Many hiring firms require workers classified as ICs to obtain workers' comp coverage for themselves. Such coverage is available in most states, even if an IC is running a one-person business.

If you don't do this, your own workers' compensation insurer might require you to cover the IC and pay additional premiums. This is because the IC may claim to be an employee and claim workers' comp benefits from your insurer if he or she is injured on the job. Your workers' comp insurer will audit your payroll and other employment records at least once a year to make sure you're paying the proper premiums.

If you require an IC to be insured, obtain a certificate of insurance from the worker. A certificate of insurance is issued by the workers' comp insurer and is written proof that the IC has a workers' comp policy. Keep it in your files and make it available to your workers' comp insurer when you're audited.

For detailed guidance on dealing with workers' compensation insurance audits, see *Comp Control: The Secrets of Reducing Workers' Compensation Costs*, by Edward J. Priz (Oasis Press).

Even if an IC has his or her own workers' comp insurance, you'll still need to have liability insurance because the IC can sue you in court if he or she is injured due to your negligence. Since you're not the worker's employer, the workers' comp provisions barring lawsuits by injured employees won't apply to you. Injured ICs or their workers' comp insurers may file these lawsuits.

3. Requiring ICs to Provide Coverage for Their Employees

It may seem unfair, but in all states except Alabama, California, Delaware, Iowa, Maine, Rhode Island and West Virginia, you can be required to provide workers' comp benefits for an IC's employees. Under state laws that define statutory employees, an IC's uninsured employees are considered to be your employees for workers' comp purposes if:

- the IC fails to obtain workers' comp insurance for them, and
- the IC's employees perform work that is part of your regular business—that is, work customarily carried out in your business and other similar businesses.

The purpose of these laws is to prevent employers from avoiding paying for workers' comp insurance by subcontracting work out to uninsured ICs.

EXAMPLE: The Diamond Development Company, a residential real estate developer, is building a housing subdivision. It hires Tom, a painting subcontractor, to paint the houses. Tom is an IC who has sole control over the painting work. Tom hires 40 painters to do the work for him. They are all Tom's employees. Tom fails to provide his employee-painters with workers' compensation coverage.

Andy, one of Tom's employees, is injured on the job. Since Tom has no workers' comp insurance, Andy can file a workers' comp claim against Diamond Development, even though he was not Diamond's employee. This is because Andy is Diamond's statutory employee under the state law and house painting is clearly a part of Diamond's regular business of constructing new housing.

Because of these statutory employee rules, it's very important for you to require any IC who uses employees to perform services for you to provide them with workers' comp insurance. Ask to see an insurance certificate establishing that an IC's employees are covered by workers' compensation insurance. In many states you can also call the state workers' comp agency to determine if an IC has coverage for his or her employees. (See Section G for contact details.)

If your own workers' comp insurer audits your company and discovers that you have hired an IC whose employees do not have workers' comp coverage, it will likely classify that worker as your own employee for workers' comp purposes and require you to pay an additional workers' comp premium.

If you are required to provide workers' comp benefits to an IC's employees, you are entitled to seek reimbursement for the cost from the IC. But if the IC has no money or can't be located, this legal right will be useless.

 California Rule for Unlicensed Construction Workers

Under California law, a construction contractor who hires unlicensed subcontractors or construction workers is automatically considered to be their employer for workers' comp purposes. (Calif. Labor Code Sec. 2750.5.) This is so even if the workers are ICs under the usual common law rules. This means the contractor has to provide the workers with workers' comp coverage. The California State License Board determines who must be licensed to perform services in the construction industry in California. If you're not sure whether the work involved requires a license, contact the Board. If a contractor's license is required, ask to see one before hiring a construction subcontractor or worker. Otherwise, you'll have to provide workers' comp coverage.

C. Determining Who Must Be Covered

To determine whether you must provide a worker with workers' comp insurance, a two-step analysis is required.

First, determine if workers' comp coverage is necessary if the worker qualified as an employee under your state workers' comp law. Most states exclude certain types of workers from workers' comp coverage. (See Section D.) You won't have to provide coverage for workers who fall within these exclusions. Some states also don't require coverage unless you have a minimum number of employees.

But if there is no exclusion for the workers involved, you'll have to determine whether they should be classified as employees or ICs under your state's workers' compensation law. If they're employees, you'll have to provide coverage; if they're ICs, you won't. States use different tests to classify workers for workers' comp purposes. (See Section E.)

D. Exclusions From Coverage

Most states exclude certain types of workers from workers' comp coverage. The nature and scope of these exclusions vary somewhat from state to state. Check the workers' compensation law of your state—or ask your workers' comp carrier to do so—to see how these exclusions operate in your state.

1. States With Employee Minimums

The workers' compensation laws of about one-third of the states exclude employers having fewer than a designated number of employees. In other words, if you have fewer than this minimum number of employees, you don't need to obtain workers' comp insurance.

STATE REQUIREMENTS FOR WORKERS' COMPENSATION COVERAGE

State	Employees Required
Alabama	5 or more
Arkansas	3 or more
Florida	3 or more
Michigan	3 or more
Minnesota	5 or more
Mississippi	5 or more
New Mexico	3 or more
North Carolina	3 or more
Pennsylvania	4 or more
Rhode Island	4 or more
Tennessee	5 or more
Virginia	3 or more
Wisconsin	3 or more

2. Casual Labor

Most states exempt casual workers from workers' comp coverage. Who qualifies as a casual worker varies from state to state. In most states, casual labor is for a brief time period and is outside the hiring firm's usual course of business. These states include Alabama, Arizona, California, Colorado, Connecticut, Delaware, Florida, Indiana, Iowa, Minnesota, Montana, Nebraska, Nevada, New Mexico, North Carolina, North Dakota, Oregon, Ohio, Pennsylvania, Rhode Island, South Carolina, South Dakota, Utah, Vermont, Virginia and Wyoming.

EXAMPLE: The Acme Widget Company hires Sue, a caterer, to cater a retirement dinner for Acme's president. Catering is clearly outside Acme's usual course of business: manufacturing widgets. And Sue is hired for a temporary period—to plan a single event. Sue would qualify as a casual laborer under most state laws and would not have to be covered by workers' comp.

This exception is narrow. For example, people hired to do temporary maintenance or repair work would generally not be casual laborers because such work is usually considered part of a firm's normal course of business.

> **EXAMPLE:** A partition broke at a soft drink distributor's place of business, smashing hundreds of bottles. The firm hired two workers for a single day to clean up the bottles. The workers were not casual laborers because such clean-up work was a regular part of a soft drink distributor's business; such breakage was an inherent risk of the business. (*Graham v. Green*, 156 A.2d 241 (1959).)

Some states have more liberal rules. Some exclude from workers' comp coverage all types of work that is not in the hiring firm's usual course of business, whether they're casual or not—that is, temporary or transitory. These states include Georgia, Illinois, Kansas, Louisiana, Maine, Massachusetts, South Dakota, Texas and Wisconsin.

Other states exempt all casual employment, whether or not it is in the usual course of business. These states include Idaho, Maryland, New Jersey and Tennessee.

3. Domestic Workers

Most states also exclude from workers' comp coverage domestic employees who work in private homes. Domestic or household workers include housekeepers, gardeners, babysitters and chauffeurs. (See Chapter 11.)

In some states, the exclusion is subject to a salary cap or time limit. For example, in California, a domestic worker is excluded from workers' comp coverage for any 90-day period only if he or she works fewer than 52 hours or earns less than $100. Other states with salary caps or time limits include Colorado, Connecticut, Hawaii, Iowa,

Kentucky, Maryland, Minnesota, New York, Ohio and Pennsylvania. Contact your state workers' comp agency for details. (See Section G.)

E. Classifying Workers for Workers' Comp Purposes

If none of the exclusions discussed above applies, you must determine whether a worker is an employee or IC under your state's workers' compensation law. If the worker qualifies as an employee, you must provide workers' comp coverage. Each state has its own workers' compensation law with its own definition of who is an employee. However, these state laws follow one of three patterns.

- Most states classify workers for workers' comp purposes using the common law right of control test. (See Section E1.)
- Other states use a relative nature of the work test, either alone or in conjunction with the common law test. (See Section E2.)
- A few states use different classification schemes. (See Section E3.)

Find your state in the chart below and read the applicable discussion. For more detailed information on your state's workers' compensation laws, contact the state workers' compensation agency. (See Section G.)

When reading about your state's law, keep in mind that most state workers' compensation agencies and state courts interpret their workers' compensation laws to require coverage. This is because the workers' compensation laws are designed to help injured workers and it's considered beneficial for society as a whole to have as many workers as possible covered. Generally, if there is any uncertainty as to how a worker should be classified for workers' comp purposes, state workers' comp agencies and courts find that the worker is an employee who should be covered.

STATE TESTS USED TO CLASSIFY WORKERS

State	Test
Alabama	Common law
Alaska	Relative nature of work
Arizona	Common law
Arkansas	Common law
California	Common law and other (economic reality)
Colorado	Common law and relative nature of work
Connecticut	Common law
District of Columbia	Common law
Delaware	Common law
Florida	Common law
Georgia	Common law
Hawaii	Common law and relative nature of work
Idaho	Common law
Illinois	Common law
Indiana	Common law
Iowa	Common law
Kansas	Common law
Kentucky	Common law
Louisiana	Common law
Maine	Common law
Maryland	Common law
Massachusetts	Common law
Michigan	Other (Economic Reality)
Minnesota	Common law and other
Mississippi	Relative nature of work

State	Test
Missouri	Relative nature of work
Montana	Common law
Nebraska	Common law
Nevada	Common law
New Hampshire	Common law
New Jersey	Common law and relative nature of work
New Mexico	Common law
New York	Common law
North Carolina	Common law
North Dakota	Common law and relative nature of work
Ohio	Common law
Oklahoma	Common law
Oregon	Other (8 factors)
Pennsylvania	Common law
Rhode Island	Common law
South Carolina	Common law
South Dakota	Common law
Tennessee	Common law
Texas	Common law
Utah	Common law
Vermont	Common law
Virginia	Common law
Washington	Other (6 factors)
West Virginia	Common law
Wisconsin	Other (9 factors)
Wyoming	Common law

1. Common Law States

A majority of state workers' comp statutes define an employee as one who works for, and under the control of, another person for hire. The right to control the details of the work is the primary test used to determine whether an employment relationship exists. This is the same common law test used by the IRS and many other government agencies. (See Chapter 3, Section D.)

The list of factors used to measure control varies somewhat from state to state. But the goal of the test is the same: to determine whether the hiring firm has the right to direct and control the worker in the way he or she works, both as to the final results, and as to the details of when, where and how the work is to be done.

Many states use a four-factor test to determine if a hiring firm has the right of control. These states ask whether:

- there is direct evidence that the hiring firm has the right to control the performance of the work itself, including how, when and where it is performed
- the hiring firm has the right to discharge the worker and the worker has the right to quit at any time
- the worker is paid by the job or on a time basis—hourly, weekly, monthly, and
- the hiring firm supplies the worker with valuable equipment.

a. Right to control work

The right to control the work is the most important of these considerations. Your state workers' comp agency will consider some or all of the control factors discussed in Chapter 3, Section D. These might include whether:

- the worker is required to comply with instructions about when, where and how the work is to be done
- the worker is provided with training to enable him or her to perform the job in a particular method or manner

- the worker must personally perform the services
- the hiring firm hires, supervises or pays for assistants to help the worker on the job
- there is a continuing relationship between the worker and hiring firm
- the hiring firm sets the work schedules
- the worker is required to work or be available full-time
- the work is performed on the hiring firm's premises
- the hiring firm directs the order or sequence in which the services are performed
- the worker can't realize a profit or loss from the activity
- the worker performs services exclusively for the hiring firm rather than making his or her services available to the general public, and
- the degree of control permitted by a written hiring agreement.

b. Right to discharge

A workers' compensation auditor who discovers that you have the right to fire a worker at any time for any reason, or for no reason at all, will likely stop the audit right there and conclude that the worker is your employee. The right to discharge a worker is very strong evidence of an employment relationship, as is a worker's right to quit at any time without incurring any liability to the hiring firm.

To protect against this snap judgment, you should enter into written agreements with all ICs providing that you can discharge the worker only if he or she breaks the agreement—for example, fails to meet the contract specifications or otherwise fails to perform adequately. Likewise, the agreement should permit the worker to terminate the relationship only if you break the agreement—for example, fail to pay the worker. (See Chapter 16.)

c.   Furnishing equipment

Furnishing equipment to a worker indicates an employment relationship, unless the equipment doesn't cost much or the worker has to use the firm's equipment—for example, where a programmer must work on a hiring firm's computer. (See Chapter 3, Section D.)

d.   Method of payment

Paying a worker by the job indicates that the worker is an IC. Paying by unit of time, such as on an hourly basis, indicates an employment relationship. However, it is customary to pay many types of ICs by the hour—for example, lawyers and accountants. (See Chapter 3, Section D.) For these types of workers, paying by the hour by itself should not result in a finding of employee status.

Payment on a piecework basis is a neutral factor; it doesn't weigh in favor of either IC or employee status.

e.   Applying the common law test

It is far harder to prove that a person is an IC than an employee for workers' comp purposes. Because the states want as many workers as possible to qualify as employees, it is not necessary for all four factors to indicate that there is an employment relationship for a worker to be deemed an employee for workers' comp purposes. Rather, one or two factors are usually sufficient.

EXAMPLE: Joanna, a driver who delivers dry cleaning for Ace Cleaners, designates her own delivery schedules and routes and is otherwise not controlled by Ace. She has a one-year contract with Ace that provides that she cannot be terminated or quit unless there is a material breach of the contract.

However, Ace provides her with a delivery truck and pays her by the hour. These two factors alone are enough to show an employment relationship for workers' comp purposes. The combination of a hiring firm providing a driver with a vehicle and paying by the hour is almost always enough to show employment for workers' comp purposes.

To establish IC status, you will usually have to satisfy all the factors discussed above, with the possible exception of the method of payment.

EXAMPLE: An Oregon country club hired Marcum, an unemployed logger, to prune dead wood from some trees on the golf course. He was injured after a few days on the job and filed a workers' comp claim alleging that he was the club's employee. The court concluded that Marcum was an IC. The court examined all four factors and found that three indicated IC status, the fourth was neutral.

- *Control:* There was no direct evidence of control over Marcum by the club. A club member testified that he simply told Marcum what trees to prune. He did not tell him how to do the work or what hours to work. Marcum hired an assistant and paid him himself. Marcum had no continuing relationship with the club—he had never worked for it before.

- *Right to fire:* The club member who hired Marcum stated that he felt he could terminate Marcum's contract only if he was not properly doing the job.
- *Equipment:* Marcum furnished all his own equipment, including saws and a pickup truck.
- *Method of payment:* Marcum was paid $25 per tree. Such piecework payment indicated neither IC nor employee status. (*Marcum v. State Accident Ins. Fund*, 565 P.2d 399 (1977).)

2. Relative Nature of the Work Test

Most states now use the common law test discussed above. However, there is a growing trend to use a test that makes it more difficult to establish that a worker is an IC rather than an employee: the relative nature of the work test. This test is based on the simple notion that the cost of industrial accidents should be borne by consumers as a part of the cost of a product or service. If a worker's services are a regular part of the cost of producing your product or service, and the worker is not conducting an independent business, this test dictates that you should provide workers' comp insurance for the worker.

On the other hand, you don't need to provide workers' comp if a worker is running an independent business and the worker's services are not a normal everyday part of your business operations—the cost of which you regularly pass along to your customers or clients.

To determine whether a worker is an employee or IC under the relative nature of the work test, ask two questions:

- Is the worker running an independent business?; and
- Are the workers' services a regular part of the cost of your product or service?

If the answer to both questions is yes, the worker is an employee for workers' comp purposes.

Many states—New Jersey, for example—use the relative nature of the work test in conjunction with the common law control test. If a worker's status is unclear under the common law test, these states use the second test. Other states— Alaska, for example—use only the relative nature of the work test.

a. Independent business

If a worker is running an independent business and has the resources to provide his or her own insurance coverage for work-related accidents, it's reasonable not to require the worker's clients or customers to provide such coverage.

It's much easier for highly skilled and well paid workers to qualify as ICs under the test than low-skill low-pay workers. Highly skilled workers are most likely to have their own independent businesses and to earn enough to be financially responsible for their own accidents.

Workers' comp agencies and courts might also examine many of the factors from the common law test. (See Chapter 3, Section D.) A worker is more likely to be viewed as operating an independent business if he or she:

- makes his or her services available to the public—for example, by advertising
- does not work full-time for you
- has multiple clients and income sources, and
- has the right to reject jobs you offer.

b. Part of the cost of your product or service

A worker's services will likely be viewed as a regular part of the cost of your product or service if:

- the worker's services are a regular part of your company's daily business operations
- the work is continuous rather than intermittent, and
- the duration of the work indicates continuous services as opposed to contracting for a particular job.

c. Applying the test

If the relative nature of the work test is used, you are likely to be considered a worker's employer where you subcontract out to the worker portions of your business's regular production or distribution process—for example, obtaining raw materials, trucking, delivery and selling.

In contrast, you're not likely to be viewed as an employer where you hire a worker to perform a single job or project that is not a part of your normal business operations.

> **EXAMPLE:** Ceradsky was killed while operating a milk truck owned by Purcell. Purcell had contracted with a cheese manufacturer to pick up milk from farmers along a specific route and deliver it to the cheese factory. Although Purcell and Ceradsky had been classified as ICs by the cheese company, Ceradsky's survivors applied for workers' compensation benefits from the company. The court held that they were entitled to benefits because both Ceradsky and Purcell were employees of the cheese company under the relative nature of the work test.
>
> The milk hauling was not an independent business, but only an aid to the cheese company's production process. Purcell and Ceradksy hauled milk exclusively for the cheese company six days a week for years. They did not earn enough money from the work to be expected to purchase their own

insurance. In addition, the milk hauling work was a regular and essential part of the company's cheese production process, the costs of which were passed on to cheese consumers. (*Ceradsky v. Mid-America Dairymen, Inc.*, 583 S.W.2d 193 (Mo. App. 1979).)

> **EXAMPLE:** Ostrem suffered an eye injury while installing a diesel engine in a piece of heavy equipment owned by a construction company. He applied for workers' comp benefits from the company and was denied them because he was an IC under the relative nature of the work test. First, the court found that he operated an independent business: he was highly skilled, established his own rate of pay and hours, took out a business license, was generally unsupervised, had multiple clients and made his services available to the public. Second, Ostrem's work was not part of the construction company's regular business. He had been hired to install one engine only and had never worked for the company before. The job should have taken only a few days. He had been hired to complete a single job, not to do regular work of the construction company. (*Ostrem v. Alaska Workmen's Compensation*, 511 P.2d 1061 (Alaska 1973).)

3. Other Tests

A few states have somewhat different tests for determining who qualifies as an employee for workers' comp purposes than the two discussed above. The tests used in Michigan, Minnesota, Oregon, Washington and Wisconsin define who is an employee much more clearly than the common law or relative nature of the work tests. If you're doing business in one of these states, consider yourself fortunate. California is another story, however.

a. California

California uses at least two tests—the common law test (see Section E) and a second economic reality test. If you pass the common law test, the California Workers' Compensation Appeal Board and courts will use the second broader economic reality test to try to find employee status for the workers involved.

Under the California version of the common law control test, a worker is more likely to be viewed as an IC if he or she:

- has the right to control the manner and performance of his or her own work
- has a monetary investment in the work
- controls when the work begins and ends
- supplies tools and instruments needed for the work
- has a license to perform the work
- is paid by the project rather than by unit of time such as hourly payment
- is engaged in a distinct occupation or business
- is highly skilled
- can't quit at any time
- was hired for a temporary and fixed, rather than indefinite, time, and
- believes, along with the hiring firm, that they were involved in IC relationship.

Beginning in 1989, California began using an economic reality test along with the common law test. This is the test used to determine IC and employee status under federal labor laws. (See Chapter 12, Section A.) The economic reality test emphasizes whether the worker functions as an independent business or is economically dependent upon the hiring firm. Under this test, a worker is more likely to be viewed as an IC if:

- the worker has the right to control the manner and performance of his or her own work
- the worker's opportunity for profit or loss depends on his or her managerial skill
- the worker supplies his or her own tools and instruments

- the services rendered require a special skill
- the working relationship is temporary rather than permanent, and
- the services rendered are not an integral part of the hiring firm's business.

(*S.G. Borello & Sons, Inc. v. Dept. of Indus. Relations*, 48 C.3d 341 (1989).)

b. Michigan

Michigan uses an economic reality test to determine a worker's status for both workers' comp and unemployment compensation purposes. (See Chapter 9, Section A.)

c. Minnesota

Minnesota uses the common law test, but has designed special rules for 34 specific occupations that are intended to serve as a safe harbor—that is, workers who come within the rules are deemed ICs. These occupations include: artisans, barbers, bookkeepers and accountants, bulk oil plant operators, collectors, consultants, domestic workers, babysitters, industrial homeworkers, laborers, orchestra musicians, several types of salespeople or manufacturer's representatives, agent drivers, photographers, models, some professional workers, medical doctors providing part-time services to industrial firms, real estate and securities salespeople, registered and practical nurses, unlicensed nurses, taxicab drivers, timber fellers, buckers, skidders and processors, sawmill operators, truck owner-drivers, waste materials haulers, messengers and couriers, variety entertainers, sports officials, jockeys and trainers. (See Minn. R. 5224 and following.)

d. Oregon

Oregon uses an eight-factor statutory test to determine a worker's status for both workers' comp and unemployment compensation purposes. (See Chapter 9, Section A.)

e. Washington

In Washington, a worker is deemed an IC for workers' comp purposes if all the following six conditions are met:

- the worker is free from control while performing the services
- the worker's services are either:
  - ▲ outside the hiring firm's usual course of business, or
  - ▲ performed outside the firm's places of business, or
  - ▲ performed at a workplace for which the worker pays
- the worker is engaged in an independent business, or has a principal place of business that is eligible for a federal income tax business deduction
- the worker is responsible for filing a Schedule C or similar form with the IRS listing the worker's business expenses
- the worker pays all applicable state business taxes, obtains any necessary state registrations and opens an account with the State Department of Revenue
- the worker maintains a separate set of books or records showing all income and expenses of the worker's business.

(Wash. Rev. Code 18.27.)

f. Wisconsin

Under Wisconsin's test, a worker is an IC for workers' comp purposes if the worker satisfies nine conditions. He or she must:

- maintain a separate business with his or her own office, equipment, materials and other facilities
- hold or have applied for a federal employer identification number
- operate or contract to perform specific services or work for specific amounts of money, with the worker controlling the means of performing the services or work

- incur the main expenses related to the service or work that he or she performs under contract
- be responsible for completing the work or services and be liable for failing to complete it
- receive compensation for work or services performed under a contract on a commission, per job or competitive bid basis and not on any other basis—for example, hourly payment
- be able to realize a profit or suffer a loss under the contracts
- have continuing or recurring business liabilities or obligations, and
- have a business set-up in which success or failure depends on the relationship of business receipts to expenditures.

(Wis. Stat. 102.07(8).)

4. Consequences of Misclassifying Workers

You are subject to harsh penalties if you misclassify an employee as an IC for workers' comp purposes and have no workers' compensation insurance.

Most state workers' comp agencies maintain a special fund used to pay benefits to injured employees whose employers failed to insure them. You will be required to reimburse this fund or pay penalties used to replenish it.

In addition, in most states, the injured worker will be entitled to sue you in court for personal injuries. Most states try to make it as easy as possible for injured employees to win such lawsuits by not allowing you to raise legal defenses you might otherwise have, such as that the injury was caused by his or her own carelessness.

You will also be subject to fines imposed by your state workers' compensation agency for your failure to insure. These fines vary widely, ranging from $250 to $5,000 per employee or may be based on the amount of workers' comp premiums that should have been paid. The workers' comp agency may also obtain an injunction—a legal order to stop—preventing you from doing business in the state until you obtain workers' comp insurance.

If you are doing business as a sole proprietor or partnership, you will be personally liable for these damages and fines. And the fact that your business may be a corporation won't necessarily shield you from personal liability. In some states, shareholders of an uninsured corporation may be personally liable for the injuries sustained by the corporation's employees. For example, in California, any shareholder of an illegally uninsured corporation who holds 15% or more of the corporate stock, or at least a 15% interest in the corporation, may be held personally liable for the resulting damages and fines.

Finally, in almost all states, failure to provide employees with workers' compensation insurance is a crime—a misdemeanor or even a felony. An uninsured employer may be criminally prosecuted and fined and, in rare cases, imprisoned for up to one year.

F. Obtaining Coverage

Some states allow an employer to self-insure—a process that typically requires the business to maintain a hefty cash reserve earmarked for workers' comp claims. Usually, this isn't practical for small businesses. Most small business buy insurance through a state fund or from a private insurance carrier.

In the following states, you must purchase coverage from the state fund: Nevada, North Dakota, Ohio, Washington and West Virginia.

In the following states, you have a choice of buying coverage from the state or a private insurance company: Arizona, California, Colorado, Hawaii, Idaho, Maryland, Michigan, Minnesota, Montana, New York, Oklahoma, Oregon, Pennsylvania and Utah.

If private insurance is an option in your state, discuss it with an insurance agent or broker who handles the basic insurance for your business. Often you save money on premiums by coordinating workers' comp coverage with property damage and public liability insurance. A good agent or broker may be able to explain the mechanics of a state fund where that's an option or is required.

For a discussion of other ways employers can reduce workers' compensation costs, see *Comp Control: The Secrets of Reducing Workers' Compensation Costs*, by Edward J. Priz (Oasis Press).

G. State Workers' Compensation Offices

A list of state Workers' Compensation Offices follows.

STATE WORKERS' COMPENSATION OFFICES

Alabama
Workers' Compensation Division
Department of Industrial Relations
Industrial Relations Building
Montgomery, Alabama 36131
205-242-2868

Alaska
Division of Workers' Compensation
Department of Labor
P. O. Box 25512
Juneau, Alaska 99802-5512
907-465-2790

Arizona
Industrial Commission
800 West Washington
P. O. Box 19070
Phoenix, Arizona 85005-9070
602-542-4411

Arkansas
Workers' Compensation Commission
Fourth & Spring Streets
P. O. Box 950
Little Rock, Arkansas 72203
501-682-3930

California
Department of Industrial Relations
Division of Workers' Compensation
455 Golden Gate Ave., Room 5182
San Francisco, California 94102
415-703-3731

Colorado
Division of Workers' Compensation
1515 Arapahoe Street
Denver, Colorado 80202
303-575-8700

Connecticut
Workers' Compensation Commission
1890 Dixwell Ave.
Hamden, Connecticut 06514
203-230-3400

Delaware
Industrial Accident Board
820 North French Street, 6th Floor
Carvel State Office Building
Wilmington, Delaware 19801
302-577-2885

Florida
Division of Workers' Compensation
Department of Labor and Employment Security
301 Forrest Building, 2728 Centerview Dr.
Tallahassee, Florida 32399-0680
904-488-2548

Georgia
Board of Workers' Compensation
South Tower, Suite 1000
One CNN Center
Atlanta, Georgia 30303-2788
404-656-3875

Hawaii
Disability Compensation Division
Department of Labor and Industrial Relations
P. O. Box 3769
Honolulu, Hawaii 96812
808-586-9151

Idaho
Industrial Commission
317 Main Street
Boise, Idaho 83720
208-334-6000

Illinois
Industrial Commission
100 West Randolph Street, Suite 8-200
Chicago, Illinois 60601
312-814-6555

Indiana
Workers' Compensation Board
402 West Washington Street
Room W196
Indianapolis, Indiana 46204
317-232-3808

Iowa
Division of Industrial Services
Department of Employment Services
1000 E. Grand Ave.
Des Moines, Iowa 50319
515-281-5934

Kansas
Division of Workers' Compensation
Department of Human Resources
800 SW Jackson Street, Suite 600
Topeka, Kansas 66612-1227
913-296-4000

STATE WORKERS' COMPENSATION OFFICES (CONTINUED)

Kentucky
Department of Workers' Claims
Perimeter Park West
1270 Louisville Rd., Bldg C
Frankfort, Kentucky 40601
502-564-5550

Louisiana
Department of Labor
Office of Workers' Compensation Administration
P. O. Box 94040
Baton Rouge, Louisiana 70804-9040
504-342-7555

Maine
Workers' Compensation Board
Deering Building
State House Station 27
Augusta, Maine 04333
207-289-3751

Maryland
Workers' Compensation Commission
6 North Liberty Street
Baltimore, Maryland 21201
410-333-4700

Massachusetts
Department of Industrial Accidents
600 Washington Street, 7th Floor
Boston, Massachusetts 02111
617-727-4300

Michigan
Bureau of Workers' Disability Compensation
Department of Labor
201 North Washington Square
P. O. Box 30016
Lansing, Michigan 48909
517-322-1296

Minnesota
Workers' Compensation Division
Department of Labor and Industry
443 Lafayette Road
St. Paul, Minnesota 55155
612-296-6107

Mississippi
Workers' Compensation Commission
428 Lakeland Drive
P. O. Box 5300
Jackson, Mississippi 39296-5300
601-987-4200

Missouri
Division of Workers' Compensation
Department of Labor and Industrial Relations
3315 West Truman Boulevard
P. O. Box 58
Jefferson City, Missouri 65102
314-751-4231

Montana
State Fund Insurance Company
P. O. Box 4759
Helena, Montana 59604-4759
406-444-6518

Employment Relations Division
P. O. Box 8011
Helena, Montana 59604-8011
406-444-6530

Nebraska
Workers' Compensation Court
State House, 12th Floor
P. O. Box 98908
Lincoln, Nebraska 68509-8908
402-471-2568

Nevada
State Industrial System
515 East Musser Street
Carson City, Nevada 89714
702-687-5284

Division of Industrial Relations
400 West King Street
Carson City, Nevada 89710
702-687-3032

New Hampshire
Department of Labor
Division of Workers' Compensation
State Office Park South
95 Pleasant Court
Concord, New Hampshire 03301
603-271-3171

New Jersey
Department of Labor
Division of Workers' Compensation
CN 381
Trenton, New Jersey 08625-0381
609-292-2414

STATE WORKERS' COMPENSATION OFFICES (CONTINUED)

New Mexico
Workers' Compensation Administration
1820 Randolph Road, SE
P. O. Box 27198
Albuquerque, New Mexico 87125-7198
505-841-6000

New York
Workers' Compensation Board
180 Livingston Street
Brooklyn, New York 11248
718-802-6666

North Carolina
Industrial Commission
Dobbs Building
430 North Salisbury Street
Raleigh, North Carolina 27611
919-733-4820

North Dakota
Workers' Compensation Bureau
500 East Front Avenue
Bismark, North Dakota 58504-5684
701-328-3800

Ohio
Bureau of Workers' Compensation
30 West Spring Street
Columbus, Ohio 43266-0581
614-466-2950

Oklahoma
Oklahoma Workers' Compensation Court
1915 N. Stiles
Oklahoma City, Oklahoma 73105
405-557-7600

Oregon
Department of Consumer and Business Services
21 Labor & Industries Bldg
Salem, Oregon 97310
503-378-4100

Pennsylvania
Bureau of Workers' Compensation
Department of Labor and Industry
1171 South Cameron Street, Room 103
Harrisburg, Pennsylvania 17104-2501
717-783-5421

Rhode Island
Department of Labor
Division of Workers' Compensation
610 Manton Avenue
P. O. Box 3500
Providence, Rhode Island 02909
401-457-1800

South Carolina
Workers' Compensation Commission
1612 Marion Street
P. O. Box 1715
Columbia, South Carolina 29202
803-737-5700

South Dakota
Division of Labor and Management
Department of Labor
Kneip Building, Third Floor
700 Governor's Drive
Pierre, South Dakota 57501-2277
605-773-3681

Tennessee
Workers' Compensation Division
Department of Labor
710 James Robertson Parkway
Gateway Plaza, Second Floor
Nashville, Tennessee 37243-0661
615-741-2395

Texas
Workers' Compensation Commission
Southfield Building
4000 South IH 35
Austin, Texas 78704
512-448-7900

Utah
Industrial Commission
P. O. Box 146600
Salt Lake City, Utah 84114-6600
801-530-6800

Vermont
Department of Labor and Industry
National Life Building
Drawer 20
Montpelier, Vermont 05620-3401
802-828-2286

STATE WORKERS' COMPENSATION OFFICES (CONTINUED)

Virginia
Workers' Compensation Commission
1000 DMV Drive
P. O. Box 1794
Richmond, Virginia 23214
804-367-8600

Washington
Department of Labor and Industries
Headquarters Building
7273 Linderson Way, SW, 5th Floor
Olympia, Washington 98504
206-956-4200

West Virginia
Bureau of Employment Programs
Workers' Compensation Division
601 Morris Street
Executive Offices
Charleston, West Virginia 25332-1416
304-558-0475

Wisconsin
Workers' Compensation Division
Department of Industry, Labor and Human Relations
201 East Washington Avenue, Room 161
P. O. Box 7901
Madison, Wisconsin 53707
608-266-1340

Wyoming
Workers' Compensation Division
Department of Employment
122 West 25th Street, 2nd Floor
East Wing, Herschler Building
Cheyenne, Wyoming 82002-0700
307-777-7159

∎

Hiring Household Workers and Family Members

This chapter provides guidance if you have hired, or intend to hire, a person to work in or around your home—or if you hire a parent, spouse or child to work at any location. It explains a host of rules that often make life a little easier for people who hire these types of workers.

A. Household Workers

Household workers include housecleaners, cooks, chauffeurs, housekeepers, nannies, babysitters, gardeners, private nurses, health aides, caretakers and others who work in the home.

1. Federal Payroll Tax Status

Federal payroll taxes include Social Security tax (FICA), federal unemployment taxes (FUTA) and federal income tax withholding (FITW). You don't have to pay or withhold any federal payroll taxes for household workers who are ICs. FICA and FUTA must be paid for employee household workers whose salaries exceed certain amounts. (See Section A2.)

You determine whether a household worker is an IC or employee the same way as for any other worker. That is, you must apply the IRS right of control test. (See Chapter 3, Section D.) Household workers are your employees if you have the right to direct and control the way they do their work, not just the final results they achieve.

Family Members Need Not Be Taxed

Special rules apply when a child, spouse or parent is paid to do domestic work. Usually, no FICA or FUTA taxes are due. (See Section B.)

Household workers qualify as ICs if they are in business for themselves. But the IRS will likely deem household workers to be in business for themselves only if they provide services for several different householders, or at least make their services available to many who might hire them— for example, by advertising. Such workers are more likely to be classified as ICs if they provide their own tools and materials—for example, cleaning or gardening equipment.

But any worker who works solely for you and makes no attempt to obtain other clients or customers will almost surely be viewed as your employee by the IRS. For example, a live-in gardener, housekeeper or child care provider is almost certainly an employee.

> **EXAMPLE:** Nate hires Jane, a neighbor, to come in twice a week and clean his house. She uses Nate's vacuum cleaner and cleaning supplies and does the work according to Nate's specific instructions. Nate is always present to supervise Jane's work and pays her $5 per hour. Nate is the only person for whom Jane performs housecleaning services. Jane is Nate's employee.

EXAMPLE: Laura hires Sam to clean her house twice a week. Sam works full-time as a housecleaner. He has many clients in addition to Laura and advertises his services in the local Yellow Pages. Sam uses his own cleaning tools. Laura pays him a set fee of $50 per week. Sam is an IC.

HOME CHILDCARE PROVIDERS ARE PROBABLY EMPLOYEES

Although there are no IRS or court rulings on the status of home childcare providers, it seems likely that any person you hire to care for your children in your home is your employee. It's hard to believe that even the most callous parent would not insist on having at least the right to control how a babysitter or similar worker cares for his or her children. Undoubtedly, most parents exercise this right. The only exception might be where you obtain such a worker through an agency, and the agency pays and controls the worker. The worker might then be considered to be the agency's employee. (See Section 1a.)

a. Workers obtained through agencies

Generally, household workers obtained through an agency are not your employees if the agency is responsible for who does the work and how it is done. A babysitter you hire through a placement agency to come to your home to care for your child is not your employee if the agency sets and collects the fee, pays the sitter and controls the terms of work—for example, provides the sitter with rules of conduct and requires regular performance reports. The agency is the sitter's employer, not you.

But if you get a babysitter from a list provided by an agency or association that merely provides the list and does not regulate the hours of work, collect the pay or set standards and methods of work, the sitter you hire may be your employee.

EXAMPLE: Anna uses a list provided by a placement agency to hire Bruno to care for her child and do some light housework. Bruno works four days a week in Anna's home. He follows specific instructions from Anna regarding the household and baby care duties. Anna provides cleaning equipment and supplies and pays Bruno directly. Bruno is Anna's employee.

b. Independent contractor agreements

It's wise to have IC household workers sign independent contractor agreements before they start work. The agreement should make clear that the worker is an IC and you have no right to control the means and manner in which the work is performed—only the final results. (See Chapter 16.)

Unfortunately, because many household worker relationships are informal, it may be difficult to get the worker to sign such an agreement. Do the best you can. It may be helpful to point out that such an agreement benefits the worker as well as you because it helps prevent possible disputes by setting forth the worker's duties and your payment obligations.

c. Relief from employment tax liability

If the IRS determines that you misclassified a household employee as an IC, you may be able to avoid paying employment taxes for the worker. A rule called Section 530, or safe harbor, permits you to avoid paying FICA and FUTA taxes for a misclassified worker if you:

- consistently treated all workers holding substantially similar household worker positions as ICs, and
- had a good reason for treating the household workers as ICs instead of employees.

(See Chapter 7, Section A.)

2. Payroll Tax Rules

Even if a household worker qualifies as an employee, you still may not have to pay federal payroll taxes.

A LITTLE HISTORY

Before 1995, people who hired household employees were supposed to pay Social Security (FICA) taxes for any such employee who was paid more than $50 in any three-month period. FICA taxes were due for all but the most temporary household employees.

However, this requirement went largely ignored—both by employers and the IRS—until Zoe Baird, President Clinton's first Attorney General nominee, admitted she had violated it by failing to pay FICA taxes for a full-time nanny and gardener she employed. In the wake of the Nannygate scandals involving Baird and several other presidential nominees, Congress passed the Social Security Domestic Employment Reform Act in 1994. The Act took effect in 1995 and eased tax reporting requirements for many of the estimated two million Americans who owe Social Security and other taxes on household employees.

Under the Social Security Domestic Employment Reform Act, FICA taxes need to be paid for a household worker who qualifies as an employee under the common law test only if the worker is paid $1,000 or more in a year, retroactive to January 1, 1994. The $1,000 limit is adjusted annually to account for inflation. For the exact amount, refer to the current edition of IRS Publication 926, *Household Employer's Tax Guide.* You can obtain a copy by calling the IRS at: 800-TAX-FORM (829-3676) or by calling your local IRS office.

Employers who pay a household worker less than $1,000 a year need not have to file federal tax forms for that worker. But household employees who earn less than $1,000 still must pay their own income, FICA and FUTA taxes unless their overall income is so low that they're not required to file a tax return.

If you do a pay household employee $1,000 or more per year, however, you must comply with a number of federal tax requirements. The following IRS chart summarizes these rules.

FEDERAL TAX REQUIREMENTS FOR HOUSEHOLD WORKERS

Type of Tax	ICs	Employees
FICA	None due	FICA tax is due if you pay cash wages of $1,000 or more during the year. But don't count wages you pay to: • your spouse • your child under age 21 • your parent (but see Section B2a for exception), or • any employee under age 18 (but see Section A2a for exception).
FUTA	None due	FUTA tax is due if you pay cash wages of $1,000 or more in any calendar quarter. But don't count wages you pay to: • your spouse • your child under age 21, or • your parent.
FITW	None due	FITW need not be withheld unless the employee requests it and you agree.

⚠ Refunds to Employers

The Social Security Domestic Employment Reform Act was made retroactively effective for all of 1994. This means that the $1,000 threshold was effective for the entire 1994 year. If you paid Social Security and Medicare taxes on 1994 household employee wages of less than $1,000, you're eligible for a refund. If you haven't done so already, you can obtain your refund by filing Form 843, Claim for Refund and Request for Abatement, with the IRS. See the Appendix for a copy of this form.

a. FICA taxes

If you pay a household employee who is over 18 years of age $1,000 or more in cash wages in any year, you must withhold FICA taxes from the employee's earnings and make a matching contribution. Currently, the employer and employee must each pay an amount equal to 7.65% of the employee's wages to the IRS.

There is an exemption from FICA taxes for household employees who were under 18 any time during the calendar year and for whom household service is not a primary occupation. But FICA must be paid if domestic service is a teenager's principal employment. In other words, FICA taxes are not due if a teenager works occasionally to earn extra money and not to earn a living. FICA must be paid, however, if a teenager does household work to earn a living. If a teenager is a student, providing household services is not considered to be his or her principal occupation.

EXAMPLE: The Bartons hire Eve, a 17-year-old high school student, to babysit their children two or three times a month. The Bartons need not pay FICA for Eve even if they pay her $1,000 or more during the year.

EXAMPLE: The Smiths hire Jane to provide childcare services in their home. Jane is a 17-year-old single mother who left school and works as a childcare giver to support her family. This is clearly her principal occupation. The Smiths must pay FICA for Jane if they pay her $1,000 or more during the year.

There is also a special exemption for family members. (See Section B.)

b. FUTA taxes

If you pay a household employee $1,000 or more in cash wages during any calendar quarter—that is, any three-month period beginning with January —you must also pay FUTA taxes. The rate varies from state to state depending on the amount of state unemployment taxes, but is usually 0.8% of the first $7,000 of annual wages paid to an employee, or $56 per year.

⚠ Beware of Changing State Laws

Most states have already amended—or are expected to amend—their unemployment taxation laws to parallel the federal rule. Check with your state labor department to find out the current requirements in your state. (See Chapter 12, Section F.)

c. FITW taxes

Federal income taxes need not be withheld from a household employee's wages unless the employee requests it and the employer agrees. The employer does not have to agree. The same rule is followed under most state income tax laws.

It's unlikely that a worker would make such a request since most workers prefer not having tax withheld from their paychecks. But if a worker does ask you to withhold income tax, it's probably not in your interest to agree since it will create extra bookkeeping headaches for you.

d. Tax filing and reporting requirements

The Social Security Domestic Employment Reform Act simplified tax filing and reporting requirements for employers of household workers. For 1995 through 1997, you simply report FICA and FUTA taxes due for household employees on a separate schedule, called Schedule H, attached to your annual personal tax return, IRS form 1040, and pay the taxes once when you file your return. No quarterly tax payments are required. Schedule H is included in the Form 1040 package the IRS sends you each year.

Starting in 1998, however, FICA and FUTA taxes for household employees must be prepaid four times a year.

For detailed guidance, refer to IRS Publication 926, *Household Employer's Tax Guide.* You can obtain a copy by calling the IRS at: 800-TAX-FORM (829-3676) or by calling your local IRS office.

3. Insurance for Injuries to Household Workers

Household workers can become injured on the job. For example, a babysitter could slip on a toy carelessly discarded by your child and suffer a back injury. After the sitter finishes yelling at your child, he or she will undoubtedly look to you to pay the medical and other expenses caused by the job-related accident.

You could be liable for such injuries. For example, you'll normally be liable for a work-related injury to a household worker that is caused by your or family members' negligence or unsafe conditions in your home. But, even if you're not liable, you could still be sued by an injured household worker and have to hire an attorney and pay other legal expenses.

Paying for these expenses out of your own pocket could prove ruinous. You should have insurance to cover them. This normally takes the form of a homeowner's insurance policy that also provides workers' compensation coverage for injuries to household employees.

a. Coverage for household ICs

If you own your home, you probably already have a homeowner's insurance policy since all lenders require them. Homeowner's policies contain liability coverage that insures you if a household worker who is an IC sues you for bodily injury or property damage occurring at your home. The homeowner's insurer will pay the costs of defending such a lawsuit and pay any damages up to the policy limits. It will also pay the injured person's medical expenses.

b. Coverage for household employees

Injuries to household employees may not be covered by your homeowner's policy. Such policies typically exclude coverage for injuries to employees. Instead, you have to purchase workers' compensation insurance. This is the type of insurance that employers normally obtain to cover injuries to their employees. (See Chapter 10.)

If you only use ICs and never hire a household employee, you don't need workers' compensation insurance. Unfortunately, it can be difficult to know for sure whether a worker is an employee or IC for workers' compensation purposes. States use different tests to classify workers for this purpose. These rules can be complex and difficult to apply. (See Chapter 10, Section E.) Don't gamble that a household worker is an IC. Your homeowner's insurer may disagree with you and claim that the worker is your employee. It will then deny coverage to an injured worker under the bodily injury and medical payment provisions of your policy.

You can usually obtain workers' compensation coverage for household employees from your homeowner's insurer. Your homeowner's policy may already include this coverage. Or you may have to specifically ask for it and pay extra. Check your policy or ask your insurance agent about it. If your policy doesn't already include this coverage, you'll need to purchase a rider or endorsement covering household employees.

c. Renters

If you're a renter, you should obtain a renter's policy with this same coverage. Don't assume you'll be covered by your landlord's insurance.

4. Federal Minimum Wage and Overtime Regulations

The federal Fair Labor Standards Act (FLSA) requires most types of employees to be paid at least the federal minimum wage and time-and-a-half for overtime. The FLSA is enforced by the Department of Labor, which may impose fines against employers who violate the FLSA.

You may be surprised to discover that the FLSA applies to household employees if they:

- receive at least $50 in cash wages in a calendar quarter from their employers, or
- work a total of more than 8 hours a week for one or more employers.

These federal wage and overtime regulations apply only to household employees, not ICs.

Unfortunately, it can be hard to know for sure whether a household worker is an employee or IC under the FLSA. (See the discussion below.) If you're not sure whether a household worker is an employee or IC, the safest course is to assume he or she is an employee and obey the minimum wage and overtime rules. (See Section 4a below.) These rules do not place a very great financial burden on you.

CLASSIFYING WORKERS UNDER THE FLSA

The Department of Labor uses an economic reality test to determine a worker's status for FLSA purposes. (See Chapter 3, Section E.) To qualify as an IC, a household worker will generally have to provide services for several different households simultaneously and be able to show some opportunity for profit or loss. Profit or loss can be shown where a worker earns a set fee instead of an hourly wage, or where a worker has business expenses that could exceed business income—for example, salaries for assistants or equipment costs.

Of course, you cannot closely supervise the work of a household worker and expect him or her to qualify as an IC. Instead, your control must be limited to accepting or rejecting the worker's final results. For example, you can tell a gardener to mow your lawn and rake leaves, but you can't supervise how he or she does the work. This lack of supervision is impractical for many types of household workers, such as most childcare providers.

Any worker who works solely for you and makes no attempt to obtain other clients or customers will almost surely be viewed as your employee by the Department of Labor. For example, a live-in housekeeper or child care provider is almost certainly an employee.

a. Minimum wage laws

The federal minimum wage is currently $4.25 per hour. However, if your state has established a higher minimum wage, you must pay that amount. In New Jersey, for example, the minimum wage is $5.05 per hour. Other states with minimum wages higher than the federal rate include Alaska, Connecticut, District of Columbia, Hawaii, Iowa, Oregon, Rhode Island and Washington. Check with your state labor department to find out what the current minimum wage is in your state. (See Chapter 12, Section F.) In the few states that have a minimum wage lower than the federal rate, the federal rate controls.

You must pay the minimum wage to any nonexempt domestic employee who:

- earns at least $50 in wages from one employer in any calendar quarter, or
- works at least eight hours a week for one or more employers.

If a household employee works less than eight hours a week for you, but works for others as well, you'll have to find out how many hours he or she works for other employers.

Casual babysitters and people who help care for people who can't care for themselves are exempt from federal minimum wage requirements if less than 20% of their hours are spent on general household work. But this exemption does not apply to trained personnel whose vocation is babysitting or caring for others—for example, registered and practical nurses.

The Department of Labor defines a casual babysitter as one who cares for others' children for less than 20 hours per week for all the people he or she works for together. The casual baby-sitter exemption also applies to a sitter who accompanies your family on vacation, provided that the vacation doesn't exceed six weeks.

You must pay a household employee the minimum wage regardless of whether payment is made by the hour or with a regular salary. You must pay minimum wage for each hour worked, including all hours an employee must be on duty at your home or at any other prescribed workplace, such as a vacation house. However, you are permitted a credit for the value of room and board you provide to a household employee.

HOW ROOM AND BOARD FIGURE INTO MINIMUM WAGE

Under the FLSA, employers may take a credit against minimum wage requirements for the reasonable cost or fair value of food and lodging or other facilities customarily furnished to an employee. But an employer may take this credit only when the employee voluntarily agrees to the arrangement.

Federal and state regulations define appropriate meal and lodging credits. In California, for example, when credit for lodging is used to meet part of the employer's minimum wage obligation, no more than $20 per week may be credited for a room occupied by one person.

---

b. Compensation for overtime

Most household employees must be paid overtime at the rate of one and one-half times their regular wage rate for all hours worked beyond a 40-hour workweek. In computing overtime pay, you must treat each workweek separately—that is, you can't average hours over two or more weeks.

You do not have to pay overtime to an au pair, housekeeper or other household employee who lives in your home. You must, however, pay the minimum wage for each hour worked.

Overtime is also not required for people who help care for people who can't care for themselves.

5. Immigration Requirements

Many household workers in the United States are immigrants. Many work illegally—that is, they are not U.S. citizens and don't have a green card or other documentation of their legal status. The Immigration and Naturalization Service (INS) is cracking down on people who illegally hire household employees.

All employers, including those who hire most types of household employees, are required to verify that the employee is either a U.S. citizen or national, or a legal alien authorized to work in the United States.

You are not required to verify citizenship when you hire an IC. The INS uses the common law right of control test to determine whether a worker is an employee or IC for immigration purposes. (See Chapter 3, Section D.) A worker who qualifies as an IC for tax purposes will likely be an IC for immigration purposes as well. (See Chapter 5, Section A.)

Verification is also not required for employees who work in your home on only a sporadic basis —for example, a babysitter you hire now and then who sits for a few hours. Nor is verification necessary for employees of domestic agencies— for example, a housekeeper you hire from an agency where the worker is the agency's employee and you pay the agency, not the worker directly. Finally, the verification requirements don't apply to any employees hired before November 7, 1986.

Although you are not required to verify the immigration status of ICs or others coming within these exceptions, it is still illegal for you to hire any worker who you know to be an illegal alien. The INS can impose a fine up to $2,000 for the first offense.

If you want to help a household worker become legal, see *How to Get a Green Card*, by Loida Nicolas Lewis and Len T. Madlansacay (Nolo Press). Also, contact the INS about any federal programs or special visas for nannies or au pairs that are available from time to time.

B. Family Members as Workers

Family members—children, spouses, parents— work with and for each other all the time, especially if they're running a small business. You never have to pay payroll taxes for family members who are independent contractors. But, even if a family member qualifies as your employee, federal and state rules may exempt you from having to pay such taxes.

1. Classifying Family Member Workers

If a family member qualifies as an IC under the IRS's version of the common law right of control test, then you don't have to pay any federal payroll taxes: Social Security taxes (FICA), federal unemployment taxes (FUTA) or federal income tax withholding (FITW). Family members are ICs if you lack the right to direct and control the way they do their work, and your control is limited to accepting or rejecting the final results they achieve.

> **EXAMPLE:** Bill, a 17-year-old, mows lawns for extra money. His customers include his own father, Jack, and several neighbors. Bill owns his own lawn mower, keeps all the money he makes and does not work under the direction and control of his father or any of his other customers. Bill is an IC. Neither Bill's father nor any of Bill's other customers need pay employment taxes of withhold federal income tax for Bill.

> **EXAMPLE:** Mary works in her father's drugstore. She is paid a regular salary and is treated just like any other drugstore employee. Mary is her father's employee.

(How to determine whether a worker qualifies as an IC or employee for federal payroll tax purposes is discussed in detail in Chapters 4 and 6.)

2. Federal Payroll Tax Rules

Even if a child, spouse or parent qualifies as an employee, you may not have to pay employment (FICA and FUTA) taxes. The rules differ depending upon who's employing which worker and why they're doing it.

a. Children employed by parents

A parent need not pay FUTA taxes for services performed by a child who is under 21 years old. This is so regardless of the type of work the child does.

FICA taxes need not be paid for a child under 18 who works for a parent in a trade or business, or a partnership in which each partner is a parent of the child. If the services are for work other than a trade or business—such as domestic work in the parents' home—they are not subject to FICA taxes until the child reaches 21.

> **EXAMPLE:** Lisa, a 16-year-old, works in a bakery owned by her mother and operated as a sole proprietorship. Although Lisa is an employee under the IRS test, her mother need not pay FUTA for Lisa until she reaches 21 and need not pay FICA taxes until she reaches 18.

However, these rules do not apply—and FICA and FUTA must be paid—if a child works for:

- a corporation, even if it is controlled by the child's parent
- a partnership, even if the child's parent is a partner, unless each partner is a parent of the child, or
- an estate, even if it is the estate of a deceased parent.

> **EXAMPLE:** Ron works in a bicycle repair shop that is half owned by his mother and half owned by her partner, Ralph, who is no relation to the family. FICA and FUTA taxes must be paid for Ron because he is working for a partnership and not all the partners are his parents.

If a child is paid regular cash wages as an employee in a parent's trade or business, they may be subject to federal income tax withholding regardless of the child's age.

b. One spouse employed by another

If one spouse pays another wages to work in a trade or business, the payments are subject to FICA taxes and federal income tax withholding, but not to FUTA taxes.

EXAMPLE: Kay's husband Simon is a lawyer with his own practice. Kay works as his secretary and is paid $1,500 per month. Simon must pay the employer's share of FICA taxes for Kay and withhold employee FICA and federal income taxes from her pay.

However, neither FICA nor FUTA need be paid if the spouse performs services in other than a trade or business—for example, domestic service in the home.

EXAMPLE: Jill is a medical doctor with a busy practice. Her husband Bob stays home and takes care of the house and children. Jill gives Bob $1,000 a month as walking around money. These payments are not subject to any federal payroll taxes—FICA, FUTA or FITW.

But these rules do not apply—and FICA, FUTA and FITW must all be paid—if a spouse works for:

- a corporation, even if it is controlled by the individual's spouse
- a partnership, even if the individual's spouse is a partner, or
- an estate, even if it is the estate of a deceased spouse.

EXAMPLE: Laura's husband Rob works as a draftsperson in Laura's architectural firm. The firm is set up as a corporation solely owned and controlled by Laura. The corporation must pay FICA, FUTA and FITW for Rob.

c. Parent employed by child

The wages of a parent employed by a son or daughter in a trade or business are subject to income tax withholding and FICA taxes.

EXAMPLE: Don owns and operates a restaurant and employs Art, his father, as a part-time waiter. Since the restaurant is a business, Don must pay the employer's share of FICA taxes for Art and withhold employee FICA and federal income taxes from his pay

FICA taxes do not have to be paid if the parent's services are not for a trade or business—for example, domestic services in the home. However, this rule is subject to one exception. Wages for domestic services by a parent for a child are subject to FICA taxes if:

- the parent cares for a child under 18 who lives with children of his or her own, or who requires adult supervision for at least four continuous weeks during a calendar quarter due to a mental or physical condition, and
- the son or daughter is a widow or widower, divorced; or married to a person who, because of a physical or mental condition, cannot care for the child.

EXAMPLE: Sally is a divorcee with two small children who live with her. Sally works during the day so she hires Martha, her mother, to care for the children during working hours. Sally pays Martha $250 a week. Sally must pay the employer's share of FICA taxes for Martha and withhold employee FICA and federal income taxes from her pay.

3. State Payroll Taxes

State payroll taxes consist of unemployment compensation which employers are required to pay directly to a state fund and state income tax that employers must withhold from employees' paychecks.

a. Unemployment compensation

Every state except New York exempts from unemployment compensation coverage services performed by a person employed by his or her child or spouse. In New York, unemployment compensation must be paid where a child employs a parent. (See Chapter 9, Section A.)

All states except New Hampshire exclude from unemployment compensation coverage minor children employed by their parents. In over half the states, a minor child is one under 21 years old. In most of the other states, a minor is a child under 18. In Wyoming, the age is 19.

b. State income taxation

All states except Alaska, Florida, Nevada, South Dakota, Texas, Washington and Wyoming have income taxation. If a family member is an employee of your business and is paid regular wages, you may have to withhold state income taxes from his or her pay. Check with your state's tax authority.

No income tax withholding is required for family members who qualify as ICs under your state's income tax law. (See Chapter 9, Section E.)

■

Labor and Anti-Discrimination Laws

Employees enjoy a wide array of rights under federal labor and anti-discrimination laws. Among other things, these laws impose:

- minimum wage and overtime pay requirements on employers
- make it illegal for employers to discriminate against employees on the basis of race, color, religion, gender and national origin
- protect employees who wish to unionize, and
- make it unlawful for employers to knowingly hire illegal aliens.

Most states have similar laws protecting employees.

In recent years, a growing number of employees have brought lawsuits against employers alleging violations of these laws. Some employers have had to pay hefty damages to their employees. In addition, various watchdog agencies, such as the U.S. Department of Labor and Equal Employment Opportunity Commission, have authority to take administrative or court action against employers they claim have violated these laws.

One of the advantages of hiring ICs is that few of these laws apply to them. You have much less exposure to these kinds of employee claims and lawsuits with workers who are ICs. However, this does not mean you can freely discriminate against ICs.

For more information on labor and anti-discrimination laws, refer to *The Employer's Legal Handbook*, by Fred S. Steingold (Nolo Press).

Government agencies and courts use different tests to determine whether workers are employees or ICs under federal and state labor and anti-discrimination laws. As a practical matter, however, it doesn't matter that much which test is used. More important is the attitude of the government agencies charged with enforcing the federal labor and employment laws. Many of these agencies bend over backwards to find that workers are employees subject to these laws.

They believe this is appropriate because they're enforcing social legislation designed to help workers. These agencies and courts are particularly likely to view low-skill, low-pay workers as people who need legal protection and so are more likely to consider them to be employees.

A. Federal Wage and Hour Laws

The main law affecting workers' pay is the federal Fair Labor Standards Act or FLSA (29 U.S.C. §§ 201 and following) which establishes a national minimum wage and a 40-hour per week overtime standard for covered employees.

Most businesses are covered by the FLSA, but not all workers are included in its coverage. ICs are not subject to this law. Nor are employees who fall within any of the several exempt categories discussed below.

1. When the FLSA May Apply

It's not likely that you pay any ICs or employees less than the $4.25 federal minimum wage; or, if your state has a higher minimum wage, that wage. One possible exception is for household workers. (See Chapter 11, Section A4.) So you probably don't need to worry about the FLSA's minimum wage requirements.

The reason you need to be concerned about the FLSA is because of overtime pay requirements. The FLSA requires that all non-exempt employees be paid an additional one-half times their regular rates of pay for all hours of work over 40 hours in a week. If you've classified as ICs workers who are really non-exempt employees under the FLSA, you will likely have to pay each misclassified worker an additional one-half of that worker's regular rate for all hours worked in excess of 40 per week during the previous two or three years.

This could be a substantial sum if your workers regularly put in long work weeks. If you refuse to pay, you could face legal action by the Labor Department or the affected workers and possible fines. Business owners can be held personally liable for FLSA violations.

The Department of Labor doesn't have the large investigative staff that the IRS does, but it doesn't need it. It relies on complaints by disgruntled workers who believe they're entitled to overtime pay. Since informants' identities are kept confidential and in any event they can't be fired for complaining to the Labor Department, workers really have nothing to lose if they think they might qualify as employees and be entitled to the protection of the FLSA.

Before trying to determine how workers will be classified by the Department of Labor (see Section A4), you should first see if either your business or workers are exempt from FLSA coverage. You don't need to worry about this particular worker classification issue or the Department of Labor if your business or workers are exempt.

2. Covered Businesses

Your business is covered by the FLSA if you take in $500,000 or more in total annual sales or if you're engaged in interstate commerce. This covers nearly all workplaces because the courts have broadly interpreted interstate commerce to include, for example, any business that regularly uses the U.S. mail to send or receive letters to and from other states or makes or accepts telephone calls to and from other states.

If your business is covered by FLSA, it makes no difference how you compensate workers. If they are employees not exempt from the FLSA, they must be paid time-and-a-half for overtime. This is so whether they are paid by the hour, week or month; paid a commission on sales; paid on a piecework basis; compensated only by tips; or paid a set fee for the work.

Businesses Exempt From the FLSA

A handful of businesses are exempt from the FLSA—for example, most small farms are not covered. It's not likely your business falls within any of these exemptions, but for details of these exemptions, check with the nearest office of the U.S. Labor Department's Wage and Hour Division. (See Section F.)

3. Workers Exempt From Overtime Requirements

Several categories of workers are exempt from the FLSA, even if they qualify as employees. It doesn't matter whether these workers are employees or ICs for FLSA purposes. Either way, they aren't covered. They can work as much overtime as they want and you won't have to pay time-and-a-half. The most common exemptions are for white collar workers and outside salespeople.

a. White collar workers

Many white collar workers are exempt from the FLSA. The FLSA divides such workers into three categories:

- **Executives.** Employees who manage two or more employees within a business or a department, and who can hire, fire and promote employees.
- **Administrators.** Employees who perform specialized or technical work related to management or general business operations.
- **Professionals.** Employees who perform original and creative work or work requiring advanced knowledge normally acquired through specialized study—for example, engineers and accountants.

To be exempt from the FLSA, these employees must be paid a minimum weekly salary or fee of $250 and spend at least 80% of the workday performing duties that require them to use discretion and independent judgment.

These exemptions are explained in a free booklet titled *Regulations Part 541: Defining the Terms—Executive, Administrative, Professional and Outside Sales*. It's available from the nearest office of the Wage and Hour Division of the U.S. Department of Labor—or call 202-219-8743.

b. Outside salespeople

An outside salesperson is exempt from FLSA coverage if he or she:

- regularly works away from your place of business while making sales or taking orders, and
- spends no more than 20% of work time doing work other than selling for your business.

Typically, an exempt salesperson will be paid primarily through commissions and will require little or no direct supervision.

c. Computer specialists

Computer system analysts and programmers whose primary duty is systems analysis, systems design or high level programming are exempt from the FLSA if they receive a salary of at least $170 a week or, if paid by the hour, receive at least 6.5 times the federal minimum wage—that is, $27.63 an hour.

d. Other workers

Several other types of workers are exempt from the overtime pay provisions of the FLSA. The most common include:

- inside salespeople whose regular rate of pay is more than one and one-half times the minimum wage and who receive more than half their pay from commissions
- taxicab drivers
- truck drivers and other trucking company employees whose maximum working hours are set by the Department of Transportation
- employees of seasonal amusement or recreational businesses
- employees of local newspapers having a circulation of less than 4,000
- newspaper delivery workers
- announcers, news editors and chief engineers of certain small radio and TV stations
- employees of motion picture theaters
- switchboard operators employed by phone companies that have no more than 750 stations
- workers on small farms, and
- seafarers on all vessels.

4. Classifying Workers Under the FLSA

If a worker does not fall into any of the exempt categories discussed above, the FLSA will apply if he or she is an employee. The Department of Labor and courts use the economic reality test to determine the status of workers for FLSA purposes. (See Chapter 3, Section E.)

The Labor Department and courts usually try to find an employment relationship whenever possible. You'll have a particularly difficult time convincing the Labor Department that low-skill, low-paid workers are ICs. These are the type of workers the Labor Department and courts believe most need the protection of federal labor laws, so they usually classify them as employees.

Two recent cases arising in Texas illustrate this. In the first case, pipe welders who were classified as ICs claimed they were really employees under the labor laws and so were entitled to overtime pay. In the other case, the Department of Labor sued a nightclub owner claiming that the topless dancers he hired should have been classified as employees, not ICs. The pipe welders were very highly skilled and well paid workers. The topless dancers were not. The court held the welders were ICs but that the dancers were employees. (*Carrell v. Sunland Constr., Inc.*, 998 F.2d 330 (5th Cir. 1993); *Reich v. Circle C. Investments, Inc.*, 998 F.2d 324 (5th Cir. 1993).)

5. Avoiding Problems

The easiest way to avoid problems with FLSA overtime pay requirements is to prevent workers from putting in more than 40 hours a week. If a person is clearly an employee, you can simply prohibit him or her from working overtime. But if you classify a worker as an IC, you should not directly specify how many hours he or she should work—either orally or in a written IC agreement. Doing so makes the worker look like an employee, not only for FLSA purposes but for IRS and other purposes as well. It's really none of your business how long an IC works. You can only be concerned with the results an IC achieves, not how the worker achieves them.

Avoid giving workers who are not clearly ICs more work than they can do in a 40-hour week. This may mean you have to plan ahead so you can lengthen deadlines or hire more ICs to do the needed work.

6. Recordkeeping Requirements

The FLSA requires you to keep records of wages and hours. Different kinds of records are required depending upon whether a worker is subject to both minimum wage and overtime provisions, or is exempt from one or the other. You must retain most records for all current employees and former employees for at least three years.

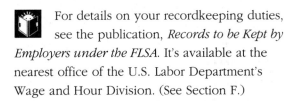 For details on your recordkeeping duties, see the publication, *Records to be Kept by Employers under the FLSA*. It's available at the nearest office of the U.S. Labor Department's Wage and Hour Division. (See Section F.)

B. Federal Labor Relations Laws

The National Labor Relations Act or NLRA (29 U.S.C. §§ 151 and following) gives most employees the right to unionize. This enables them to negotiate collective employment contracts through union representatives rather than having to deal with employers individually.

The National Labor Relations Board (NLRB) administers the law and interprets its provisions. The NLRB conducts union elections and enforces the NRLA's rules of conduct, determining whether employers have engaged in unfair labor practices.

1. Only Employees Covered

The NRLA applies only to employees; it specifically excludes coverage for ICs. ICs have the right to form a union if they wish to do so, but they are not protected by the NRLA. You can decline to use the services of ICs who form a union or simply express support for a union. You can't do this with employees who are covered by the NRLA.

Union membership has declined dramatically in recent years to about 11% of private sector workers and is expected to fall to only 7% by the year 2001. So the fact that ICs are not protected by the NRLA is not as important as it was 20 or 30 years ago when unions were much stronger and companies in many industries—trucking, for example—hired ICs mainly to avoid having to deal with unions. Nevertheless, this is still one advantage of using ICs rather than employees.

2. Employees Exempt From the NRLA

Not all private sector employees are covered by the NRLA. Exempt employees include:

- managers and supervisors
- confidential employees—such as company accountants
- farm workers
- members of an employer's family
- most domestic workers, and
- workers in certain industries—such as the railroad industry—that are covered by other labor laws.

3. Determining Worker Status

If a worker does not fall within one of the classes of NRLA-exempt employees, you need to decide whether he or she is an employee or IC for NRLA purposes. The common law right of control test is used for this purpose. You can safely assume that if a non-exempt worker is an employee for IRS purposes he or she is also covered by the NRLA. (See Chapter 3, Section D.)

C. Anti-Discrimination Laws

The federal government and most states have laws prohibiting discrimination in the workplace. Most of these laws apply only to employees, not ICs.

1. Federal Anti-Discrimination Laws

The main federal law barring workplace discrimination is Title VII of the federal Civil Rights Act of 1964. Title VII applies to businesses that have 15 or more full-time or part-time employees. It outlaws discrimination in employment based on race, color, religion, gender and national origin. Sexual harassment in the workplace is also prohibited as a variety of illegal gender discrimination.

Other federal laws barring workplace discrimination include:

- the Age Discrimination in Employment Act, which prohibits discrimination in employment on account of age against people who are 40 or more years old and applies to employers with 20 or more employees
- the Pregnancy Discrimination Act, which bars employers from discriminating against employees on account of pregnancy, birth or related conditions and applies to employers with 15 or more employees

- the Immigration Reform and Control Act, which makes it illegal to discriminate against people who aren't U.S. citizens but who have been legally admitted to the United States
- the Equal Pay Act, which requires employers to provide equal pay and benefits to men and women who do the same job or jobs requiring equal skill, effort and responsibility, and
- the Americans with Disabilities Act, which protects disabled people from employment discrimination and applies to employers with 15 or more employees.

With the exception of some Title VII cases, none of these anti-discrimination laws apply to ICs. An IC has no legal right to bring a lawsuit against you claiming that you have discriminated in violation of these statutes. And the federal agencies charged with enforcing these laws, such as the Equal Employment Opportunity Commission, have no power to handle claims where ICs are concerned.

But you are not free to discriminate against ICs. First of all, a worker you've classified as an IC might be able to convince a court that he or she is really an employee. The anti-discrimination laws would then apply. A court or federal agency would likely bend over backwards to find an employment relationship if you have engaged in blatant discrimination.

In addition, an IC might be able to sue you under state anti-discrimination laws and you might be subject to administrative action by a state anti-discrimination agency. Some of these state laws may apply to ICs. (See Section C2.)

BEWARE OF STATE TWISTS

Federal courts in some parts of the country—the western United States, for example—have found that in certain situations Title VII can apply to an IC. This is where discrimination against an IC results in damage to the IC's job opportunities.

For example, a doctor was permitted to bring a Title VII action alleging discrimination on the basis of national origin. The doctor, clearly an IC, had submitted a bid to run a hospital's emergency room. The doctor claimed that the bid was rejected because he was Hispanic and that the rejection had adversely affected his job opportunities. (*Gomez v. Alexian Bros. Hosp.*, 698 F.2d 1019 (9th Cir. 1983).)

Until recently, courts almost always used the economic reality test to determine whether a worker was an employee or IC for purposes of federal anti-discrimination statutes. However, many courts are now switching to the common law right of control test. (See Chapter 3, Section D.)

2. State Anti-Discrimination Laws

All states except Alabama, Arkansas, Georgia and Mississippi have their own civil rights laws that prohibit discrimination in private employment based on race, color, gender and national origin. Most states also prohibit discrimination based on religion or disability. In addition, many states and localities prohibit forms of discrimination that aren't covered by federal law—for example, discrimination based on marital status.

These laws may be enforced by a special state administrative agency, the state labor department or state attorney general. Covered workers can also bring lawsuits alleging job discrimination against employers in state court.

Most of these state laws apply only to employees, not ICs. Different state courts use both the economic reality and common law tests to determine worker status under these laws. Regardless of what test is used, state agencies and courts often take a very broad view of who qualifies as an employee under these anti-discrimination laws. It's possible, therefore, that a worker might be viewed as an IC under federal anti-discrimination laws but an employee under a similar state law.

Beware that the civil rights laws of a few states—Louisiana, North Dakota and Vermont, for example—might include ICs as well as employees.

D. Worker Safety Laws

The federal Occupational Safety and Health Act or OSHA (29 U.S.C. Sections 651 to 678) requires employers to keep their workplaces safe and free from recognized hazards that are likely to cause death or serious harm to employees. Employers must also provide safety training to employees, inform them about hazardous chemicals, notify government administrators about serious workplace accidents and keep detailed safety records.

OSHA applies to businesses that affect interstate commerce. The legal definition of interstate commerce is so broad that almost all businesses are covered.

OSHA is enforced by the federal Occupational Safety and Health Administration, or OSHA, a unit of the Department of Labor. OSHA can impose heavy penalties for legal violations and set additional workplace standards. Employees may not sue their employers for OSHA violations.

1. ICs Excluded

OSHA applies only to employees, not ICs. OSHA uses the economic reality test to determine if workers are employees or ICs. (See Chapter 3, Section E.) OSHA has interpreted the test broadly to include, for example, supervisors, partners, corporate officers, former employees and applicants for employment. (29 C.F.R. 1977.5(b).)

OSHA regulations requiring employers to notify workers about hazardous chemicals appear to apply to ICs as well as employees. (29 C.F.R. 1910.1200(c).)

2. Importance of Maintaining a Safe Workplace

Even though OSHA cannot impose penalties against you if you have no employees, it's important for you to maintain a safe workplace. ICs who perform services at your workplace may be able to sue you for negligence and obtain monetary damages if they are injured because of hazardous or unsafe conditions. (See Chapter 10, Section B.)

E. Immigration Laws

Many workers in the United States are immigrants. And many work illegally—that is, they are not U.S. citizens and don't have a green card or other documentation of their legal status. The Immigration and Naturalization Service (INS) has recently stepped up efforts to crack down on people who hire illegal aliens.

All employers are required to verify that their employees are either U.S. citizens or nationals, or legal aliens authorized to work in the U.S. Penalties for failing to comply can run up to $1,000 for each employee.

You are not required to verify citizenship when you hire an IC. The INS uses the common law right of control test to determine whether a worker is an employee or IC for immigration purposes. (See Chapter 3, Section D.) A worker who qualifies as an IC for tax purposes will likely be an IC for immigration purposes as well. (See Chapter 4, Section A.)

In addition, the verification requirements do not apply to any employees hired before November 7, 1986.

However, although you are not required to verify the immigration status of ICs or others coming within these exceptions, it is still illegal for you to hire any worker who you know to be an illegal alien. The INS can impose a fine up to $2,000 for the first offense.

F. Labor Departments

U.S. Department of Labor
200 Constitution Avenue, NW
Washington, DC 20210
202-219-6666

Check government pages of the telephone book for nearest location.

STATE LABOR DEPARTMENTS

Alabama
Labor Department
1789 Dickenson Drive, 2nd Floor
Montgomery, AL 36130
205-242-3460

Alaska
Labor Department
P.O. Box 21149
Juneau, AK 99802-1149
907-465-2700

Arizona
Labor Division
800 West Washington Street, Suite 102
Phoenix, AZ 85007
602-542-4515

Arkansas
Labor Department
10421 West Markham Street
Little Rock, AR 72205
501-682-4500

California
Industrial Relations Department
455 Golden Gate Avenue
P.O. Box 420603
San Francisco, CA 94142-0603
415-703-4281

Colorado
Labor Division
1120 Lincoln Street
Denver, CO 80203
303-837-3800

Connecticut
Labor Department
200 Folly Brook Boulevard
Wethersfield, CT 06109
203-566-4384

Delaware
Labor Department
820 North French Street; 6th Floor
Wilmington, DE 19801
302-577-2710

District of Columbia
Wage and Hour Office
950 Upshur Street, NW; 2nd Floor
Washington, DC 20011
202-576-6942

Florida
Labor Employment & Training Division
Atkins Building, Suite 300
Tallahassee, FL 32399-0667
904-488-7228

Georgia
Labor Department
148 International Blvd, NE, Suite 600
Atlanta, GA 30303
404-656-3011

Hawaii
Labor & Industrial Relations Department
830 Punchbowl Street
Honolulu, HI 96813
808-586-8842

Idaho
Labor & Industrial Services Department
277 North 6th Street
State House Mail
Boise, ID 83720
208-334-3950

Illinois
Labor Department
160 North LaSalle Street, 13th Floor
Chicago, IL 60601
312-793-2800

Indiana
Labor Department
402 West Washington, Room W-195
Indianapolis, IN 46204
317-232-2655

Iowa
Labor Services Commission
1000 East Grand Avenue
Des Moines, IA 50319
515-281-8067

Kansas
Public Employee Relations Board
512 West 6th
Topeka, KS 66603
913-296-3094

Kentucky
Labor Cabinet
US Hwy. 127, South Building
Frankfort, KY 40601
502-564-3070

STATE LABOR DEPARTMENTS (CONTINUED)

Louisiana
Labor Department
P.O. Box 94094
Baton Rouge, LA 70804-9094
504-342-3011

Maine
Labor Department
20 Union Street
P.O. Box 309
Augusta, ME 04332-0309
207-287-3788

Maryland
Labor & Industry Division
501 Saint Paul Place
Baltimore, MD 21202
410-333-4179

Massachusetts
Labor & Industries Department
100 Cambridge Street, Room 1100
Boston, MA 02202
617-727-3454

Michigan
Labor Department
Victor Office Building, 201 North Washington Square
P.O. Box 30015
Lansing, MI 48909
517-373-9600

Minnesota
Labor & Industry Department
443 Lafayette Road
St. Paul, MN 55155
612-296-2342

Mississippi
Employment Security Commission
1520 West Capitol
P.O. Box 1699
Jackson, MS 39215
601-354-8711

Missouri
Labor & Industrial Relations Department
3315 West Truman Boulevard
Jefferson City, MO 65109
314-751-4091

Montana
Labor & Industry Department
1327 Lockey Avenue
P.O. Box 1728
Helena, MT 59624
406-444-3555

Nebraska
Labor Department
P.O. Box 94600
Lincoln, NE 68509
402-471-9000

Nevada
Labor Commission
1445 Hot Springs Road, Suite 108
Carson City, NV 89710
702-687-4850

New Hampshire
Labor Department
95 Pleasant Street
Concord, NH 03301
603-271-3171

New Jersey
Labor Department
John Fitch Plaza, CN 110
Trenton, NJ 08625
609-292-2323

New Mexico
Labor & Industrial Division
1596 Pacheco Street
Santa Fe, NM 87501
505-827-6808

New York
Labor Department
State Campus, Bldg. 12
Albany, NY 12240
518-457-2741

North Carolina
Labor Department
4 W. Edenton Street
Raleigh, NC 27601
919-733-7166

North Dakota
Labor Department
600 East Boulevard
Bismarck, ND 58505
701-224-2660

STATE LABOR DEPARTMENTS (CONTINUED)

Ohio
Industrial Relations Department
2323 West 5th Avenue
P.O. Box 825
Columbus, OH 43216
614-644-2223

Oklahoma
Labor Department
4001 Lincoln Boulevard
Oklahoma City, OK 73105
405-528-1500

Oregon
Labor & Industries Bureau
800 NE Oregon
Portland, OR 97232
503-731-4200

Pennsylvania
Labor & Industry Department
Labor & Industry Building
Harrisburg, PA 17120
717-787-3756

Rhode Island
Labor Department
610 Manton Avenue
Providence, RI 02909
401-457-1800

South Carolina
Labor Department
P.O. Box 11329
Columbia, SC 29211-1329
803-734-9594

South Dakota
Labor Department
700 Governor's Drive
Pierre, SD 57501
605-773-3101

Tennessee
Labor Department
710 James Robertson Parkway, 2nd Floor
Nashville, TN 37243-0655
615-741-2582

Texas
Licensing & Regulation Department
P.O. Box 12157, Capitol Station
Austin, TX 78711
512-463-5522

Utah
Labor Division
160 E. 300 South, 3rd Floor
P.O Box 146630
Salt Lake City, UT 84114-6630
801-530-6921

Vermont
Labor & Industry Department
National Life Building, Drawer 20
Montpelier, VT 05620-3401
802-828-2286

Virginia
Labor & Industry Department
13 South 13th Street
Richmond, VA 23219
804-786-2377

Washington
Labor & Industries Department
P.O. Box 44001
Olympia, WA 98504-4001
206-956-4213

West Virginia
Labor Division
1800 Washington Street E
Charleston, WV 25305
304-558-7890

Wisconsin
Industry, Labor & Human Relations Department
P.O. Box 7946
Madison, WI 53707
608-266-7552

Wyoming
Labor & Statistics Department
U.S. West Building
6101 Yellowstone Road, Room 259C
Cheyenne, WY 82002
307-777-7261

Intellectual Property Ownership

This chapter explains the rights and responsibilities of those who hire ICs to help create intellectual property. This includes not only high technology companies and publishers, but any company that has information it wants to keep from its competitors.

A. What Is Intellectual Property

Intellectual property is a generic term describing products of the human intellect that have economic value. It includes works of authorship such as writings, films and music, inventions and information or know-how not generally known.

Intellectual property is considered property because over the past 200 years, a body of laws has been created giving the owners of such works legal rights similar to owners of real estate or tangible personal property such as automobiles. Intellectual property may be owned and bought and sold the same as other personal property. However, although intellectual property has been called the real estate of the '90s, in some important respects owning intellectual property is very different from owning a house or car. If you pay an IC to build a house, you own the house. But you can pay an IC to create intellectual property and yet not own the finished product.

B. Laws Protecting Intellectual Property

When you hire an IC to create intellectual property on your behalf, the rules determining who owns it differ, depending upon what form of intellectual property is involved. There are three separate bodies of law that protect most types of intellectual property: copyright, patent and trade secret law.

1. Copyright Law

The federal copyright law (17 U.S.C. §§ 101 and following) protects all original works of authorship. A work of authorship is any work created by a human being that other humans can understand or perceive, either by themselves or with the help of a machine such as a film projector or television. This includes, but is not limited to, all kinds of written works, plays, music, artwork, graphics, photos, films and videos, computer software, architectural blueprints and designs, choreography and pantomimes.

The copyright law gives the owner of a copyright a bundle of exclusive rights over how the work may be used. These include the exclusive right to copy and distribute the protected work, to create derivative works based upon it—updated editions of a book, for example—and to display and perform it. Copyright owners typically profit from their works by selling or licensing all or some of these rights to others—publishers, for example.

For a detailed discussion of copyright, see *The Copyright Handbook: How to Protect and Use Written Works* and *Copyright Your Software*, both by Stephen Fishman (Nolo Press).

2. Patent Law

The federal patent law (35 U.S.C. §§ 100 and following) protects inventions. To obtain a patent, an inventor must file an application with the U.S. Patent and Trademark Office in Washington, DC. If the Patent Office determines that the invention meets the legal requirements, it will issue the inventor a patent. A patent gives an inventor a monopoly to use and commercially profit from the invention for 20 years. In other words, anyone who wants to use or sell the invention must obtain the patent owner's permission. A patent may protect the functional features of a machine, process, manufactured item or composition of matter, or the ornamental design of a nonfunctional feature. A patent also protects improvements of any such items.

 For a detailed discussion of patents, see *Patent It Yourself,* by David Pressman (Nolo Press).

3. Trade Secret Law

A trade secret is information or know-how that is not generally known by others and that provides its owner with a competitive advantage in the marketplace. The information can be an idea, written words, a formula, process or procedure, technical design, customer list, marketing plan or any other secret that gives the owner an economic advantage.

If a trade secret owner takes reasonable steps to keep the confidential information or know-how secret—for example, does not publish it or otherwise make it freely available to the public—the laws of most states will protect the owner from disclosures of the secret by:

- the owner's employees
- people who agree not to disclose it
- industrial spies, and
- competitors who wrongfully acquire the information.

 For detailed information, see *Trade Secrets* by James H.A. Pooley (Amacom).

C. Copyright Ownership

A work of authorship is automatically protected by copyright the moment it is created. At that same moment, someone becomes the owner of the copyright. If you pay an IC to create a copyrightable work on your behalf, you normally want to be the copyright owner. That will give you the exclusive right to copy, distribute and otherwise economically exploit the work. Without these rights, your ability to use the work will be very limited, even though you paid for it.

There are two ownership possibilities. Either:

- the work will be a work made for hire, in which case you will automatically be the copyright owner, or
- the work will not be a work made for hire, in which case the IC will initially own the copyright and you will have no ownership rights unless you specifically obtain them from the IC.

1. Works Made for Hire

When you pay someone to create a work made for hire, you automatically own all the copyright rights in the work. Indeed, you are considered to be the work's author for copyright purposes, even though you didn't create it. The actual creator of a work made for hire has no copyright rights at all. All the creator receives is whatever compensation you give him or her.

As the author, you're entitled to register the work with the Copyright Office, and you own all the exclusive rights that make up a copyright, such as the right to copy and distribute the work. You can exercise these rights yourself, sell or license them to others or do whatever else you want with them. The person or people you paid to create the work have no say over what you do with your copyright rights in the work.

There are two types of works made for hire. They include:

- works created by employees within the scope of their employment, and
- certain types of specially commissioned works created by ICs.

a. Works by employees

All works of authorship created by your employees within the scope of employment are works made for hire. This means you automatically own all the copyright rights in such works. You aren't legally required to have your employees sign agreements relinquishing their copyright rights in works made for hire. However, costly disputes can develop concerning whether a work is created within the scope of employment. For example, if an employee creates a work partly at home outside working hours, he or she might claim it is not a work for hire because the work was done outside the scope of employment.

For this reason, it is a very good idea to have a written agreement describing the employee's job duties so it will be clear whether a work is created within the scope of employment. It's also wise to include in the agreement a provision assigning or transferring to you the copyright rights in any job-related works that for some reason are not works made for hire.

For sample employment agreements for employees involved in the software industry, see *Software Development: A Legal Guide,* by Stephen Fishman (Nolo Press).

b. Specially commissioned works by ICs

Certain types of specially commissioned or ordered works created by ICs are also considered to be works made for hire in which the hiring firm automatically owns all copyright rights. However,

you and the IC must both sign an agreement stating that the work is made for hire. (See Chapter 16.)

Nine categories of works can be IC-created works made for hire. They include:

- a contribution to a collective work—for example, a work created by more than one author, such as a newspaper, magazine, anthology or encyclopedia
- a part of an audiovisual work—for example, a motion picture screenplay
- a translation
- supplementary works—for example, forewords, afterwords, supplemental pictorial illustrations, maps, charts, editorial notes, bibliographies, appendixes and indexes
- a compilation—for example, an electronic database
- an instructional text
- a test
- answer material for a test, and
- an atlas.

EXAMPLE: The editor of *The Egoist Magazine* asks Gloria, a freelance writer, if she would be interested in writing an article for the magazine on night life in Palm Beach. Gloria agrees and the editor sends Gloria an agreement to sign setting forth such terms as Gloria's compensation, the deadline for the article and its length, and stating that the article "shall be a work made for hire." Gloria signs the agreement, writes the article and is paid by the magazine. Since the article qualifies as a work made for hire, the magazine is the initial owner of all the copyright rights in the article.

Gloria owns no copyright rights in the article. As the copyright owner, the magazine is free to sell reprint rights in the article, to sell film and television rights, translation rights and any other rights anyone wants to buy. Gloria is not entitled to license or sell any rights in the article because she doesn't own any, she gave up all her copyright rights by signing the work for hire agreement.

SPECIAL RULES FOR CALIFORNIA

California law provides that a person who commissions a work made for hire is considered to be the employer of the creator of the work for purposes of the workers' compensation, unemployment insurance and unemployment disability insurance laws. (Cal. Labor Code § 3351.5(c); Cal. Unemployment Insurance Code § 621 and § 686)

No one is sure what impact this has on those who commission works made for hire in California. Neither the California courts nor state agencies have addressed the question. However, it may mean that the hiring firm has to obtain workers' compensation coverage for the person who created the work and might be liable for any injuries sustained in the course of the work. It might also mean that special penalties could be assessed against a hiring firm that does not pay the creator money due after he or she is discharged or resigns.

In addition, it's possible that the IRS could use these California laws as an excuse to classify creators as employees for federal tax purposes. At least one California publisher has had this experience where it paid workers' compensation and unemployment compensation for freelance writers who created specially commissioned works under work for hire agreements. This was so even though the writers appeared to qualify as ICs under the common law test. (See Chapter 3, Section D.)

These potential requirements and liabilities are good reasons why it might be desirable for those commissioning work in California not to enter into work made for hire agreements, and instead have the one who created the work assign the desired copyright rights to the hiring firm in advance. (See Section C2.)

2. IC Works That Are Not Made for Hire

Works of authorship created by ICs that do not fall within the list of nine specially commissioned works discussed above can never be works made for hire. This means that the IC, not the hiring firm, initially owns the copyright in such a work. As the copyright owner, the IC has the exclusive right to copy, distribute and create new works based on the work. Even though you paid the IC to create the work, you won't own any of these exclusive rights. You may end up only with a limited right to use the work.

EXAMPLE: Tom hires Jane, a freelance programmer, to create a computer program. Tom and Jane have an oral work agreement and Jane clearly qualifies as an IC. She works at home under her own direction, sets her own hours and uses her own computer. Jane completes her work, delivers her code and Tom pays her.

The program is not a work for hire because Jane is an IC, not Tom's employee; and a computer program does not fall within one of the categories of works created by ICs that can be works made for hire. And, in any event, Jane never signed a work for hire agreement. This means that Jane owns all the copyright right in the program. As the copyright owner, Jane has the exclusive right to sell the program to others or permit them to use it. Even though Tom paid Jane to create the program, he doesn't own it and can't sell or license it to others.

Fortunately, it's easy to avoid this unhappy result. Simply require all ICs who create copyrightable works for you to sign written agreements assigning, or transferring, to you the copyright rights you need before they begin work on a project.

An assignment is simply a transfer of copyright ownership. You can obtain all the copyright rights in the work, or part of them. It's up to the IC and you to decide which rights to transfer. As discussed above, a copyright is really a number of rights including the exclusive rights to copy, distribute, perform, display and create derivative works from a work. Each of these rights can be sold or licensed together or separately. They can also be divided and sub-divided by geography, time, market segment or any other way you can think up. For example, you could obtain the right to copy and distribute a work in North America for ten years.

An assignment can be made either before or after a work is created, but must be in writing to be valid. (See Chapter 16.)

> **EXAMPLE:** Tom hires Jane, a freelance programmer, to create a computer program. Before Jane starts work, Tom has her sign an independent contractor agreement providing, among other things, that she transfers all her copyright rights in the program to Tom. Jane completes her work, delivers the program and Tom pays her. Tom owns all the copyright rights in the program.

When you obtain copyright ownership through an assignment, it is legally not the same as owning a work made for hire created by an employee or a specially commissioned work created by an IC under a work for hire agreement. When you own a work for hire you are considered to be the work's author, even though you didn't create it. You automatically own all the copyright rights in the work. You are not considered the author when you obtain a copyright through an assignment, and you only acquire those rights covered by the assignment.

However, you'll usually want the assignment to transfer all the IC's copyright rights. When you do this, the only practical difference between an assignment and a work made for hire is that the IC or his or her heirs can terminate the assignment 35 to 40 years after it was made. However, in most cases this is meaningless because very few works have a useful economic life of more than 35 years.

FAILING TO OBTAIN COPYRIGHT TRANSFERS FROM ICS

If you fail to obtain a copyright transfer from an IC, the best thing that can happen is that you will be considered a co-author of the work the IC helps create. For this to occur, you or somebody who works for you must actually help the IC to create the work. Giving suggestions or supervision is not enough to be a co-author. If you qualify as a co-author, you and the IC will jointly share copyright ownership in the work. As a co-author, you're entitled to use or let other people use the work without obtaining approval of the other co-author. But any profits you make must be shared with the other co-author or co-authors.

If you don't qualify as a co-author, at most you will have a nonexclusive right to use the work. For example, if you hired an IC to create a computer program, you will be able to use the program without asking the IC for permission. But you won't be allowed to sell or license any copyright rights in the work because you won't own any. The IC will own all the rights and will be able to sell or license them without your permission and without sharing the profits with you.

---

3. Determining Whether Workers Are Employees or ICs

It should be clear by now that it is very important to know whether any person you hire to create a work of authorship qualifies as an employee or IC for copyright ownership purposes. You automatically own the copyright in works created by employees within the scope of employment, but this is emphatically not the case with works created by ICs. The special steps discussed above must be taken to own IC-created works.

The common law right of control test is used to determine whether a worker is an IC or employee for copyright purposes. (See Chapter 3, Section D.) The main distinguishing feature of an employment relationship is that the employer has the right to control both the manner and means by which the work is created. A worker is more likely to be considered an IC if he or she:

- is highly skilled
- provides his or her own equipment and tools
- doesn't have a long relationship with the hiring firm
- doesn't have to accept additional projects from the hiring firm
- determines his or her own working hours
- is paid by the project rather than by the hour
- decides what assistants will be hired and pays them himself or herself
- performs work not in the hiring firm's ordinary line of business
- is in business for himself or herself
- does not receive employee benefits from the hiring firm, and
- is treated like an IC for tax purposes by the hiring firm.

(See Chapter 3 for a detailed analysis of all these factors.)

EXAMPLE: Marco, a professional photographer, took photographs for several issues of *Accent Magazine*, a trade journal for the jewelry industry, over a six-month period. Marco had an oral agreement with the magazine and was paid a fee of about $150 per photograph. Marco made no agreement with the magazine concerning copyright ownership of the photos. Marco, who had not signed a work for hire agreement, claimed that he owned all the copyright rights in the photos.

The court concluded that Marco was an IC. Marco was an experienced and skilled photographer. He used his own equipment, and worked at his own studio, on days and times of his choosing, without photography assistants hired by the magazine. No income tax was withheld from his payments and he received no employee benefits. He performed discrete assignments for the magazine, rather than hourly or periodic work. Since Marco owned the copyright in the photos, the court held that the magazine had to pay him a licensing fee when it re-used them. (*Marco v. Accent Publishing Co., Inc.*, 969 F.2d 154 (3d Cir. 1992).)

YOU CAN'T HAVE IT BOTH WAYS

Courts don't look favorably upon hiring firms that don't treat workers evenhandedly for copyright ownership purposes. In one recent case, for example, a federal court held that a part-time programmer employed by a swimming pool retailer was not the company's employee for copyright purposes and the programmer was therefore entitled to ownership of a program he wrote for the company. The court stated that the company's failure to provide the programmer with health, unemployment or life insurance benefits, or to withhold Social Security, federal or state taxes from his pay was a virtual admission that the programmer was an independent contractor. The court stressed that the company could not treat the programmer as an independent contractor for tax purposes and then turn around and claim he was an employee for copyright ownership purposes. (*Aymes v. Bonelli*, 980 F.2d 857 (2d Cir. 1992).)

The moral is that if you treat a worker as an IC for IRS purposes, you had better assume he or she is an IC for copyright ownership purposes as well.

D. Trade Secret and Patent Ownership

The rules for determining ownership of trade secrets and patentable inventions by ICs are essentially the same.

1. Inventions and Trade Secrets Created by ICs

Whenever you hire any worker to create or contribute to the creation of a patentable invention or information or know-how you wish to maintain as a trade secret, it's vital that the worker sign an agreement transferring his or her ownership rights to your company. This is so whether the worker is an employee or IC.

Such an intellectual property ownership transfer is called an assignment. It should be in writing and signed before work begins. It is common practice among high technology firms and other businesses that create patentable inventions or valuable trade secrets to have creative workers sign such assignments. (See Chapter 16.)

In the absence of a signed assignment, you can still obtain ownership of any inventions or trade secrets an IC creates on your behalf, but you may be in for a costly legal dispute. You'll have to prove that the worker was hired to develop a specific product or to help create inventions for you.

2. Revealing Trade Secrets to Third Parties

When you hire ICs to perform services for you, it is sometimes necessary for you to reveal to them sensitive business information that you don't want your competitors to know. For example, it may be necessary to reveal highly valuable customer lists to an IC salesperson.

Even in the absence of a written agreement saying so, ICs probably have a duty to keep such information confidential. But just to make sure, it's wise to include a confidentiality clause in an IC agreement providing that the IC has a duty to keep your proprietary information confidential. (See Chapter 16.) ■

Planning to Avoid Government Audits

This chapter explains how, with careful planning, you can hire outside workers and lessen your chances of being audited or losing if you are audited. These methods have been known to legal and employment professionals for years. But you don't have to hire a highly paid expert to use them.

A. Hiring Incorporated Independent Contractors

Most experts believe that the single most effective thing you can do to avoid IRS and other government audits is to hire ICs who have formed corporations, rather than those who operate as sole proprietors or partnerships.

To understand why this is so, you need to know a little about the various legal forms a business can take. ICs can legally operate their businesses as:

- sole proprietors
- partnerships, or
- corporations.

Find out which category ICs fall into before hiring them, since it could affect the outcome of an IRS or other government audit.

There Is Nothing in a Name

ICs may call themselves by a variety of names: consultants, independent business people, freelancers, self-employed workers and entrepreneurs are just a few examples. None of these names have any legal significance; ICs can use any of them no matter how their businesses are organized. What's important is whether they're sole proprietors, partners or corporations.

1. Sole Proprietorships

A sole proprietorship is simply a one-owner business. Any person who starts a business and does not incorporate or have one or more partners is automatically a sole proprietor.

A sole proprietor is neither an employee nor an IC of the proprietorship. The owner and the sole proprietorship are treated as a single entity for tax purposes. The business does not pay FICA or FUTA taxes on the owner's income or withhold income tax. Instead, business income and losses are reported on the sole proprietor's individual federal tax return, Form 1040, Schedule C. Sole proprietors must pay all their FICA taxes themselves in the form of self-employment taxes. These taxes are reported on Schedule SE.

> **EXAMPLE:** Imelda operates a computer consulting business as a sole proprietorship. She is the sole owner of the business. Tax-wise, Imelda and her proprietorship are one in the same. All money the business receives is paid to Imelda personally. She must report all the income she receives from her clients on her individual Form 1040, Schedule C. No separate tax return is filed for her business.

A sole proprietorship is by far the simplest and easiest way to legally operate a business, and it costs virtually nothing to start. For this reason, the vast majority of ICs—at least 90%—are sole proprietors.

Many sole proprietors qualify as ICs. You likely won't have problems having IC status verified if a sole proprietor is clearly running an independent business—for example, offers services to the public, has multiple clients, substantial ongoing business expenses such as workplace rental and insurance, is paid by the project and hires and pays assistants.

But in borderline cases, the fact that a worker is a sole proprietor is never helpful. Sole proprietors who don't hire assistants can look a lot like employees. They're working on their own, just like employees. They're selling their personal services to you, just like employees do. You pay them directly, just like you do employees. They may deposit the money in a personal account, just like employees do. And like employees, they don't have corporate meetings, partnership agreements or other business formalities.

The bottom line is that an IRS or other government auditor is more likely to question the status of a sole proprietor you've hired than a corporation or partnership. Unfortunately, you may not be able to avoid hiring a sole proprietor because this is how most ICs do business.

2. Partnerships

A partnership is formed automatically whenever two or more people go into business together and do not form a corporation. This form of business is similar to a sole proprietorship, except there are two or more owners. Like a sole proprietorship, a partnership is legally inseparable from the owners—the partners.

Partners share in profits or losses in the manner in which they've agreed. Partnerships do not themselves pay taxes, although they file an annual tax form. Instead, partnership income and losses are passed through the partnership directly to the partners and reported on the partners' individual federal tax returns, Form 1040, Schedule E.

Partners are neither employees nor ICs of their partnership; they are self-employed business owners. A partnership does not pay FICA and FUTA taxes on the partners' income, nor does it withhold income tax. Like sole proprietors, partners pay their own FICA taxes.

> **EXAMPLE:** Brenda, Dave and Mike start their own computer consulting business. They form a partnership in which all three are partners. Tax-wise, their lives are pretty much the same as if they were sole proprietors. Each partner must pay his or her own FICA and FUTA taxes, and each must report their share of partnership income and losses on an individual tax return. Brenda, Dave and Mike are not employees of their partnership; each is a business owner.

Relatively few ICs do business as partnerships. But if you have the choice between hiring a sole proprietor and a partnership, you're usually better off hiring a partnership. Partnerships simply look more like independent businesses than most sole proprietorships. Partnerships involve two or more people in business together, not a single person. Partners' relationships with each other are governed by state partnership laws and partnership agreements, which can be extremely complex and expensive legal documents. Also, partnerships can have their own bank accounts and own property. This means you can pay the partnership for the work, rather than paying the partners directly.

However, even though workers call themselves partners, the IRS will decide they are really employees of the hiring firm if they are under the hiring firm's control—that is, the firm has the right to control how they do their work. (See Chapter 3, Section D.) This is so even if the remuneration is paid to the partnership, rather than directly to the individual partners. (Rev. Rul. 69-183, 1969-1 C.B. 255.)

3. Corporations

A corporation is created by filing articles of incorporation with the appropriate state agency—usually the secretary of state or corporations commissioner. Once this is done and the appropriate fees paid, the corporation becomes a separate legal entity—distinct from its owners, the shareholders. It can hold title to property, sue and be sued, have bank accounts, borrow money and hire employees and ICs.

a. Corporate officers, directors and shareholders

In theory, corporations consist of three groups:
- those who direct the business—called directors

- those who run the business—called officers, and
- those who invest in it—called shareholders.

In the case of small business corporations, these three groups are often the same person.

All corporate officers—the president, vice president, treasurer and any others—are automatically considered employees for employment tax purposes. (See Chapter 6, Section B.) Corporate shareholders who are not officers, but who perform full or part-time services for the corporation, are also employees of the corporation. (Rev. Rul. 71-86, 1971-1 C.B. 285.)

Usually, the owners of a typical incorporated small business are employees of the corporation, either because they serve as officers or perform services for the corporation. The corporation must deduct federal income tax withholding from the owners' wages and pay employment taxes and state payroll taxes as well.

> **EXAMPLE:** Suzy has been operating a one-person sales and marketing business as a sole proprietor. She incorporates the business. Suzy will be the sole shareholder, director and president of Suzy's Sales Services, Inc. After she files articles of incorporation and pays the incorporation fees, she will no longer be self-employed in the eyes of the tax law. Instead, she is a full-time employee of her corporation. As an employee, she earns wages from her corporation, just as if she didn't own the business. The corporation must withhold Suzy's federal income taxes, pay her FUTA and half her FICA taxes and also pay state payroll taxes.

b. Benefits of hiring incorporated outside workers

When you hire incorporated outside workers, you enter into a three-sided relationship with yourself in the top rung. You pay the worker's corpora-

tion, which pays the worker, who is an employee of the corporation. Legally, you have no direct relationship with the worker at all—only with the worker's corporation which cannot be classified as an employee.

> **EXAMPLE:** Acme Widget Company hires Sam's Sales Services, Inc. to sell widgets. Acme pays no money to Sam directly, even though he is the sole shareholder and president of Sam's Sales Services, Inc. and is the person doing all the work. Instead, Acme pays Sam's corporation, which is Sam's employer. It's the corporation's responsibility to pay state and federal payroll taxes for Sam.

Having a legal entity, the corporation, between you and the worker is the main benefit of hiring an incorporated worker. Legally, the corporation is the worker's employer, not you. It is supposed to pay state and federal payroll taxes and provide

workers' compensation insurance, not you. If the corporation fails to pay these taxes, IRS and state auditors will likely concentrate on the corporation and its owners, not you, unless the corporation is a sham. (See Section 3c.)

Even if you're audited, you'll usually have an easier time proving that an incorporated worker is an IC. Forming a corporation is expensive and time-consuming, and operating one can be burdensome as well. Auditors are usually greatly impressed by the fact that a worker has gone to the time and trouble to form and operate a corporation. This is something that only people who are running their own businesses do. And people who are running their own businesses can't be your employees.

In one case, for example, the New Jersey Labor Department audited a carpet company that hired 39 carpet installers and classified them as ICs. One of the installers was incorporated. Only two of the installers were eventually found to be ICs, one of whom was the incorporated installer. (*Carpet Remnant Warehouse, Inc. v. New Jersey Dept. of Labor*, 593 A.2d 1177 (1991).)

Another benefit of hiring incorporated outside workers is that you don't have to file a Form 1099-MISC reporting to the IRS payments to corporations—eliminating a very important IRS audit lead. (See Chapter 15, Section C.) You will not have the advantage of this benefit, however, where you make payments to medical corporations.

c. Problems with corporations

Incorporating is not a panacea. Simply filing articles of incorporation will not magically insulate a hiring firm or worker from the IRS. You're most likely to have problems where an outside worker's corporation fails to pay federal or state payroll taxes. If this is coupled with evidence that the corporation is not being operated as an independent business, it's quite possible that the IRS will disregard the corporation as a sham and determine that the worker is an employee of the hiring firm.

EXAMPLE: Bill, a delivery truck driver, forms a corporation called Bill's Trucking, Inc. with himself as the sole shareholder and president. The corporation has no assets and no employees other than Bill. Acme Press hires Bill's Trucking to make deliveries. Bill is treated just like an Acme employee; Acme provides him with a truck, gives him health and pension benefits and controls him on the job. Acme pays a monthly check to Bill's Trucking. However, Bill deposits the funds in his personal account and pays no federal or state payroll taxes. It's likely the IRS would conclude that the corporation is a sham and that Bill is Acme's employee.

d. Finding incorporated ICs

Skilled workers such lawyers, doctors and accountants often form their own corporations. You may not have much trouble hiring incorporated workers in these fields.

However, it's much more unusual for lower skilled and less highly paid workers to be incorporated. For example, it's rare for a trucker or delivery person to be incorporated. So you simply may not be able to find an incorporated worker to perform these types of services.

⚠ When to Steer Clear of Incorporators

You should not help a worker form a corporation or pay him or her to do so, since this makes the corporation look like a sham. True ICs who are in business for themselves form their corporations on their own initiative with their own money.

In addition, you may have to pay more to hire an incorporated worker because operating a corporation is more expensive and burdensome than being a sole proprietor or partner. For example, if there is more than one shareholder, certain formalities must be adhered to such as holding annual meetings and keeping corporate minutes. And in many states, a corporation must pay a minimum annual tax even if it didn't earn any money for the year.

B. Employee Leasing

Instead of hiring workers directly, many companies lease or rent them from outside leasing companies. Such workers may be referred to as temporary employees, temps, contract employees or contingent or casual workers. This chapter refers to them as leased employees.

Using leased employees is sometimes referred to as outsourcing or outside staffing. Whatever the practice is called, over the past ten years, leasing employees has become an increasingly popular method for hiring firms to obtain the services of outside workers.

Worker leasing arrangements take a variety of forms. For example, you may lease workers from an employment agency which locates the workers for you or already has them on staff. This is what temp agencies do. In other cases, the leasing company may hire your employees and lease them back to you for a fee.

Employee leasing can give you many of the benefits that can be obtained by hiring ICs directly. You can obtain the services of highly trained and experienced workers who have been screened and selected by the leasing company. You use them only when needed and then dispense with their services without going through the trauma and expense of laying off your own employees. You do not have to pay and withhold federal and state payroll taxes for leased workers or provide them with workers' compensation or employee benefits; the leasing company is supposed to do all this. Another benefit is that you have reduced exposure to government audits.

It can cost more to lease workers through leasing companies than hiring them directly since leasing companies have to pay the leased employees salaries plus earn a profit, but many companies feel it's worth it. Almost all companies use leased employees from time to time. However, although employee leasing arrangements can work well, there are some serious pitfalls you should be aware of that require careful planning to avoid.

A LOOK AT OTHER ALTERNATIVE WORK ARRANGEMENTS

Besides leasing employees, there are many other alternative work arrangements that don't require full-time year-round work in a hiring firm's workplace. They include:
- hiring part-time workers
- hiring short-term workers
- having workers work at home and communicate with the office via phone and computer—also known as telecommuting, and
- using seasonal workers.

Some hiring firms believe that workers involved in such work arrangements can never be their employees. This is not the case. The fact that workers work part-time, short-term or at home has relatively little impact on their status. If you have the right to control such workers on the job, they will be your employees. (See Chapter 3, Section D.)

---

1. Leased Workers' Employment Status

The idea behind worker leasing is that the leased workers are supposed to be the leasing firm's employees, not yours. In the ideal worker leasing arrangement, the leasing firm is responsible for supervising and controlling the worker's job performance, paying the leased workers' salaries and paying and withholding federal and state payroll taxes, paying for unemployment compensation, providing workers' compensation coverage and any employee benefits. Ideally, all you do is pay the leasing firm a fee.

Whenever you're on the top rung of a three-sided relationship like this, you have much less chance of being audited. As long as the leasing firm pays all applicable taxes, there is little likelihood that you'll have any problems with the IRS. However, you may have IRS problems if your company has a pension plan.

PROBLEMS WITH RETIREMENT PLANS

If your company leases workers full-time for work that used to be performed by employees, the IRS may view the leased workers as company employees for retirement and profit-sharing plan purposes.

The leased workers would be counted in determining whether the nondiscrimination and minimum participation rules governing tax-qualified retirement plans are satisfied. This is important because a minimum number of employees must be included in a retirement plan for it to be tax-qualified—that is, for company contributions to the plan to be deductible by the company and nontaxable to the recipients until retirement. (See Chapter 8, Section G.)

If any of your plans are found not to comply with the requirements for tax-qualified status, then all previous tax deductions for benefits or contributions to the plan can be thrown out. Your business can lose the deductions, and the benefit recipients will have to pay taxes on the benefits.

There are ways to avoid this problem. But this is a very complex area of the law, so it's best to discuss this issue with a retirement plan administrator, or to seek advice from a retirement plan consultant or an attorney or CPA specializing in this field.

---

a. The problem of joint employment

Unfortunately, things don't always work out as described above. If you control a leased worker's performance on the job, you can be considered the worker's employer along with the leasing company. This is called joint employment. If you're a joint employer of a leased employee, you lose all the benefits of employee leasing. You have the same duties and liabilities as if you were the worker's sole employer.

> **EXAMPLE:** The Merrill Lynch securities firm leased the services of Amarnare through an employment agency. Amarnare's pay and benefits were paid by the agency, not Merrill Lynch. Amarnare was fired after two weeks on the job and then sued Merrill Lynch, but not the employment agency, for unlawful discrimination claiming that she was fired because of her sex and race. Merrill Lynch claimed it was not liable because it was not Amarnare's employer, the employment agency was.
>
> The court disagreed. It held that Merrill Lynch was Amarnare's joint employer, along with the employment agency, because it completely controlled Amarnare on the job. Merrill Lynch controlled Amarnare's work assignments, working hours and manner of performance; directly supervised her; and had the right to discharge her and request a replacement if it found her work unsatisfactory. (*Amarnare v. Merrill, Lynch, Pierce, Fenner & Smith, Inc.*, 611 F.Supp. 344 (S.D.N.Y. 1984).)

If you're found to be a joint employer of a leased worker, you'll not only be liable for labor and anti-discrimination law violations, but can have a legal duty to provide the worker with unemployment insurance and workers' compensation. If the leasing company fails to provide them, you'll have to and will be subject to penalties for the leasing company's failure to do so in the first place.

b. Avoiding joint employer status

To avoid being a joint employer of a leased worker, you must give up all control over the worker. The leasing firm, not you, must control the leased worker's performance on the job.

Carefully follow these guidelines.

- Don't ever deal or negotiate with a leased worker about such matters as time, place and type of work, working conditions or the quality and price of the services to be provided by the worker. The leasing company should handle all these negotiations for you—that is, you tell the leasing company what you want and it tells the worker.
- The leasing company should have the sole right to determine whether to assign or reassign workers to perform needed tasks.
- The leasing company should set the rate of pay for the leased workers.
- The leasing company should pay the leased workers from its own account.
- The leasing company, not you, should have the right to hire or fire the leased workers; if the company fails to provide you with high quality workers, don't fire them. Instead, hire a new leasing company.
- The leasing company should have the authority to assign or reassign a worker to other clients or customers if you feel the worker is not acceptable.

It's also very helpful if the leasing company provides its own supervisor or on-site administrator to manage and supervise the leased workers. This will significantly reduce your control over the workers and reduce the chances that you'll be a joint employer.

If you're unable or unwilling to relinquish all control over leased workers, you can still go ahead with a leasing arrangement. But be aware that you may be considered to be the leased workers' joint employer. As such, you'll need to make certain that the leasing firm is paying all required payroll taxes, providing workers' compensation insurance and not engaging in behavior that could get you sued, such as discriminating against workers on the basis of race or age.

c. Problems with workers' compensation insurance

Another problem area with which you need to be concerned when you lease workers is workers' compensation insurance. The employee leasing company, not you, is supposed to provide the leased workers with workers' comp coverage.

In the past, some shady hiring firms saved money on workers' comp insurance premiums by having equally shady leasing firms hire their employees and lease them back to them. The leasing firm would purchase workers' comp insurance for the employees at a lower rate than the hiring firm because it was newly in business and few or no workers' comp claims had been filed against it. Workers' comp premiums are based in part on how many claims are filed against a company. This factor is called the experience modifier. Companies that have many claims filed by employees pay more than companies that don't. These leasing companies continually changed their names and formed new business entities. Each new entity would have a clean workers' comp record and so would pay a lower workers' comp premium.

This scam is no longer possible in most states. Most now require employee leasing companies to use the same experience modifier as their client firms use for similar workers. To make sure that a leasing company is paying the proper workers' comp premium, ask to see a copy of its workers' comp policy showing the classifications and experience modifier used. If these are different from those in your own policy, question the leasing company closely.

Also, make sure your agreement with the leasing company requires it to notify you in writing if its workers' compensation insurance is canceled for any reason. You may end up having to pay premiums for leased employees if the leasing firm's insurance is canceled.

2. Dealing With Established Leasing Companies

It's very important that you deal with a reputable leasing firm that is an established business with its own offices and management. Such a firm is more likely to make all required payroll tax and insurance payments. Remember, if the leasing firm doesn't pay for these items, you may have to pay for them.

Don't take a leasing firm's word it's paying payroll taxes and insurance premiums. Require any leasing firm to provide you with proof that it is withholding and paying federal and state payroll taxes and paying for workers' compensation insurance for your leased employees.

3. Using Written Agreements

Sign a written lease agreement with a leasing company. Among other things, such an agreement should provide that:

- the leased workers are the leasing company's employees
- the leasing company is responsible for paying the leased workers' wages and withholding and paying all state and federal payroll taxes, including unemployment compensation

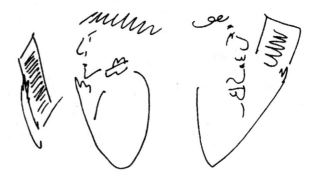

- the leasing company will provide the leased workers with workers' compensation insurance, and
- the leasing company will indemnify you—that is, repay you—for all losses you might suffer as a result of its failure to comply with any legal requirements, including the costs of defending against charges of alleged violations. For example, if the leasing company fails to withhold and pay employment taxes, it will pay any IRS assessments and penalties and your legal fees incurred in defending yourself against the IRS.

The agreement should also provide that the leasing company has the sole authority to hire, fire, schedule, supervise and discipline the leased workers. (See Section 1b above.)

Most leasing companies have their own lease agreements. It's wise to have an attorney review any leasing agreement before you sign it. ■

Procedures for Hiring Independent Contractors

Assume that sooner or later you will be audited by the IRS and other government agencies and the status of workers you've classified as ICs will be questioned. Long before you're audited, you should have in your files all the information and documentation you need to prove that a worker is an IC. Don't wait until you're audited to start thinking about how to prove a worker is an IC; by then it may be too late.

A. Before Hiring an IC

Someone in your company should be in charge of:
- interviewing prospective ICs
- determining whether applicants qualify as ICs
- authorizing workers to be hired as ICs, and
- preparing an IC data file containing the information and documentation you'll need to prove the worker is an IC if you're audited.

This individual, who may be called a Contract Administrator, should be fully trained regarding the laws and rules used to determine a worker's status. If you're running a one-person business, this person is you.

1. Interviewing Prospective ICs

All prospective ICs should fill out the Independent Contractor Questionnaire contained in the Appendix and provide the required documentation. Do not have an IC fill out an employment application; this makes the worker look like an employee.

The Contract Administrator should review the Questionnaire and documentation with the IC during an initial interview. The goal is to determine whether you can prove that the IC is in business for himself or herself.

QUESTIONS YOU SHOULDN'T ASK

Federal and state laws bar employers from asking certain types of questions in interviews or on employment applications. It's wise to also follow these rules when you interview ICs. For example, the Americans With Disabilities Act prohibits pre-employment questions about a disability. In addition, the Civil Rights Act forbids you to ask about an applicant's race, marital status, height, weight, gender, birthplace or national origin. There are also restrictions concerning questions about an applicant's age, arrest record, citizenship and affiliations. For detailed information, see *The Employer's Legal Handbook* by Fred Steingold (Nolo Press).

2. Required Documentation

Ask any worker you plan to hire as an IC to provide the following documentation:
- copies of the IC's business license if required and any professional licenses the IC has, such as a contractor's license
- certificates showing that the IC has insurance, including general liability insurance and workers' compensation insurance if the IC has employees
- the IC's business cards and stationery
- copies of any advertising the IC has done, such as a Yellow Pages listing
- a copy of the IC's white pages business phone listing, if there is one
- if the IC is operating under an assumed name, a copy of the fictitious business name statement
- the IC's invoice form to be used for billing purposes
- a copy of any office lease and a photograph of the IC's office or workplace will also be helpful

- the names and salaries of all assistants that the IC will use on the job
- the names and salaries of all assistants the IC has used on previous jobs for the past two years and proof that the IC has paid them, such as copies of canceled checks or copies of payroll tax forms
- a list of all the equipment and materials the IC will use in performing the services and how much it costs; proof that the IC has paid for the equipment, such as copies of canceled checks, is very helpful
- the names and addresses of other clients or customers for whom the IC has performed services during the previous two years; but don't ask for the identities of any clients the IC is required to keep confidential, and
- if the IC is a sole proprietor and will agree to do so, copies of the IC's tax returns for the previous two years showing that the IC has filed a Schedule C, Profit or Loss From a Business; this will show that the IC has been operating an independent business.

THE IMPORTANCE OF IC'S FORM OF BUSINESS

How an IC's business is legally organized plays an important role in avoiding and winning IRS and other government audits. (See Chapter 8, Section B.) You'll have the most trouble proving that ICs who are sole proprietors are in business for themselves. Unfortunately, that is the way the vast majority of ICs do business.

From your point of view, by far the best form of legal organization for an IC is a corporation. Don't take an IC's word that he or she is incorporated. Obtain a copy of the articles of incorporation—a document that must be filed with the Secretary of State or similar official in the state where the corporation is organized as proof that the corporation exists. Also, call the Secretary of State's office to make sure that the corporation is in good standing—that is, not dissolved or defunct.

3. Determining Whether Workers Qualify as ICs

The Contract Administrator must examine the answers the worker provided on the Independent Contractor Questionnaire, the documentation and the task the IC is being hired to perform to see if the worker can qualify as an IC.

This can be difficult because there is no single definition of an IC. Mechanical rules won't work. For example, some firms will hire any worker as an IC so long as he or she is incorporated and works no longer than six months for the firm. While both these factors are very helpful, they are no guarantee that the worker will not be reclassified as an employee by the IRS or other government auditors. All the facts and circumstances must be examined and weighed on a case-by-case basis. (See Chapter 3, Section A.)

ONE IMPORTANT QUESTION TO ASK

One very important question to ask yourself is whether in the past your company has used employees to perform services similar to those the IC will be asked to do. While it may be theoretically possible for employees and ICs to perform the same services, it can pose practical problems. For one thing, you will not be permitted to use the Section 530 safe harbor, one of your most important defenses in an IRS audit. (See Chapter 7.) You're much better off if you keep the work your employees and ICs do separate.

---

4. Drafting and Signing an IC Agreement

If you determine that the worker qualifies as an IC, complete and sign an independent contractor agreement before the IC starts work. (See Chapter 16.) However, the IC may have his or her own agreement. If so, ask for a copy and use it as your starting point in drafting the agreement. This will show that the agreement is a real negotiated contract, not a standard form you forced the worker to sign. Pay particular attention to whether the IC's agreement contains any provisions that should be deleted or amended, or whether new provisions should be added. (See Chapter 16, Section C.)

5. Obtaining the IC's Taxpayer ID Number

If you pay an unincorporated IC $600 or more during a year, you must obtain the IC's taxpayer identification number. If you don't, you are required to withhold 31% of all payments over $599 you make to the IC and remit the money to the IRS. This is called backup withholding. If you fail to backup withhold, on audit the IRS will impose an assessment against you equal to 31% of what you paid the IC.

Backup withholding is not required for corporations. You only need to do it when you fail to obtain the taxpayer identification number from an IC who is a sole proprietor or member of a partnership.

a. How to avoid backup withholding

It's very easy to avoid backup withholding. Have the IC fill out and sign IRS Form W-9, Request for Taxpayer Identification Number, and retain it in your IC file. (See the Appendix for a copy of the form.) You don't have to file the W-9 with the IRS. This simple form merely requires the IC to list his or her name and address and taxpayer ID number. Corporations, partnerships and sole proprietors must have a federal employer identification number (EIN), which is obtained from the IRS. In the case of sole proprietors without employees, the taxpayer ID number is either the IC's Social Security number or an EIN if the IC has obtained one.

If the IC doesn't already have an EIN, you don't have to backup withhold for 60 days after he or she applies for one. It usually takes several weeks to obtain.

WHICH IS BETTER, A SOCIAL SECURITY NUMBER OR EIN?

A sole proprietor IC who doesn't have employees can use either his or her Social Security number or a separate federal employer identification number as the taxpayer ID number. It's better for you if the IC obtains an EIN. This helps show that the IC is running an independent business. Employees don't have EINs. Encourage any sole proprietor IC you hire to obtain an EIN.

Obtaining one is easy and costs nothing. The IC simply files IRS Form SS-4 with the IRS center listed in the instructions on the form. The IC can obtain an SS-4 by calling the IRS at: 800-TAX-FORM (829-3676).

---

b. Backup withholding procedure

If you are unable to obtain an IC's taxpayer ID number or the IRS informs you that the number the IC gave you is incorrect, you'll have to do backup withholding. Backup withholding must begin after you pay an IC $600 or more during the year. You need not backup withhold on payments totaling less than $600.

For this procedure, you withhold 31% of the IC's compensation and deposit it every quarter with your bank or other payroll tax depository. These deposits must be made separately from the payroll tax deposits you make for employees.

You report the amounts withheld on IRS Form 945, Annual Return of Withheld Federal Income Tax. This is an annual return you must file by January 31 of the following year. See the instruc-

tions to form 945 for details. You can obtain a copy of the form by calling the IRS at: 800-TAX-FORM (829-3676) or by contacting your local IRS office.

6. Keeping Records

Create a file for each IC you hire. Keep these files separate from the personnel files you use for employees. Each file should contain:

- the Independent Contractor Questionnaire completed by the IC (see the Appendix and forms disk at QUEST)
- the signed final IC agreement and copies of any interim drafts
- the IRS W-9 form signed by the IC containing the IC's taxpayer identification number
- all the documentation provided by the IC, such as proof of insurance, business cards and stationery, copies of advertisements, professional licenses, copies of articles of incorporation
- all the invoices the IC submits for billing purposes, and
- copies of all Form 1099s you file reporting your payments to the IC. (See Section C.)

Keep your IC files for at least six years.

B. During the IC's Work Period

Treat the worker as an IC while he or she works for you—much the way you would the accountant who does your company's taxes or the lawyer who handles your legal work.

There are a number of work habits you must avoid:

- Don't supervise the IC or his or her assistants. The IC should perform the services without your direction. Your control should be limited to accepting or rejecting the final results the IC achieves.
- Don't let the IC work at your offices unless the nature of the services absolutely requires

it—for example, where a computer consultant must work on your computers or a carpet installer is hired to lay carpet in your office.

- Don't give the IC employee handbooks or company policy manuals.
- Don't establish the IC's working hours.
- Avoid giving ICs so much work or such short deadlines that they have to work full-time for you. It's best for ICs to work for others at the same time they work for you.
- Don't provide ongoing instructions or training. If the IC needs special training, he or she should not obtain it in-house and should pay for it himself or herself.
- Don't provide the IC with equipment or materials unless absolutely necessary.
- Don't give an IC business cards or stationery to use that has your company name on them.
- Don't give an IC a title within your company.
- Don't pay the IC's travel or other business expenses. Pay the IC enough to cover these expenses out of his or her own pocket.
- Don't give an IC employee benefits such as health insurance. Pay ICs enough to provide their own benefits.
- Don't require formal written reports. An occasional phone call inquiring into the work's progress is acceptable. But requiring regular written status reports indicates the worker is an employee.
- Don't invite an IC to employee meetings or functions.
- Don't refer to an IC as an employee, or to your company as the IC's employer, either verbally or in writing.
- Don't pay ICs on a weekly, bi-weekly, or monthly basis as you pay employees. Rather, require all ICs to submit invoices to be paid for their work. Pay the invoices at the same time you pay other outside vendors.

- Obey the terms of your IC agreement. Among other things, this means that you can't fire the IC. You can only terminate the IC's contract according to its terms—for example, if the IC's services fail to satisfy the contract specifications.
- Don't give the IC new projects after the original project is completed without signing a new IC agreement.

C. After the IC's Services End

A hiring firm's work is never done. Even after an IC's services end, there is paperwork to complete. Failing to do so may mean severe penalties if you're audited.

1. Filing 1099s

The single most important thing to do after an unincorporated IC's services end is to provide the worker and IRS with an IRS Form 1099-MISC reporting the compensation you paid the worker. Your failure to do so will result in severe penalties if the IRS later audits you and determines you misclassified the worker.

First, you'll be required to pay the IRS twice as much for the misclassification. (See Chapter 8, Section C.)

You'll also lose the right to claim Section 530 relief for any payments not reported on Form 1099; this means you'll lose one of your best defenses against the IRS. (See Chapter 7.)

And finally, the IRS may impose a $50 fine for each 1099-MISC you failed to file.

a. When 1099s must be filed

The basic rule is that you must file a 1099-MISC whenever you pay an unincorporated IC—that is, an IC who is a sole proprietor or member of a partnership—$600 or more in a year for work done in the course of your trade or business.

EXAMPLE: The Acme Widget Company hires Thomas to install a new computer system. Acme classifies Thomas as an IC and pays him $2,000 during 1995. Thomas is a sole proprietor. Since Acme paid him more than $599, it must file a Form 1099 with the IRS reporting the payment.

In calculating whether the payments made to an IC total $600 or more during a year, you must include payments for parts or materials used by the IC in performing the services.

EXAMPLE: The Old Reliable Insurance Company pays $1,000 to an unincorporated auto repair shop to repair one of its insured's cars. The repair contract states that $300 is for labor and $700 is for parts. Old Reliable must report the entire $1,000 on Form 1099 because the parts were used by the repair shop to perform the car repair services.

b. Services in the course of your trade or business

A 1099-MISC need be filed only when an IC's services are performed in the course of your trade or business. A trade or business is an activity carried on for gain or profit. You don't have to file a 1099-MISC for payments for non-business related services. This includes payments you make to ICs for personal or household service—for example, payments to babysitters, gardeners and housekeepers. Running your home is not a profit-making activity.

EXAMPLE: Eddy owns several homes he rents out to tenants. He is in the business of renting houses. Eddy pays Linda, who operates a painting business as a sole proprietor, $1,750 to paint one of his rental houses. Eddy must report the $1,750 payment to Linda on Form 1099-MISC.

EXAMPLE: Eddy pays Linda $1,750 to paint his own home. He lives in this home with his wife and family and it is not a part of his home rental business. Eddy need not report this payment on Form 1099-MISC because this work was not done in the course of his business.

Although nonprofit organizations are not engaged in a trade or business, they are still required to report payments made to ICs. Payments to ICs by federal, state or local government agencies must also be reported.

EXAMPLE: Leslie, owner of an unincorporated home repair business, is paid $1,000 for repair work on a church. Even though the church is a tax-exempt nonprofit organization and is not engaged in business, it must report the $1,000 payment to Leslie on Form 1099-MISC.

c. Payments exempt from 1099 filing requirement

You don't need to report payments solely for merchandise or inventory. This includes raw materials and supplies that will become a part of merchandise you intend to sell.

EXAMPLE: The Acme Widget Company pays $5,000 to purchase 100 used widgets from Joe's Widgets, a sole proprietorship owned by Joe. Acme intends to fix up and resell the widgets. The payment to Joe need not be reported on Form 1099 because Acme is purchasing merchandise from Joe, not IC services.

In addition, you need not file a Form 1099 when you pay for:
- freight, storage and similar items
- telephone, telegraph and similar services, or
- rent to real estate agents.

You need not file 1099s for wages paid to your employees, or for payments for their traveling or business expenses. These amounts are reported on Form W-2.

d. No 1099s needed for corporations

Subject to one exception, you need not file a Form 1099 for payments made to an incorporated IC. This is one of the main advantages of hiring incorporated ICs because the IRS uses 1099s as an audit lead. (See Chapter 8, Section B.)

EXAMPLE: The Acme Sandblasting Company pays $5,000 to Yvonne, a CPA, to perform accounting services. Yvonne has formed her own one-person corporation called Yvonne's Accounting Services, Inc. Acme pays the corporation, not Yvonne personally. Since Acme is paying a corporation, it need not report the payment on Form 1099-MISC.

The only exception to this rule is for payments to medical corporations; these must be reported on Form 1099-MISC.

EXAMPLE: The Acme Sandblasting Company pays $2,000 to Dr. Smith to perform physicals for its employees. Smith has formed his own medical corporation, and the $2,000 is paid to the corporation, not to Smith personally. Nevertheless, the payment must be reported on Form 1099-MISC because Smith is operating a medical corporation.

e. Filing procedures

One 1099-MISC must be filed for each IC to whom you paid $600 or more during the year. You must obtain original 1099 forms from the IRS. You cannot photocopy this form because it is a multi-copy form. Each 1099 form contains three parts and can be used for three different workers. All your 1099s must be submitted together along with one copy of Form 1096, which is a transmittal form—the IRS equivalent of a cover letter. (See below for a sample.) You must obtain an original Form 1096 from the IRS, you cannot submit a photocopy. These forms can be obtained by calling the IRS at: 800-TAX-FORM (829-3676) or by contacting your local IRS office.

Filling out Form 1099-MISC is easy. Follow this step-by-step approach:
- List your name and address in the first box titled "Payer's name."
- Your taxpayer identification number must be listed in the box entitled "Payer's Federal identification number."
- The IC is called the "Recipient" on this form, meaning the person who received payment from you. You must provide the IC's taxpayer identification number, name and address in the boxes indicated. For sole proprietors, you must list the individual's

name first, and then may list a different business name, though this is not required. You may not enter only a business name for a sole proprietor.

- The amount of your payments to the IC must be entered in Box 7, entitled "Non-employee compensation." Be sure to fill in the right box or the 1099-MISC will be deemed invalid by the IRS.

- Finally, if you've done backup withholding for an IC who has not provided you with a taxpayer ID number, enter the amount withheld in Box 4.

The 1099-MISC form contains five copies. These must be filed as follows:

- Copy A, the top copy, must be filed with the IRS no later than February 28 of the year after payment was made to the IC;

don't cut or separate this page, even though it has spaces for three workers.

- Copy 1 must be filed with your state taxing authority if your state has a state income tax. The filing deadline is probably February 28, but check with your state tax department to make sure. Your state may have a specific transmittal form you must obtain.

- Copy B and Copy 2 must be given to the worker no later than January 31 of the year after payment was made.

- Copy C is for you to retain for your files.

All the IRS copies of each 1099-MISC are filed together with Form 1096, a simple transmittal form. You must add up all the payments reported on all the 1099s and list the total in the box indicated on Form 1096. File the forms with the IRS Service Center listed on the reverse of Form 1096.

FORM 1099-MISC

9595 ☐ VOID ☐ CORRECTED		
PAYER'S name, street address, city, state, and ZIP code	1 Rents $	OMB No. 1545-0115
	2 Royalties $	19**95** **Miscellaneous Income**
	3 Other income $	Form **1099-MISC**
PAYER'S Federal identification number / RECIPIENT'S identification number	4 Federal income tax withheld $	5 Fishing boat proceeds $	**Copy A** For **Internal Revenue Service Center**
RECIPIENT'S name	6 Medical and health care payments $	7 Nonemployee compensation $	**File with Form 1096.**
Street address (including apt. no.)	8 Substitute payments in lieu of dividends or interest $	9 Payer made direct sales of $5,000 or more of consumer products to a buyer (recipient) for resale ▶ ☐	For Paperwork Reduction Act Notice and instructions for completing this form, see **Instructions for Forms 1099, 1098, 5498, and W-2G.**
City, state, and ZIP code	10 Crop insurance proceeds $	11 State income tax withheld $	
Account number (optional)	2nd TIN Not. ☐	12 State/Payer's state number	

Form **1099-MISC**   Cat. No. 14425J   Department of the Treasury - Internal Revenue Service

Do NOT Cut or Separate Forms on This Page

FORM 1096

DO NOT STAPLE 6969

Form **1096** Department of the Treasury Internal Revenue Service	**Annual Summary and Transmittal of U.S. Information Returns**	OMB No. 1545-0108 19**95**

A T T A C H I R S L A B E L H E R E

FILER'S name

Street address (including room or suite number)

City, state, and ZIP code

If you are not using a preprinted label, enter in box 1 or 2 below the identification number you used as the filer on the information returns being transmitted. Do not fill in both boxes 1 and 2.	Name of person to contact if the IRS needs more information Telephone number ( )	**For Official Use Only**

1 Employer identification number	**2** Social security number	**3** Total number of forms	**4** Federal income tax withheld $	**5** Total amount reported with this Form 1096 $

Enter an "X" in only one box below to indicate the type of form being filed.   If this is your FINAL return, enter an "X" here ▶ ☐

W-2G 32	1098 81	1099-A 80	1099-B 79	1099-C 85	1099-DIV 91	1099-G 86	1099-INT 92	1099-MISC 95	1099-OID 96	1099-PATR 97	1099-R 98	1099-S 75	5498 28
☐	☐	☐	☐	☐	☐	☐	☐	☐	☐	☐	☐	☐	☐

Please return this entire page to the Internal Revenue Service. Photocopies are NOT acceptable.

Under penalties of perjury, I declare that I have examined this return and accompanying documents, and, to the best of my knowledge and belief, they are true, correct, and complete.

Signature ▶   Title ▶   Date ▶

When in Doubt, File a 1099

If you're not sure whether a Form 1099-MISC must be filed for a worker, go ahead and file one anyway. You lose nothing by doing so and will save yourself the severe consequences of not filing if you were in fact required to do so.

2. IRS Form 4669

If the IRS determines that you intentionally misclassified a worker as an IC, it will impose a 20% income tax assessment. You will be required to pay the IRS an amount equal to 20% of all the payments you made to the worker.

However, this assessment will be reduced or eliminated if you can prove the worker reported and paid income taxes on the payments. Such a reduction is called an offset or abatement.

To obtain this abatement, you must file IRS Form 4669, Employee Wage Statement. This form states how much tax the worker paid on the wages in question. The worker must sign the form under penalty of perjury. You must file a Form 4669 for each worker involved along with

Form 4670, Request for Relief From Payment of Income Tax Withholding, which is used to summarize and transmit the Forms 4669.

 Copies of both Form 4669 and Form 4670 are contained in the Appendix.

Unfortunately, by the time your company is audited, typically one to three years after you hired the worker, it may be impossible for you to locate the worker or persuade him or her to complete and sign a Form 4669. This means you'll be unable to get the abatement.

A better approach is to be proactive and ask workers to sign a Form 4669 as soon as their services end. Retain the signed 4669s in your IC files. This way you'll be sure to be able to obtain an abatement if the worst happens: You're audited by the IRS and it claims you have intentionally misclassified the worker.

By April 15 of the year following the year an IC performed services for you, send him or her a blank Form 4669 to fill out and sign. Your IC agreement should contain a provision obligating the worker to provide the information required in the form. (See Chapter 16.) ■

Independent Contractor Agreements

This chapter explains why you should use written agreements with independent contractors, describes what such agreements should contain and provides sample language for you to use.

There are a number of ways you can use the suggested text offered here.

- You can draft contracts using the files contained on the Forms Disk. Using the suggested language from the disk gives you the greatest flexibility, as you will be able to pick and choose the clauses that apply to your situation. You can then use your final draft as a starting point of negotiations with the IC and tailor your final agreement to both of your needs.

- If you do not have access to a computer, you can retype the language suggested in this chapter to assemble your final agreement. Again, this will allow you to tailor your document to your specific needs.

- You can complete and use the tear-out sample forms in the Appendix. While this may be the easiest option available to you, it is the least desirable. This is because IRS examiners and other government officials may be looking into your business matters. They are likely to look askance at a fill-in-the-blank form, since that implies that you and the IC did not negotiate the agreement, but that you coerced him or her to sign according to your terms.

A. Using Written Agreements

Sign a written agreement with an IC before he or she starts work. An IC agreement serves two main purposes:

- it avoids later disputes by providing a written description of the services the IC is supposed to perform and how much the IC will be paid, and

- it describes the relationship between you and the IC to help make clear that the IC is not your employee.

1. Oral Agreements

Courts are crowded with lawsuits filed by people who entered into oral agreements with one other and later disagreed over what was said. Costly misunderstandings can develop if an IC performs services for you without a writing clearly stating what he or she is supposed to do and what will happen if it isn't done. Such misunderstandings may be innocent; you and the IC may have simply misinterpreted one another. Or they may be purposeful; without a writing to contradict him or her, an IC can claim that you orally agreed to anything.

Consider a good written IC agreement to be your legal lifeline. If disputes develop, the agreement will provide ways to solve them. If you and the IC end up in court, a written agreement will establish your legal duties to one another.

2. Establishing IC Status

If your business is audited, an auditor will first ask to see your agreements with all workers you've classified as independent contractors. A well-drafted agreement that indicates that the IC is in business for himself or herself will help make clear to the auditor that the worker is an independent contractor. The document will help demonstrate that you and the worker intended to create an independent contractor relationship. And because written agreements with ICs have become a routine fact of business life, if you don't have one, you will immediately look suspect.

However, a written IC agreement is not a magic legal bullet. It will never by itself make a worker an IC. What really counts is the substance of how you treat a worker. If the agreement is accurate when it says the worker is in business, that will be helpful. But it won't help a bit if the worker is treated like an employee.

> **EXAMPLE:** AcmeSoft, Inc. hires Pat to perform computer programming. It requires her to sign a document called an Independent

Contractor Agreement. The agreement states that Pat is an IC and that AcmeSoft will exercise no control over Pat on the job. However, in reality Pat is treated just like an AcmeSoft employee: her work is closely supervised, she is paid bi-weekly, she has set hours of work and she works only for AcmeSoft. Pat is an AcmeSoft employee, despite what the agreement says.

B. Drafting Agreements

You don't need to hire a lawyer to draft an independent contractor agreement. All you need is a brain and a little common sense. This chapter gives you guidance and suggested language to use as a starting point in fashioning your agreement to meet your needs.

1. Standard Form Agreements

There are various standard form IC agreements you can obtain from stationery stores and other sources. These forms contain standard one-size-fits-all legalese and are not tailored for any particular occupation.

IRS and state auditors are well aware that hiring firms often have workers sign such generic IC agreements before they start work. The worker may not even bother to read the agreement and certainly makes no changes in it to reflect the real work situation.

The more an IC agreement is custom-tailored for each worker or group of workers performing similar tasks and reflects the true relationship between the hiring firm and workers, the more helpful it will be.

2. The Drafting Process

Either you or the IC should begin the process of drafting an agreement by offering the other person proposed language to include. Then both of you can negotiate and make changes until you agree on a final version.

a. Using the IC's agreement

Many ICs have their own agreements they've used in the past. If so, it's often wise to use that agreement as the starting point. This avoids giving government auditors the impression that the agreement is simply a company-drafted standard form the worker was forced to sign.

Read the IC's agreement carefully because it may contain provisions unduly favorable to the IC and harmful to you. Make sure it contains all the necessary provisions discussed here. (See Section C.) If not, add them. You may also wish to add some provisions of your own or other optional provisions discussed below. (See Section D.)

Keep copies of the IC's original agreement and all the changes. These will help show auditors that the agreement was negotiated, not a contract you imposed on the IC.

b. Using your own agreement

If the IC does not have an agreement you can use, you'll have to provide one of your own. You can use the general IC agreement provided here and adapt it for almost any kind of work.

A copy of the General Independent Contractor Agreement is included in the Appendix. You can also find it on the Forms Disk under GENAGREE. (See Section E.)

Again, feel free to add provisions of your own or other options discussed below. (See Section D.)

In addition, because large numbers of ICs traditionally work in certain occupations, this chapter discusses five different agreements, each tailored for specific types of service providers, including:

- household workers (see Section F1)
- direct sellers (see Section F2)
- real estate salespeople (see Section F3)
- independent consultants (see Section F4), and
- contributors to a work made for hire (see Section F5).

Copies of all of these agreements are included in the Appendix. You can also find them on the Forms Disk, as discussed in the appropriate section.

Generally, independent contractor agreements for the development of computer software must contain a number of complex provisions concerning intellectual property, software testing, source code escrows and other matters outside the scope of this book. For a detailed discussion of software development agreements and sample forms, see *Software Development: A Legal Guide,* by Stephen Fishman (Nolo Press).

C. Essential Provisions

A number of provisions should be included in most IC agreements. All of these sample clauses are included in the General Independent Contractor Agreement. (See Section E for a sample of how an entire agreement might look when assembled.)

The entire text of the following agreement is on the Forms Disk in the back of this book under GENAGREE.

This information can be used as:

- a checklist when you review an IC agreement provided by a worker to make sure nothing important has been left out, or
- a starting point to draft your own agreement.

These provisions may be all you need for a simple IC agreement. Or you may need to combine them with some of your own clauses or one or more of the optional clauses discussed here. (See Section D.)

Title of agreement. Deceptively simple things such as what you call an IC agreement and yourself and the IC can have a big impact. You need not have a title for an IC agreement, but if you want one, call it Independent Contractor Agreement or Consulting Agreement. Consulting Agreement may sound a little more high-toned than Independent Contractor Agreement and is often used when contracting with skilled professionals to provide services. For example, IC agreements with computer software experts are often called consulting agreements. Do not use Employment Agreement as a title.

SUGGESTED LANGUAGE:

INDEPENDENT CONTRACTOR AGREEMENT

 This text is on the Forms Disk under TITLE.

Names of IC and hiring firm. Do not refer to an IC as an employee or to yourself as an employer.

Initially, it's best to refer to the IC by his or her full name. If an IC is incorporated, use the corporate name, not the IC's own name—for example: "John Smith, Incorporated" instead of "John Smith." If the IC is unincorporated but is doing business under a fictitious business name, use that name. A fictitious business name or assumed name is a name sole proprietors or partners use to identify their businesses. For example, if consultant Al Brodsky calls his one-person marketing research business "ABC Marketing Research," use that name. This shows you're contracting with a business, not a single individual.

For sake of brevity, it is usual to identify yourself and the IC by shorter names in the rest of the agreement. You can use an abbreviated version of the IC's full name—for example, ABC for ABC Marketing Research. Or you can refer to the IC simply as Contractor or Consultant.

Refer to yourself initially by your company name and subsequently by a short version of the name or as Client or Firm.

Also include the addresses of the principal place of business of the IC and yourself. If you or the IC have more than one office or workplace, the principal place of business is the main office or workplace.

> **Names of IC and Hiring Firm**
> This Agreement is made between [Your company name] (Client) with a principal place of business at [Your business address] and [IC's name] (Contractor), with a principal place of business at [IC's address].

 The text of this clause is on the Forms Disk under NAMES.

1. Term of Agreement

The term of the agreement should be as short as possible. A good outside time limit is six months. A longer term makes the agreement look like an employment agreement, not an IC agreement. If the work is not completed at the end of six months, you can negotiate and sign a new agreement.

The date the agreement begins can be the date you sign it or another date either before or after you sign.

> **Term of Agreement**
> This Agreement will become effective on _____, 19__ and will end no later than _____, 19__.

 The text of this clause is on the Forms Disk under TERMAGR.

2. Services to Be Performed

The agreement should describe in as much detail as possible what the IC is expected to do. You must word the description carefully to concentrate on the results he or she is expected to achieve. Don't tell the IC how to achieve the result; that would indicate that you have the right to control how the IC performs the work. Such a right of control is the hallmark of an employment relationship. (See Chapter 3, Section D.)

> **EXAMPLE:** Jack hires Jill to prepare an index for his multi-volume history of ancient Sparta. Jack should describe the results Jill is expected to receive, like this: Contractor agrees to prepare an index of Client's *History of Sparta* of at least 100 single-spaced pages. Contractor will provide Client with a printout of the finished index and a 3.5 inch computer disk version in ASCII format.
>
> Jack should not tell Jill how to create the index like this: Contractor will prepare an alphabetical three-level index of Client's *History of Sparta*. Contractor will first prepare 3 by 5 inch index cards listing every index entry beginning with Chapter One. After each chapter is completed, Contractor will deliver the index cards to Client for Client's approval. When index cards have been created for all 50 chapters, Contractor will create a computer

version of the index using Complex Software Version 7.6. Contractor will then printout and edit the index and deliver it to Client for approval.

It's perfectly okay for you to establish very detailed specifications for the IC's finished work product. But the specs should only describe the end results the IC must achieve, not how to obtain those results.

You can include the description in the main body of the Agreement. Or if it's a lengthy explanation, put it on a separate attachment.

SUGGESTED LANGUAGE: ALTERNATIVE A

Services to Be Performed

Contractor agrees to perform the following services: [Briefly describe services you want performed by IC.]

SUGGESTED LANGUAGE: ALTERNATIVE B

Services to Be Performed

Contractor agrees to perform the services described in Exhibit A, which is attached to this Agreement.

The text of these clauses is on the Forms Disk under SERVICES. Choose Alternative A if you include the explanation of services in the contract. Choose Alternative B if the explanation of the services is attached to the main contract.

3. Payment

Independent contractors are usually paid in one of two ways:
- a fixed fee, or
- by unit of time.

a. Fixed fee

Paying an IC a fixed sum for the entire job, rather than an hourly or daily rate strongly supports a

finding of independent contractor status. If paid a fixed sum, the IC risks losing money if the project takes longer than expected, or may earn a substantial profit if the project is completed quickly. Having the opportunity to earn a profit or suffer a loss is a very strong indication of IC status. (See Chapter 3, Section D.)

SUGGESTED LANGUAGE: ALTERNATIVE A

Payment

In consideration for the services to be performed by Contractor, Client agrees to pay Contractor $[State amount] according to the terms set out below.

The text of this clause is on the Forms Disk under PAYMENT. Choose Alternative A If you will pay the IC a fixed fee.

b. Unit of time

Paying a worker by the hour or other unit of time usually indicates that the worker is an employee because the worker has no real risk of loss. However, it's customary for ICs in some occupations—for example, lawyers and accountants—to charge hourly. Government auditors would likely not challenge the IC status of workers in these occupations as long as they are in business for themselves. (See Chapter 3, Section D.)

SUGGESTED LANGUAGE: ALTERNATIVE B

Payment

In consideration for the services to be performed by Contractor, Client agrees to pay Contractor at the rate of $[State amount] per [Hour, day, week or other unit of time] according to the terms of payment set out below.

The text of this clause is on the Forms Disk under PAYMENT. Choose Alternative B if you will pay the IC by the hour.

If you pay by the hour, you may wish to place a cap on the IC's total compensation. This may be a particularly good idea if you're unsure of the IC's reliability or efficiency.

ADDITIONAL OPTION

> **Payment**
> Unless otherwise agreed in writing, Client's maximum liability for all services performed during the term of this Agreement shall not exceed $[State the top limit on what you will pay].

The text of this clause is on the Forms Disk under PAYMENT. Choose Additional Option if you wish to cap the IC's payments.

4. Terms of Payment

Since an IC is running an independent business, he or she should submit an invoice setting out the amount you have to pay.

a. Fixed fee agreements

The following provision requires you to pay the IC's fixed fee within a reasonable time after the work is completed. If you wish, you can delete "reasonable time" and add a specific time period for payment—for example, 30, 60 or 90 days.

SUGGESTED LANGUAGE: ALTERNATIVE A

> Upon completing Contractor's services under this Agreement, Contractor shall submit an invoice. Client shall pay Contractor the compensation described within a reasonable time after receiving Contractor's invoice.

The text of this clause is on the Forms Disk under TERMPAY. Choose Alternative A if you will pay the IC a fixed fee.

b. Divided payments

You can also opt to pay part of a fixed fee when the agreement is signed and the remainder when the work is finished.

The following provision allows you to pay a specific amount when the IC signs the agreement and then the rest when the work is finished. The amount of the up-front payment is subject to negotiation. It could be as little as 10% or less of the entire fixed fee.

SUGGESTED LANGUAGE: ALTERNATIVE B

> Contractor shall be paid $[State amount] upon signing this Agreement and the rest of the sum described above when the Contractor completes services and submits an invoice.

The text of this clause is on the Forms Disk under TERMPAY. Choose Alternative B if you will pay the IC in divided payments.

c. Installment payments

ICs may balk at accepting a fixed fee for complex or long term projects due to difficulties in accurately estimating how long the job will take. One way to deal with this problem is to break the job into phases or milestones and pay the IC a fixed fee when each phase is completed. If, after one or two phases are completed, it looks like the fixed sum won't be enough to complete the entire project, you can always renegotiate the agreement.

This type of arrangement is far more supportive of an IC relationship than hourly payment, since the IC still has some risk of loss.

To do this, draw up a schedule of installment payments tying each payment to the IC's completion of specific services and attach it to the agreement. The main body of the agreement should simply refer to the attached payment schedule.

SUGGESTED LANGUAGE: ALTERNATIVE C

Terms of Payment

Client shall pay Contractor according to the following schedule of payments

1. $[State sum] when an invoice is submitted and the following services are complete:

   [Describe first stage of services]

2. $[State sum] when an invoice is submitted and the following services are complete:

   [Describe second stage of services]

3. $[State sum] when an invoice is submitted and the following services are complete:

   [Describe third stage of services]

The text of this clause is on the Forms Disk under TERMPAY. Choose Alternative C if you will pay the IC in installments.

d. Payments by unit of time

Even ICs who are paid by the hour or other unit of time should submit invoices. Do not automatically pay an IC weekly or bi-weekly the way you pay employees. It's best to pay ICs no more than once a month since this is how businesses are normally paid.

SUGGESTED LANGUAGE: ALTERNATIVE D

Terms of Payment

Contractor shall submit an invoice to Client on the last day of each month for the work performed during that month. The invoice should include: an invoice number, the dates covered by the invoice, the hours expended and a summary of the work performed. Client shall pay Contractor's fee within a reasonable time after receiving the invoice.

The text of this clause is on the Forms Disk under TERMPAY. Choose Alternative D if you will pay the IC according to the number of hours worked.

5. Expenses

The IRS considers payment of a worker's business or traveling expenses to be a strong indication of an employment relationship. (See Chapter 5, Section A.) An IC should usually not be reimbursed for expenses. Instead, compensate the IC well enough so that he or she can pay the expenses directly out of his or her own pocket.

However, it sometimes is customary to pay the expenses of certain types of ICs. For example, attorneys typically charge their clients separately for photocopying charges, deposition fees and travel. Where there is an otherwise clear IC relationship and payment of expenses is customary in the IC's trade or business, you can probably get away with doing it.

SUGGESTED LANGUAGE

Expenses

Contractor shall be responsible for all expenses incurred while performing services under this Agreement. This includes license fees, memberships and dues; automobile and other travel expenses; meals and entertainment; insurance premiums; and all salary, expenses and other compensation paid to employees or contract personnel the Contractor hires to complete the work under this Agreement.

 The text of this clause is on the Forms Disk under EXPENSE.

6. Independent Contractor Status

One of the most important functions of an independent contractor agreement is to help establish that the worker is an IC, not your employee. The key to doing this is to make clear that the IC, not the hiring firm, has the right to control how the work will be performed.

You will need to emphasize the factors the IRS and other agencies consider in determining whether an IC controls how the work is done. (See Chapter 5, Section A.)

SUGGESTED LANGUAGE

Independent Contractor Status

Contractor is an independent contractor, not Client's employee. Contractor's employees or contract personnel are not Client's employees. Contractor and Client agree to the following rights consistent with an independent contractor relationship.

- Contractor has the right to perform services for others during the term of this Agreement.
- Contractor has the sole right to control and direct the means, manner and method by which the services required by this Agreement will be performed.
- Contractor has the right to perform the services required by this Agreement at any place, location or time.
- Contractor will furnish all equipment and materials used to provide the services required by this Agreement.
- Contractor has the right to hire assistants as subcontractors, or to use employees to provide the services required by this Agreement.
- The Contractor or Contractor's employees or contract personnel shall perform the services required by this Agreement; Client shall not hire, supervise or pay any assistants to help Contractor.
- Neither Contractor nor Contractor's employees or contract personnel shall receive any training from Client in the skills necessary to perform the services required by this Agreement.
- Client shall not require Contractor or Contractor's employees or contract personnel to devote full time to performing the services required by this Agreement.

 The text of this clause is on the Forms Disk under STATUS.

 Less May Be Just Enough
When you draft your own agreement, include only those provisions that apply to your particular situation. The more that apply, the more likely will the worker be viewed as an IC.

7. Business Permits, Certificates and Licenses

The IC should have all business permits, certificates and licenses needed to perform the work. For example, if you hire an IC to perform construction work, the IC should have a contractor's license if one is required by your state's law. Lack of such licenses and permits makes a worker look like an employee, not an IC in business for himself or herself. The IC should obtain such licenses and permits on his or her own; you should not pay for them.

SUGGESTED LANGUAGE

Business Permits, Certificates and Licenses

Contractor has complied with all federal, state and local laws requiring business permits, certificates and licenses required to carry out the services to be performed under this Agreement.

The text of this clause is on the Forms Disk under PERMIT.

8. State and Federal Taxes

Do not pay or withhold any taxes on an IC's behalf. Doing so is a very strong indicator that the worker is an employee. Indeed, some courts have held that workers were employees based upon this factor alone.

Include a straightforward provision, such as the one suggested below, to help make sure the IC understands that he or she must pay all applicable taxes.

SUGGESTED LANGUAGE

State and Federal Taxes

Client will not:

- withhold FICA (Social Security and Medicare taxes) from Contractor's payments or make FICA payments on Contractor's behalf
- make state or federal unemployment compensation contributions on Contractor's behalf, or
- withhold state or federal income tax from Contractor's payments.

Contractor shall pay all taxes incurred while performing services under this Agreement—including all applicable income taxes and, if Contractor is not a corporation, self-employment (Social Security) taxes. Upon demand, Contractor shall provide Client with proof that such payments have been made.

 The text of this clause is on the Forms Disk under TAXES.

9. Fringe Benefits

Do not provide either ICs or their employees with fringe benefits that you provide your own employees such as health insurance, pension benefits, childcare allowances or even the right to use employee facilities such as an exercise room.

SUGGESTED LANGUAGE

Fringe Benefits

Contractor understands that neither Contractor nor Contractor's employees or contract personnel are eligible to participate in any employee pension, health, vacation pay, sick pay or other fringe benefit plan of Client.

 The text of this clause is on the Forms Disk under FRINGE.

10. Workers' Compensation

If a worker qualifies as an IC under your state's workers' compensation law, do not provide the IC with workers' compensation coverage.

If the IC has employees, the IC should provide them with workers' compensation coverage. If an IC's employees lack workers' compensation coverage, it's likely your own workers' comp insurer will require you to provide coverage under your own policy and pay an additional workers' comp premium. To avoid this, require ICs to provide you with a certificate of insurance establishing that an IC's employees are covered by workers' compensation insurance. A certificate of insurance is issued by the workers' comp insurer and is written proof that the IC has a workers' comp policy.

Whether an IC has employees or not, you may want to require the worker to have his or her own workers' comp coverage. Self-employed people who have no employees are usually not required to have workers' comp coverage, but they usually can obtain it. More and more hiring firms are requiring this because their own workers' comp insurers may require them to cover ICs who don't have their own workers' comp insurance. (See Chapter 10, Section B.)

SUGGESTED LANGUAGE

> **Workers' Compensation**
>
> Client shall not obtain workers' compensation insurance on behalf of Contractor or Contractor's employees. If Contractor hires employees to perform any work under this Agreement, Contractor will cover them with workers' compensation insurance and provide Client with a certificate of workers' compensation insurance before the employees begin the work.

 The text of this clause is on the Forms Disk under WORKCOMP.

OPTIONAL LANGUAGE

> **Workers' Compensation**
>
> If not operating as a corporation, Contractor shall obtain workers' compensation insurance coverage for Contractor. Contractor shall provide Client with proof that such coverage has been obtained before starting work.

 The text of this clause is on the Forms Disk under WORKCOMP. Choose Optional Language if you want the worker to provide his or her own workers' comp coverage. This clause is best suited to workers who have no employees of their own.

11. Unemployment Compensation

If the worker qualifies as an IC under your state's unemployment compensation law, do not pay unemployment compensation taxes for him or her. (See Chapter 9, Section A.) The IC will not be entitled to receive unemployment compensation benefits when the work is finished or the agreement terminated.

SUGGESTED LANGUAGE

> **Unemployment Compensation**
>
> Client shall make no state or federal unemployment compensation payments on behalf of Contractor or Contractor's employees or contract personnel. Contractor will not be entitled to these benefits in connection with work performed under this Agreement.

 The text of this clause is on the Forms Disk under UNEMPL.

12. Insurance

An IC should have his or her own liability insurance policy just like any other business; you need not provide it. This type of coverage insures the IC against personal injury or property damage claims by others. For example, if an IC accidentally injures a bystander while performing services for you, the IC's liability policy will pay the costs of defending a lawsuit and pay damages up to the limits of the policy coverage. This helps eliminate an injured person's motivation to attempt to recover from you as well as the IC for fear the IC won't be able to pay. Also, having insurance helps show that the IC is in business.

The IC should also agree to indemnify—that is, repay—you if somebody he or she injures decides to sue you.

> **Insurance**
>
> Client shall not provide any insurance coverage of any kind for Contractor or Contractor's employees or contract personnel. Contractor agrees to maintain an insurance policy of at least $[State amount] to cover any negligent acts committed by Contractor or Contractor's employees or agents while performing services under this Agreement.
>
> Contractor shall indemnify and hold Client harmless from any loss or liability arising from performing services under this Agreement.

 The text of this clause is on the Forms Disk under INSURE.

13. Terminating the Agreement

The circumstances under which you may terminate the agreement are important. You should not retain the right to fire or terminate an IC for any reason or no reason at all as you would with an employee under the generally prevailing employment at will doctrine. This type of unfettered termination right strongly indicates an employment relationship. (See Chapter 3, Section D.) Instead, you should be able to terminate the agreement only if you have a reasonable cause to do so.

a. Termination for reasonable cause

You should have the limited right to terminate the IC only if you have a reasonable cause to do so. There are two types of reasonable cause. The first is a serious violation of the agreement by the IC. It would include, for example, the IC's failure to produce results or meet the deadline specified in the agreement.

You can also terminate the agreement if the IC does something to expose you to liability for personal injury or property damage—for example, if the IC's negligence injures your employees, damages your property or damages someone else's property. You don't have to terminate the agreement if this happens, but you have the option of doing so. You may not want to continue dealing with an IC who is extremely careless.

If you fire an IC who performs adequately and otherwise satisfies the terms of the agreement, you'll be liable to him or her for breaking the agreement. The IC can sue you in court and obtain a judgment against you for money damages.

> **Terminating the Agreement**
>
> With reasonable cause, either Client or Contractor may terminate this Agreement, effective immediately upon giving written notice.
>
> Reasonable cause includes:
> - a material violation of this Agreement, or
> - any act exposing the other party to liability to others for personal injury or property damage.

 The text of this clause is on the Forms Disk under TERMIN. Choose Alternative A if you wish to allow either you or the worker to end the agreement based on reasonable cause.

b. Termination on 30 days notice

If you just can't live with a restricted termination right, your best approach is to add a provision giving you the right to terminate the agreement for any reason upon 30 days written notice. You can lengthen the notice period if you wish, but 30 days is the absolute minimum to avoid a strong implication of employee status. Think twice before you do this since, from the point of view of establishing the worker's IC status, you're much better off without this provision.

Terminating the Agreement
Either party may terminate this Agreement any time by giving thirty days written notice to the other party of the intent to terminate.

 The text of this clause is on the Forms Disk under TERMIN. Choose Alternative B if you wish to allow either you or the worker to end the agreement by giving written notice.

14. Exclusive Agreement

Business contracts normally contain a provision stating that the written agreement is the complete and exclusive agreement between those involved. This reinforces the idea that what is written in the contract is all the agreement entails. Neither you nor the IC can later bring up side letters, oral statements or other material not covered by the contract. A clause such as this avoids later claims that promises not contained in the written contract were made and broken.

Because of this provision, you must make sure that all documents containing any representations made by the IC upon which you are relying are attached to the agreement as exhibits. This may include the IC's proposal or bid, sales literature, side letters and so forth. If they aren't attached, they won't be considered to be part of the agreement.

Exclusive Agreement
This is the entire Agreement between Contractor and Client.

The text of this clause is on the Forms Disk under EXCLUS.

15. Severability

This standard contract provision permits the agreement as a whole to continue even if portions of it are found invalid by a court or arbitrator. For example, if for some reason a court found the provision requiring the IC to obtain workers' compensation coverage to be invalid, the rest of the contract would remain in force.

Severability
If any part of this Agreement is held unenforceable, the rest of the Agreement will continue in effect.

 The text of this clause is on the Forms Disk under SEVERAB.

16. Applicable Law

If you and the IC have offices in the same state, that state's law will apply. This law will determine, for example, how long you have to file a lawsuit if the IC breaks the agreement. But if your offices are in different states, you'll need to decide which state's law should govern the agreement. There is some advantage to having the law of your own state govern, since your local attorney will likely be more familiar with that law.

Applicable Law
This Agreement will be governed by the laws of the state of [Indicate state in which you have main office].

 The text of this clause is on the Forms Disk under APPLLAW.

17. Notices

When you want to do something important involving the agreement—terminate it, for example—you need to tell the IC about it. This is called giving notice. The following provision gives you several options for providing the IC with notice: by personal delivery, by mail, or by fax or telex followed by a confirming letter.

If you give notice by mail, it is not effective until three days after it's sent. For example, if you want to end the agreement on 30 days notice and mail your notice of termination to the IC, the agreement will not end until 33 days after you mailed the notice.

SUGGESTED LANGUAGE

> **Notices**
>
> All notices and other communications in connection with this Agreement shall be in writing and shall be considered given as follows:
> - when delivered personally to the recipient's address as stated on this Agreement
> - three days after being deposited in the United States mail, with postage prepaid to the recipient's address as stated on this Agreement, or
> - when sent by fax or telex to the last fax or telex number of the recipient known to the person giving notice. Notice is effective upon receipt provided that a duplicate copy of the notice is promptly given by first class mail, or the recipient delivers a written confirmation of receipt.

 The text of this clause is on the Forms Disk under NOTICE.

18. No Partnership

You want to make sure that you and the IC are separate legal entities, not partners or co-venturers. If an IC is viewed as your partner, you'll be liable for his or her debts and the IC will have the power to make contracts that obligate you to others without your consent.

SUGGESTED LANGUAGE

> **No Partnership**
>
> This Agreement does not create a partnership relationship. Contractor does not have authority to enter into contracts on Client's behalf.

 The text of this clause is on the Forms Disk under NOPART.

19. Assignment

As a general rule, either party may assign its rights and obligations under the contract unless you expressly prohibit it. Assignment means the IC may get another person with whom you may have never dealt directly to perform some of even all of the work.

a. Assignment allowed

Allowing an unrestricted right of assignment is strong evidence of an IC relationship because it shows you're only concerned with results, not who achieves them. It also demonstrates lack of control over the IC.

SUGGESTED LANGUAGE: ALTERNATIVE A

> **Assignment**
>
> Either Contractor or Client may assign or subcontract any rights or obligations under this Agreement.

The text of this clause is on the Forms Disk under ASSIGNM. Choose Alternative A If you wish to allow the IC to assign contractual rights to others.

b.   Approval required

There may be some situations in which you really don't want an IC to assign his or her contractual duties without your consent. This is usually where you hire a particular IC because of his or her special expertise, reputation for performance or financial stability and don't want some other IC performing the services. Unfortunately, using such a provision tends to indicate an employment relationship, so don't include it your agreement unless absolutely necessary.

SUGGESTED LANGUAGE: ALTERNATIVE B

> **Assignment**
> Contractor may not assign or subcontract any rights or obligations under this Agreement without Client's prior written approval.

The text of this clause is on the Forms Disk under ASSIGNM. Choose Alternative B if you wish to restrict the IC's right to assign contractual rights to others.

20. Signatures

The end of the main body of the agreement should contain spaces for you to sign, write in your title and date—and in which the IC can also sign and provide a Taxpayer ID Number.

If either you or the IC is a corporation, the agreement should be signed on the corporation's behalf. For example, if Joe Jones is president of Acme Corporation, he should sign on Acme's behalf like this:

Acme Corporation,

By: *Joe Jones*

Joe Jones, President

It's best that a corporation's president or chief executive officer (CEO) sign the agreement, since he or she will have clear authority to sign on the corporation's behalf. For the same reason, if either party is a partnership, it's best that a part-

ner sign. If this is not possible, the signature should be accompanied by a corporate resolution or partnership resolution stating that the person signing the agreement has the authority to do so.

The Importance of Numbers

Be sure to obtain the IC's Social Security number, or taxpayer ID number if the IC is a corporation or partnership. If you don't, you'll have to withhold federal income taxes from the IC's pay. (See Chapter 4, Section A.)

Traditionally, each party to a contract signs it personally. They need not be together when they sign and it isn't necessary for them to sign at the same time. Prepare at least two copies of the final agreement. Make sure that each copy contains all the needed exhibits and attachments. Both you and the IC should sign both copies, both are originals. Both you and the IC should keep one original signed copy of the agreement. It should be placed in your IC file. (See Chapter 15, Section A.)

SUGGESTED LANGUAGE

> **Signatures**
> Client: _____
> Name of Client
>
> By: _____
> Signature
>
> _____
> Typed or Printed Name
>
> Title: _____
>
> Date: _____
>
> Contractor: _____
> Name of Contractor
>
> By: _____
> Signature
>
> _____
> Typed or Printed Name
>
> Title: _____
>
> Taxpayer ID Number: _____
>
> Date: _____

The text of this clause is on the Forms Disk under SIGNS.

SIGNING BY FAX

It is increasingly common to use faxed signatures to finalize contracts. The validity of a faxed signature is unclear in most states, so if you sign by fax you should replace the faxed signatures with original signatures some time in the future. If you use faxed signatures, you should include a specific provision at the end of the agreement.

OPTIONAL LANGUAGE IF FAXED

> **Signatures**
> Contractor and Client agree that this Agreement will be considered signed when the signature of a party is delivered by facsimile transmission. Signatures transmitted by facsimile shall have the same effect as original.

 The text of this clause is on the Forms Disk under SIGNS. Add this clause if you wish to have the parties sign by fax.

D. Optional Provisions

The following provisions are not absolutely necessary to include in every IC agreement, but you may want to include one or more in your agreement depending on the circumstances.

1. Attorney Fees

If either person has to sue the other in court to enforce the agreement and wins—that is, becomes the prevailing party—the loser is required to pay the other person's attorney fees and expenses. This can help make filing a lawsuit economically feasible and will give the IC an additional reason to settle if you have a strong case.

However, there may be cases in which you do not want to include an attorney fees provision. An IC who has little or no money won't be able to pay the fees, so the provision is useless as far as you're concerned. What's worse, an attorney fees provision could help the IC convince a lawyer to file a case against you without the IC providing an up front cash retainer. If you think it's more likely you'll break the contract than the IC will, an attorney fees provision is not in your interests.

SUGGESTED LANGUAGE

> **Attorney Fees**
> If any legal action is necessary to enforce this Agreement, the prevailing party shall be entitled to reasonable attorney fees, costs and expenses in addition to any other relief to which it may be entitled.

 The text of this clause is on the Forms Disk under FEES.

2. Modifying the Agreement

Unless a contract provides otherwise, it normally can be amended by an oral agreement that is actually carried out.

EXAMPLE: Art signs a contract with Zeno to build an addition to his house. Halfway through the project, Art decides that he wants Zeno to do some extra work not covered by their original agreement. Art and Zeno have a telephone conversation in which Zeno agrees to do the extra work for extra money. Nothing is put in writing.

Once Zeno completes the extra work, the oral agreement between Zeno and Art is enforceable—that is, Art will be legally obligated to pay for the work under the terms orally agreed upon. Before the extra work is commenced, however, Art could change his mind and call the extra work off with no liability to Zeno.

In the real world, people make changes to their contracts all the time and never write them down. The flexibility afforded by such an informal approach to contract amendments might be just what you want. However, you should be aware that misunderstandings and disputes can arise from this approach. It's always best to have some sort of writing showing what you've agreed to do. You can do this informally. For example, you can simply send a confirming letter following a telephone call with an IC summarizing the changes you both agreed to make. Be sure to keep a copy for your files. Or if the amendment involves a contract provision that is very important—the IC's payment, for example—you can insist on a written amendment signed by you and the IC.

You may if you wish, however, add a provision to the contract requiring that all amendments be in writing signed by you and the IC before they become effective. You can still negotiate changes by phone or fax, but they won't take effect until you and the IC sign a formal amendment to the agreement. This eliminates even the possibility of orally amending the agreement. This approach requires more time and paperwork, but provides you with the security of knowing that it

will be impossible for the IC to legally enforce any claimed oral amendment to the agreement.

SUGGESTED LANGUAGE

Modifying the Agreement

This Agreement may be amended only by a writing signed by both Client and Contractor.

 The text of this clause is on the Forms Disk under MODIFY.

3. Work at Your Premises

An IC should not work at your office or other premises you maintain unless the nature of the work absolutely requires it. (See Chapter 5, Section B.) For example, a computer consultant may have to perform work on your computers at your office. In these situations, it's a good idea to add the following provision to the agreement making it clear that the IC is working at your premises because the work requires it.

> **Work at Your Premises**
> Because of the nature of the services to be provided by Contractor, Client agrees to furnish space on its premises for Contractor while performing these services.

 The text of this clause is on the Forms Disk under PREMISE.

4. Indemnification

If the IRS or another government agency determines that you have misclassified a worker as an IC, you may have to pay back taxes, fines and penalties. This is one of the greatest risks of hiring ICs. Some hiring firms try to shift this risk to the IC's shoulders by including an indemnification clause in their IC agreements. Such a provision requires the IC to repay the hiring firm for any losses it suffers if the IC is reclassified as an employee.

This may sound attractive at first, but there are several reasons why it's usually not a good idea to include such a clause in an IC agreement.

- You are prohibited by law from recovering from a worker any taxes and penalties the IRS assesses against you if it determines that you unintentionally classified the worker as an IC. (See Chapter 8, Section C.)
- The clause is practically useless if you're unable to locate the IC when you're audited or the IC has no money to repay you for your losses.
- The clause makes it look as if you're not sure whether the worker is really an IC and may also make an auditor doubt whether the worker is an IC.
- Many intelligent ICs will refuse to sign an agreement containing such a clause.
- The Department of Labor does not permit employers to use such clauses to shift liabil-

ity for failure to pay workers time-and-a-half for overtime.

- Even if you can locate the IC and he or she has the money to repay you for your losses, you'll still have to go to the expense and trouble of going to court to collect if the IC refuses to pay. There is a chance you'll lose because a court might conclude that the indemnification clause goes against public policy and so is unenforceable.

> **Indemnification**
> Contractor agrees to indemnify and hold Client harmless against all losses Client incurs if Contractor or Contractor's employees or contract personnel are deemed to be Client's employee.

 The text of this clause is on the Forms Disk under INDEMN.

5. Resolving Disputes

Mediation and arbitration—often lumped together under the term alternative dispute resolution—are two methods for settling disputes without resorting to expensive court litigation.

a. Mediation

In mediation, a neutral third person called a mediator meets with the parties and makes suggestions as to how to resolve their controversy. Typically, the mediator either sits the parties down together and tries to provide an objective view of their disputes, or shuttles between the parties as a hopefully cool conduit for what may be hot opinions.

Where the real problem is a personality conflict or simple lack of communication, a good mediator can often help the parties find their own compromise settlement which will avoid shattering their relationship. Where the argument is more serious, a mediator may at least be able to lead the parties to a mutually satisfactory ending of both the dispute and their relationship that will obviate time-consuming and expensive litigation.

Mediation is nonbinding. That means that if either party to the dispute doesn't like the outcome of the mediation, he or she can ask for binding arbitration or go to court.

b. Arbitration

If the parties cannot resolve their dispute by mediation, they often submit it to arbitration by a neutral arbitrator. The arbitrator is either selected directly by the parties or is designated by an arbitration agency. The arbitrator acts as both judge and jury in hearing the dispute and issues a decision called an award. The award is final and binding on the parties.

Arbitration can be either binding or nonbinding. If arbitration is nonbinding, either party can take the case to court if he or she doesn't like the outcome. Binding arbitration is usually final.

If you don't like the arbitrator's decision, you can't go to court and retry the dispute except in unusual cases where you can show the arbitrator was guilty of fraud, misconduct or bias. There are a number of organizations which conduct arbitrations, notably the American Arbitration Association which has offices in most major cities.

c. Agreeing to mediation and arbitration

No one can be forced into arbitration or mediation; you must agree to it, either in the contract or later when a dispute arises. Business contracts today commonly include an arbitration provision and many also require mediation. This is primarily because both procedures are usually much faster and cheaper than court litigation.

However, a mediation or arbitration provision is included only as one of the optional provisions you may add to your contract because it may not always be in your best interests. If your financial resources are much greater than the IC's, you'll have an enormous advantage if mediation or arbitration isn't permitted and you and the IC have to resort to expensive court litigation to resolve disputes. The IC may not have the money to challenge you in court.

This advantage is more or less neutralized if you agree to cheap mediation or arbitration. By agreeing to arbitration, you're basically giving up your right to go to court to enforce the contract. Companies that don't like the results they achieve in binding arbitration often wish they had never agreed to it. If you're not sure whether mediation and arbitration are best for you, discuss the matter with an attorney.

SUGGESTED LANGUAGE

Resolving Disputes

If a dispute arises under this Agreement, the parties agree to first try to resolve the dispute with the help of a mutually agreed-upon mediator. If it proves impossible to arrive at a mutually satisfactory solution through mediation, the parties agree to submit their dispute to binding arbitration under the rules of the American Arbitration Association.

 The text of this clause is on the Forms Disk under RESOLVE.

6. Intellectual Property Ownership

Where an IC is hired to create intellectual property—for example, writings, music, software programs, designs or inventions—you should include a provision controlling the arrangement. Unless you include a specific provision about the assignment or transfer of intellectual property rights to you by an IC, you can never be sure that you will own the work you pay the IC to create. (See Chapter 13.)

Intellectual Property Ownership

To the extent that the work performed by Contractor under this Agreement (Contractor's Work) includes any work of authorship entitled to protection under the copyright laws, the parties agree to the following provisions.

- Contractor's Work has been specially ordered and commissioned by Client as a contribution to a collective work, a supplementary work or other category of work eligible to be treated as a work made for hire under the United States Copyright Act.

- Contractor's Work shall be deemed a commissioned work and a work made for hire to the greatest extent permitted by law.

- Client shall be the sole author of Contractor's Work and any work embodying the Contractor's Work according to the United States Copyright Act.

- To the extent that Contractor's Work is not properly characterized as a work made for hire, Contractor grants to Client all right, title and interest in Contractor's Work, including all copyright rights, in perpetuity and throughout the world.

- Contractor shall help prepare any papers Client considers necessary to secure any copyrights, patents, trademarks or intellectual property rights at no charge to Client. However, Client shall reimburse Contractor for reasonable out-of-pocket expenses incurred.

- Contractor agrees to require any employees or contract personnel Contractor uses to perform services under this Agreement to assign in writing to Contractor all copyright and other intellectual property rights they may have in their work product. Contractor shall provide Client with a signed copy of each such assignment.

The text of this clause is on the Forms Disk under INTPROP.

Having paid the IC to create intellectual property for you, you probably won't want the IC to use the material for others without your permission and will probably want to include the following paragraph. However, this is always subject to negotiation.

Intellectual Property Ownership

Contractor agrees not to use any of the intellectual property mentioned above for the benefit of any other party without Client's prior written permission.

The text of this clause is on the Forms Disk under INTROP. Add this clause if you wish to require that the worker obtain your written permission before using the intellectual property involved.

7. Confidentiality

If, during the course of his or her work, an IC may have access to your valuable trade secrets—for example, customer lists, business plans, business methods and techniques not known by your competitors—it is reasonable for you to include a nondisclosure provision in the agreement. Such a

provision means that the IC may not disclose your trade secrets to others without your permission. (See Chapter 13, Section D.)

SUGGESTED LANGUAGE

> ### Confidentiality
>
> Contractor will not disclose or use, either during or after the term of this Agreement, any proprietary or confidential information of Client without Client's prior written permission except to the extent necessary to perform services on Client's behalf.
>
> Proprietary or confidential information includes:
>
> - the written, printed, graphic or electronically recorded materials furnished by Client for Contractor to use
> - business plans, customer lists, operating procedures, trade secrets, design formulas, know-how and processes, computer programs and inventories, discoveries and improvements of any kind, and
> - information belonging to customers and suppliers of Client about whom Contractor gained knowledge as a result of Contractor's services to Client.
>
> Contractor shall not be restricted in using any material which is publicly available, already in Contractor's possession or known to Contractor without restriction, or which is rightfully obtained by Contractor from sources other than Client.
>
> Upon termination of Contractor's services to Client, or at Client's request, Contractor shall deliver to Client all materials in Contractor's possession relating to Client's business.

 The text of this clause is on the Forms Disk under CONFID.

8. Non-Solicitation

If you're concerned about an IC getting to know your clients or customers and perhaps stealing business away from you, you can include the following non-solicitation clause in the agreement. (See Chapter 15, Section C.)

SUGGESTED LANGUAGE

> ### Non-Solicitation
>
> For a period of [Fill in period from two months to three years] after termination of this Agreement, Contractor agrees not to call on, solicit or take away Client's customers or potential customers of which Contractor became aware as a result of Contractor's services for Client.

 The text of this clause is on the Forms Disk under NONSOLIC.

E. Sample General IC Agreement

The text of a General Independent Contractor Agreement is in the Appendix and on the Forms Disk under GENAGREE.

Note that the provisions in the sample agreement below are numbered to coincide with the discussion in Section C. You should be able to craft some form of this agreement to meet your needs if you hire any type of general independent contractor.

INDEPENDENT CONTRACTOR AGREEMENT

This Agreement is made between Acme Widget Co. (Client) with a principal place of business at 123 Main Street, Marred Vista, CA 90000 and ABC Consulting, Inc. (Contractor), with a principal place of business at 456 Grub Street, Santa Longo, CA 90001.

1. Term of Agreement

This Agreement will become effective on May 1, 19XX and will end no later than June 1, 19XX.

2. Services to Be Performed

Contractor agrees to perform the following services: Install and test Client's DX9-105 widget manufacturing press so that it performs according to the manufacturer's specifications.

3. Payment

In consideration for the services to be performed by Contractor, Client agrees to pay Contractor $20,000 according to the terms out below.

4. Terms of Payment

Upon completing Contractor's services under this Agreement, Contractor shall submit an invoice. Client shall pay Contractor the compensation described within a reasonable time after receiving Contractor's invoice.

5. Expenses

Contractor shall be responsible for all expenses incurred while performing services under this Agreement. This includes license fees, memberships and dues; automobile and other travel expenses; meals and entertainment; insurance premiums; and all salary, expenses and other compensation paid to employees or contract personnel the Contractor hires to complete the work under this Agreement.

6. Independent Contractor Status

Contractor is an independent contractor, not Client's employee. Contractor's employees or contract personnel are not Client's employees. Contractor and Client agree to the following rights consistent with an independent contractor relationship.

- Contractor has the right to perform services for others during the term of this Agreement.
- Contractor has the sole right to control and direct the means, manner and method by which the services required by this Agreement will be performed.
- Contractor has the right to perform the services required by this Agreement at any place, location or time.
- Contractor will furnish all equipment and materials used to provide the services required by this Agreement.

- Contractor has the right to hire assistants as subcontractors, or to use employees to provide the services required by this Agreement.
- The Contractor or Contractor's employees or contract personnel shall perform the services required by this Agreement; Client shall not hire, supervise or pay any assistants to help Contractor.
- Neither Contractor nor Contractor's employees or contract personnel shall receive any training from Client in the skills necessary to perform the services required by this Agreement.
- Client shall not require Contractor or Contractor's employees or contract personnel to devote full time to performing the services required by this Agreement.

7. Business Permits, Certificates and Licenses

Contractor has complied with all federal, state and local laws requiring business permits, certificates and licenses required to carry out the services to be performed under this Agreement.

8. State and Federal Taxes

Client will not:

- withhold FICA (Social Security and Medicare taxes) from Contractor's payments or make FICA payments on Contractor's behalf
- make state or federal unemployment compensation contributions on Contractor's behalf, or
- withhold state or federal income tax from Contractor's payments.

Contractor shall pay all taxes incurred while performing services under this Agreement—including all applicable income taxes and, if Contractor is not a corporation, self-employment (Social Security) taxes. Upon demand, Contractor shall provide Client with proof that such payments have been made.

9. Fringe Benefits

Contractor understands that neither Contractor nor Contractor's employees or contract personnel are eligible to participate in any employee pension, health, vacation pay, sick pay or other fringe benefit plan of Client.

10. Workers' Compensation

Client shall not obtain workers' compensation insurance on behalf of Contractor or Contractor's employees. If Contractor hires employees to perform any work under this Agreement, Contractor will cover them with workers' compensation insurance and provide Client with a certificate of workers' compensation insurance before the employees begin the work.

11. Unemployment Compensation

Client shall make no state or federal unemployment compensation payments on behalf of Contractor or Contractor's employees or contract personnel. Contractor will not be entitled to these benefits in connection with work performed under this Agreement.

12. Insurance

Client shall not provide any insurance coverage of any kind for Contractor or Contractor's employees or contract personnel. Contractor agrees to maintain an insurance policy of at least $500,000 to cover any negligent acts committed by Contractor or Contractor's employees or agents while performing services under this Agreement.

Contractor shall indemnify and hold Client harmless from any loss or liability arising from performing services under this Agreement.

13. Terminating the Agreement

With reasonable cause, either Client or Contractor may terminate this Agreement, effective immediately upon giving written notice.

Reasonable cause includes:

- a material violation of this Agreement, or
- any act exposing the other party to liability to others for personal injury or property damage.

14. Exclusive Agreement

This is the entire Agreement between Contractor and Client.

15. Severability

If any part of this Agreement is held unenforceable, the rest of the Agreement will continue in effect.

16. Applicable Law

This Agreement will be governed by the laws of the state of California.

17. Notices

All notices and other communications in connection with this Agreement shall be in writing and shall be considered given as follows:

- when delivered personally to the recipient's address as stated on this Agreement
- three days after being deposited in the United States mail, with postage prepaid to the recipient's address as stated on this Agreement, or
- when sent by fax or telex to the last fax or telex number of the recipient known to the person giving notice. Notice is effective upon receipt provided that a duplicate copy of the notice is promptly given by first class mail, or the recipient delivers a written confirmation of receipt.

18. No Partnership

This Agreement does not create a partnership relationship. Contractor does not have authority to enter into contracts on Client's behalf.

19. Assignment

Either Contractor or Client may assign or subcontract any rights or obligations under this Agreement.

20. Signatures

Client:

Acme Widget Co.

By: *Basilio Chew*
(Signature)

   Basilio Chew
(Typed or Printed Name)

Title: President

Date: April 30, 19XX

Contractor:

ABC Consulting, Inc.

By: *George Bailey*
(Signature)

   George Bailey
(Typed or Printed Name)

Title: President

Taxpayer ID Number: 123-45-6789

Date: April 30, 19XX

F. Agreements for Specialized ICs

This book provides five IC agreements that are tailored for specific types of service providers, including:

- household workers (see Section F1)
- direct sellers (see Section F2)
- real estate salespersons (see Section F3)
- independent consultants (see Section F4), and
- contributors to a work made for hire (see Section F5).

1. Household Workers

The text of a Household Worker Agreement is in the Appendix and on the Forms Disk under HOUSEH.

Household workers are people who perform services in and around your home such as gardeners, housekeepers, cooks and nannies. The following agreement is tailored to use with those household workers who qualify as ICs. (See Chapter 11.)

This agreement is as simple and short as possible. It contains a series of boxes for you to check off to indicate exactly what services the worker is required to perform. You can add to these short descriptions if you wish.

The agreement states that the worker will provide all equipment and materials, since this strongly supports IC status. However, if you will be providing any equipment—a lawn mower or vacuum cleaner, for example—delete that reference in the agreement.

Since the worker will be working in and around your home, you need to set up a work schedule. This agreement provides that you and the worker will set up a mutually agreeable schedule. You don't need to set forth the schedule in the agreement. Instead, simply state where the work will be performed.

2. Direct Sellers

The text of a Direct Sellers Agreement is in the Appendix and on the Forms Disk under DIRSELL.

This agreement is for direct sellers such as traveling salespeople who are paid by commission only. Such salespeople are statutory ICs for IRS purposes if they sign an IC agreement. This

means you don't have to withhold or pay employment taxes for them. (See Chapter 6, Section C.)

You need to describe in the agreement what product or merchandise the salesperson will sell. You can't give the worker other duties besides selling on commission, or the worker will lose his or her statutory IC status.

These salespeople are statutory ICs only if they are paid solely by commission, not on the number of hours worked. The agreement here provides for this type of payment.

The agreement also provides that the worker will provide all necessary equipment, but you are permitted to provide sales forms.

Traveling salespeople usually travel by car. This agreement requires the salesperson to have car insurance and to list you as a named insured on the policy. This can make it easier for you to collect if there is an accident. The salesperson also agrees to indemnify you—that is, repay you—if he or she gets into an accident and the victim sues you.

Since salespeople often have to be given access to your valuable customer lists, the agreement requires the salesperson to keep such information confidential.

3. Real Estate Salespeople

The text of a Real Estate Salesperson's Agreement is in the Appendix and on the Forms Disk under REALEST.

Real estate salespeople—called real estate agents in some states—who are paid by commission only qualify as statutory ICs if they sign an IC agreement. (See Chapter 6, Section C.)

This agreement provides that the salesperson will be paid by commission only and will be responsible for all expenses incurred in showing and selling real estate including travel and other expenses involved in showing properties.

Most states require that real estate salespeople work for a licensed real estate broker who is

responsible for their actions. The broker usually maintains a real estate office and has several salespeople working for him or her. The broker provides clerical and other support staff, while the salespeople are required to be at the office at certain hours to field customer inquiries. The agreement here provides for this type of arrangement and requires the salesperson to agree upon a schedule of times when the salesperson must be in the office. The schedule doesn't have to be set forth in the agreement.

Real estate salespeople are required to be licensed in most states. Include the state and date of issuance of the salesperson's license on the agreement.

Since real estate salespeople usually travel by car to and from properties, it's important that they have car insurance. This is required in the agreement. The salesperson also agrees to indemnify you—that is, repay you—if he or she gets into an accident and the victim sues you.

4. Consultants

The text of a Consultants Agreement is in the Appendix and on the Forms Disk under CONSULT.

Skilled professionals who provide advice and assistance to businesses are often called consultants. This can include software experts, engineers, marketing, accounting and finance experts and anyone else who calls himself or herself a consultant.

The agreement to be used for consultants is basically the same as the general IC agreement except that provisions regarding intellectual property ownership and confidentiality have been added.

Many consultants are hired to create or contribute to the creation of intellectual property—for example, computer software, important business documents, marketing plans, inventions and trademarks. This agreement provides that the consultant assigns—transfers—all ownership rights in such material to you. This avoids any possible dispute over who owns such material.

In addition, consultants often have access to valuable company trade secrets such as marketing plans, product information and financial information. You probably don't want the consultant to blab about these things to your competitors. This agreement requires the consultant to keep your trade secrets confidential.

5. Works Made for Hire

The text of a Work Made for Hire Agreement is in the Appendix and on the Forms Disk under FORHIRE.

You can use this agreement only when you hire an IC to create or contribute to a work of authorship that falls within one of the following categories:

- a contribution to a collective work—a work created by more than one author, such as a newspaper, magazine, anthology or encyclopedia
- a part of an audiovisual work—for example, a motion picture screenplay
- a translation
- supplementary works such as forewords, afterwords, supplemental pictorial illustrations, maps, charts, editorial notes, bibliographies, appendixes and indexes
- a compilation—for example, an electronic database

- an instructional text
- a test
- answer material for a test, or
- an atlas.

Do not use this agreement for any work that does not fall within one of these categories. (See Chapter 13.)

When an IC signs this agreement, he or she gives up all copyright rights in the work he or she creates. Moreover, you are considered the author of the work for copyright purposes. (See Chapter 13.)

You need to describe in the agreement or on a separate attachment the work the IC will create.

The agreement also provides that the work will be a work made for hire. This means that you, the Client, will be considered the work's author for copyright purposes and own all the copyright rights in the work. However, if for some reason the work fails to qualify as a work made for hire, this agreement contains an assignment from the IC to you of all copyright rights in the work. This will mean you will still own all the copyright rights in the work.

However, in this event, the work won't be a work made for hire and you won't be considered the author. The only practical result of this is that the IC can revoke the assignment 35 years after it's made. There's nothing you can do to prevent this, but in most cases it's meaningless because few works have a useful economic life of more than 35 years. ■

Help Beyond This Book

The legal issues involved in hiring ICs are complex and varied. You may have questions that aren't answered by this book. This chapter provides guidance on how to find and use more specific legal resources including lawyers and other knowledgeable experts. It also explains the basics of doing your own legal research.

A. Finding and Using a Lawyer

An experienced attorney may help answer your questions and allay your fears about setting up and running your business.

1. What Type of Lawyer Do You Need

Many different areas of law are involved when you hire ICs, including:

- federal tax law
- state tax law
- workers' compensation law
- federal and state employment and anti-discrimination laws, and
- general business law.

Unfortunately, you may find it difficult or impossible to find a single attorney to competently advise you about all these legal issues. For example, an attorney who knows the fine points of tax law may know nothing about your state's workers' compensation and employment laws.

However, there are attorneys who specialize in advising businesses, both large and small. And some of them have experience dealing with the legal issues faced by businesses that hire ICs. These lawyers are a bit like general practitioner doctors: they know a little about a lot of different areas of law.

A lawyer with plenty of experience working with businesses like yours may know enough to answer your questions. For example, if you run a software company, a lawyer who customarily represents software firms may be familiar with the laws as they apply to the software industry and should also know about the legal problems that other software companies that hire ICs have encountered.

But if you can't find a lawyer with this type of experience, you may need to consult more than one attorney or consult other types of experts. For example, a CPA may be able to help you research IRS Rulings, while a business lawyer can help you deal with unemployment compensation, employment and other state laws.

HIRING A TAX ATTORNEY TO HANDLE IRS AUDITS

If you're facing an IRS field audit with the possibility of having to pay several thousands of dollars in assessments or penalties, it makes sense to hire a tax attorney. A tax attorney is a lawyer with either a special tax law degree, an LL.M. in taxation, or a tax specialization certification from a state bar association. Tax attorneys specialize in representing taxpayers before the IRS and in court.

---

2. Finding a Lawyer

When you begin looking for a lawyer, try to find someone with experience representing businesses similar to yours.

Don't start your search by consulting phone books, legal directories or advertisements. Lawyer referral services operated by bar associations are usually equally unhelpful. Often, they simply supply the names of lawyers who have signed onto the service, accepting the lawyer's own word for what types of skills he or she has.

The best way to locate a lawyer who is experienced in advising businesses about hiring ICs is through referrals from other businesses in your community that use ICs. Industry associations and trade groups are also excellent sources of referrals. If you already have or know a lawyer, he or she might also be able to refer you to an experienced person who has the qualifications you need. Other people, such as your banker, accountant or insurance agent may know of good business lawyers.

3. Paying a Lawyer

Whenever you hire a lawyer, insist upon a written explanation of how the fees and costs will be paid.

Most business lawyers charge by the hour. Hourly rates vary, but in most parts of the United States, you can get competent services for your business for $150 to $250 an hour. Comparison shopping among lawyers will help you avoid overpaying. But the cheapest hourly rate isn't necessarily the best. A novice who charges only $80 an hour may take three hours to review a consultant's contract. A more experienced lawyer who charges $200 an hour may do the same job in half an hour and make better suggestions. If a lawyer will be delegating some of the work on your case to a less experienced associate, paralegal or secretary, that work should be billed at a lower hourly rate. Be sure to get this information recorded in your initial written fee agreement.

Sometimes, a lawyer may quote you a flat fee for a specific job. For example, a lawyer may offer to represent you for $3,000 in a dispute with the labor department. You pay the same amount regardless of how much time the lawyer spends. This can be cheaper than paying an hourly fee, but not always.

Alternatively, some businesses hire lawyers on retainer—that is, they pay a flat annual fee in return for the lawyer handling all their routine legal business. However, few small businesses can afford to keep a lawyer on retainer.

4. Using a Lawyer as a Legal Coach

One way to keep your legal costs down is to do as much work as possible yourself and simply use the lawyer as your coach. For example, you can draft your own IC agreements, giving your lawyer the relatively quick and inexpensive task of reviewing them. In an IRS audit or unemployment compensation case, you can assemble needed documents and line up witnesses.

But get a clear understanding about who's going to do what. You don't want to do the work and get billed for it because the lawyer duplicated your efforts. And you certainly don't want any crucial elements to fall through cracks because you each thought the other was attending to the work.

B. Help From Other Experts

Lawyers aren't the only ones who can help you deal with the legal issues involved in hiring ICs. Tax professionals, insurance brokers and trade groups can also be very helpful.

1. Tax Professionals

Attorneys are usually the most expensive, but not always the most knowledgeable, professionals you can go to for advice on tax law. You can get outstanding tax advice at lower cost from many non-attorney tax professionals such as enrolled agents and certified public accountants. These tax professionals can help you research IRS Rulings and answer other tax-related questions.

a. Enrolled agents

Enrolled agents are tax advisors and preparers licensed by the IRS. They earn the designation of enrolled agent by either passing a difficult IRS test or working for the IRS for at least five years. There are approximately 24,000 enrolled agents in the United States. An enrolled agent is generally the least expensive of the tax pros, and is very adequate for most small business tax advice and reporting.

b. Accountants

Certified public accountants, or CPAs, are licensed and regulated by each state, like attorneys. They perform sophisticated accounting and business-related tax work and prepare tax returns. CPAs shine in giving business tax advice but generally are not as aggressive as tax lawyers when facing IRS personnel. Some states license accountants other than CPAs, such as public accountants. Many of these workers may also be able to give you competent advice on the tax effects of using ICs in your business.

2. Insurance Brokers

Insurance brokers and agents who sell workers' compensation insurance and business liability insurance should be knowledgeable about your state's workers' compensation laws. They can also help you save money when you buy such insurance.

3. Industry and Trade Associations

Business or industry trade associations or similar organizations can be a fount of information on IC issues. Many such groups track federal and state laws, lobby Congress and state legislatures and even help members fight the IRS and other federal and state agencies. Find out if there is such an organization for your business or industry and get in touch with it.

C. Doing Your Own Legal Research

If you decide to investigate the law on your own, your first step should be to obtain a good guide to help you understand legal citations, use the

law library and understand what you find there. There are a number of sources that provide a good introduction to legal research, including:

- *Legal Research: How to Find and Understand the Law,* by Stephen Elias and Susan Levinkind (Nolo Press). This nontechnical book simply explains how to use all major legal research tools and helps you frame your research questions.
- *Legal Research Made Easy: A Roadmap Through the Law Library Maze,* by Robert C. Berring (Legal Star/Nolo Press). This is a videotape with a six-step strategy for legal research. It's available from many public and law library video collections—or directly through Nolo Press.

Next, you need to find a law library that's open to the public. Your county should have a

public law library, often at the county courthouse. Public law schools often contain especially good collections and generally permit the public to use their libraries. Some private law schools grant access to their libraries—sometimes for a modest fee. The reference department of a major public or university library may have a fairly decent legal research collection. Finally, don't overlook the law library in your own lawyer's office. Most lawyers, on request, will share their books with their clients.

1. Researching Federal Tax Law

Many resources are available to augment and explain the tax information in this book: IRS publications, self-help tax preparation guides, textbooks, court decisions and periodicals. Some are free, and others are reasonably priced. Tax publications for professionals are expensive, but are often available at public or law libraries.

a. IRS booklets

The IRS publishes over 350 free booklets explaining the tax code, and many are clearly written and useful. These booklets, called IRS Publications, range from several pages to several hundred pages in length. The following IRS Publications contain useful information for businesses that hire ICs:

- Publication 15, *Circular E, Employer's Tax Guide*
- Publication 937, *Employment Taxes and Information Returns*
- Publication 334, *Tax Guide for Small Businesses*
- Publication 505, *Tax Withholding and Estimated Tax*
- Publication 926, *Household Employer's Tax Guide*
- Publication 51, Circular A, *Agricultural Employer's Tax Guide*

IRS Publications are available in IRS offices, or by calling 800-TAX-FORM (829-3676), or by sending in an order form. There is no charge, not even for postage.

⚠ Don't Rely Exclusively on the IRS

IRS publications are useful to obtain information on IRS procedures and to get the IRS's view of the tax law. But keep in mind that they only present the IRS's interpretation of the law, which may be very one-sided and even be contrary to court rulings. So don't rely exclusively on IRS Publications for information.

b. The Internal Revenue Manual

The Internal Revenue Manual, or IRM, is a series of handbooks that serve as internal guides to IRS employees on points of tax law and procedure. The IRM tells IRS employees, such as auditors or collectors, how specific tax code provisions should be enforced. Section 5(10) of the IRM deals with employment tax examinations and provides useful guidance on how IRS auditors handle worker classification questions. It also explains how employment tax audits are conducted. It will be particularly helpful if you're handling an IRS audit yourself.

The manual is for IRS internal use, but most of it is public and reprinted by private tax book publishers. It is also available to the public in larger IRS offices that have Freedom of Information Act reading rooms, and in law libraries and some tax professionals' offices. If you're unable to locate the IRM elsewhere, you can purchase a copy of Section 5(10) of the IRM from Urquhart Business Publishing for around $20; the telephone number is: 714-752-5544.

c. Internal Revenue Code

All federal tax laws are in the Internal Revenue Code, or IRC, which is written by Congress and often referred to as the code or the tax code. The IRC is found in Title 26 of the United States Code, abbreviated as USC. Title simply refers to the place within the massive USC where the IRC is found. The IRC is divided up into sections, which are subdivided and resubdivided into more parts. A reference to IRC §3121(d)(3)(C) means that this particular tax law is found in Title 26 of the USC, the Internal Revenue Code, Section 3121, subsection (d), paragraph 3, subparagraph C.

The tax code is extremely long, complex and difficult to understand. Fortunately, you probably don't need to read it. Few sections of the IRC deal with ICs and they have all been summarized in this book.

d. IRS pronouncements on tax law

The IRS makes written statements of its position on various tax matters. They do not have the force of law, but guide IRS personnel and taxpayers as to how specific tax laws should be interpreted and applied. Over the years, the IRS has issued thousands of rulings on how workers in almost every conceivable occupation should be classified.

Reviewing IRS Rulings can help you predict how the IRS is likely to classify a worker if you're audited. However, IRS Rulings are not always consistent and may even conflict with each other. Even IRS auditors don't always follow IRS rulings, since they don't have the force of law.

But, if you can find a favorable ruling, it can supply a reasonable basis for classifying a worker as an IC. Such a ruling might enable you to successfully use the employer's safe harbor against employment taxes, also known as Section 530. This can be your best defense in an IRS audit. (See Chapter 8.) Unfortunately, the majority of IRS rulings find that the workers involved are employees, not ICs, and will be of little help.

The IRS makes its opinions and legal summaries known in a number of publications.

- *Revenue Rulings* (Rev. Rul.) are IRS written statements of how the tax law applies to a specific set of facts. These are published as general guidance to taxpayers. The rulings are reprinted and indexed by IRC section and subject matter. A Revenue Ruling usually contains a hypothetical set of facts, followed by an explanation of how the tax code applies to those facts. For example: Rev. Rul. 87-41 refers to IRS Revenue Ruling number 41, issued in 1987.

- *IRS Letter Rulings* are IRS answers to specific written questions and hypothetical situations posed by taxpayers. There are thousands of IRS Letter Rulings dealing with how to classify workers. Letter rulings are published in the Internal Revenue Cumulative Bulletin, and in private tax service publications found in larger public and law libraries. For example: Ltr. Rul. 892012 refers to a ruling issued in 1989, in the 20th week and which was the 12th letter ruling issued that week.

- *IRS Revenue Procedures* (Rev. Procs.) are another way the IRS tells taxpayers how to comply with certain tax provisions, although they are primarily written to guide tax professionals and preparers. Revenue Procedures often explain when and how to report tax items. They are published in the Internal Revenue Cumulative Bulletin, found in larger public and law libraries and widely reprinted in professional tax publications. For example: Rev. Proc. 91-15 refers to a published Revenue Procedure number 15, issued in 1991.

- *IRS Regulations*, also called Treasury Regulations or Regs, are the IRS's most authoritative statement on how to interpret the IRC. Regs are usually found in a four-volume set, called Treasury Regulations, found in most larger libraries and some bookstores. Regulations are somewhat easier to read and comprehend than the tax code However, few Regs concern IC issues.

DIRECTORIES OF IRS RULINGS

Finding an IRS Ruling dealing with a situation similar to yours can be very difficult. Fortunately, tax experts have culled through thousands of IRS rulings on worker classification and categorized them by occupation. By using their publications you can find citations to IRS Rulings involving workers similar to yours. Two such publications are available:

- *Employment Status—Employee v. Independent Contractor*, 391-2nd T.M., by Helen Marmoll, summarizes and provides citations to IRS rulings on classification of workers in 374 different occupations—everything from accountants to yacht sales agents. This guide is expensive, around $80. You may be able to find a copy in a good law library; if not, it's well worth buying. It's published by Tax Management Inc.; telephone number: 800-372-1033.

- Many state Chambers of Commerce publish guides for companies that hire ICs that list IRS Rulings for various occupations. For example, the California Chamber of Commerce publishes a guide called *Independent Contractors: A Manager's Guide and Audit Reference.* It categories thousands of IRS Rulings by occupation and also covers rulings by California state agencies. Call your state Chamber of Commerce to see if it publishes such a guide for your state; it probably has an office in your state capitol.

An industry trade group or association may also be aware of, or even have copies of, helpful IRS Rulings and court decisions.

e. Tax cases

Federal courts have interpreted the tax law in thousands of court cases, many of which involve worker classification issues. A favorable court decision can also provide you with a reasonable basis for claiming the employer's safe harbor against employment taxes. (See Chapter 7.) You may rely on decisions by any federal tax court, federal district court, federal court of appeals or the U.S. Supreme Court.

Employment Status—Employee v. Independent Contractor, the guide mentioned above, lists by occupation many court decisions on worker classification. It is the best starting point for this type of legal research.

f. Trade association publications

Every business or trade has its own publications and newsletters that closely track tax issues of common interest, including worker classification issues. By reading them, you can learn about recent IRS and court rulings affecting other employers in your industry.

COMPUTERIZED LEGAL RESEARCH

One quick way to find IRS Rulings and many court decisions is to use computer databases. There are two main commercially-owned legal databases: Westlaw and Lexis. Unfortunately, if you are not connected with a large law office or law school, you will likely find it difficult to get access to either of these systems. A small but growing number of public law libraries offer these services. Those that do offer them usually require a sizable advance deposit or a credit card; you pay as you go.

If you wish to use one of these systems, either ask a law librarian where the nearest publicly accessible terminal is located, or write to the companies at the addresses below. If you do find an available service, be prepared to pay as much as $300 per hour.

For more information about Westlaw, write to: West Publishing Co., 50 West Kellogg Boulevard, P.O. Box 3526, St. Paul, MN 55165. For Lexis, write to: Lexis, Mead Data Central, 200 Park Avenue, New York, NY 10017.

Westlaw and Lexis provide almost complete coverage of all federal and state laws, IRS Rulings and court decisions. However, a far from complete, but growing, number of court decisions are available on the internet for free or at nominal cost. Finding these decisions can be difficult, however. For detailed guidance, see *Law on the Net*, by James Evans (Nolo Press).

2. Researching Other Areas of Law

Many fields of law other than federal tax law are involved when you hire ICs. These include other federal laws that apply throughout the country and the laws of your particular state.

a. Federal laws

The best starting point for further research into federal employment and anti-discrimination laws that affect your business is *The Employer's Legal Handbook* by Fred Steingold (Nolo Press). This guide will likely answer your questions, or at least tell you where to go for more information.

In addition, the U.S. Labor Department publishes a free pamphlet on worker classification for purposes of the federal labor laws called Publication 17, *Employee Relationship Under the Fair Labor Standards Act*. You can get a copy by calling the Labor Department at: 202-219-6666.

b. State laws

If you have questions about your state workers' compensation, unemployment compensation, tax law or employment laws, first contact the appropriate state agency for more information. Many of these agencies publish useful information pamphlets. This book contains contact information for state workers' compensation agencies see Chapter 10), unemployment compensation agencies (see Chapter 9), tax departments (see Chapter 9) and labor departments (see Chapter 12).

More in-depth research into your state law will require that you review:

- legislation, also called statutes, passed by your state legislature; your state unemployment compensation, workers' compensation and income tax withholding laws will probably be most important to you
- administrative rules and regulations issued by state administrative agencies such as

your state unemployment compensation agency, and

- published decisions of your state courts.

Many states, particularly larger ones, have legal encyclopedias or treatises that organize the state case law and some statutes into narrative statements organized alphabetically by subject. Through citation footnotes, you can locate the full text of the cases and statutes. These works are a good starting point for in-depth state law research.

HOW TO READ A CASE CITATION

To locate a published court decision, you must understand how to read a case citation. A citation provides the names of the people or companies involved on each side of the case, the volume of the legal publication—called a reporter—in which the case can be found, the page number on which it begins and the year in which the case was decided. Here is an example of what a legal citation looks like: *Smith v. Jones Int'l*, 123 F.3d 456 (1995). Smith and Jones are the names of the people having the legal dispute. The case is reported in volume 123 of the Federal Reporter, Third Series, beginning on page 456; the court issued the decision in 1995.

Federal court decisions. There are several different federal courts and the decisions of each are published in a different reporter. Opinions by the federal district courts are in a series called the Federal Supplement, or F.Supp.

Any case decided by a federal court of appeals is found in a series of books called the Federal Reporter. Older cases are contained in the first series of the Federal Reporter, or F. More recent cases are contained in the second or third series of the Federal Reporter, F.2d or F.3d.

Cases decided by the U.S. Supreme Court are found in three publications: United States Reports (identified as U.S.), the Supreme Court Reporter (identified as S.Ct.) and the Supreme Court Reports, Lawyer's Edition (identified as L.Ed.). Supreme Court case citations often refer to all three publications.

There are also federal courts that specialize in handling tax disputes, including the United States Tax Court and United States Claims Court—formerly Court of Claims. Published decisions of the United States Tax

How to Read a Case Citation (continued)

Court can be found in the Tax Court Reports, or TC, published by the U.S. Government Printing Office. Tax Court decisions can also be found in a reporter called Tax Court Memorandum Decisions, or TCM, published by Commerce Clearing House, Inc.

Decisions from all federal courts involving taxation can be found in a reporter called U.S. Tax Cases, or USTC, published by Commerce Clearing House, Inc.

State court decisions. Most states publish their own official state reports. All published state court decisions are also included in the West Reporter System. West has divided the country into seven regions—and publishes all the decisions of the supreme and appellate state courts in the region together. These reporters are:

A. and A.2d. Atlantic Reporter (First and Second Series), which includes decisions from Connecticut, Delaware, the District of Columbia, Maine, Maryland, New Hampshire, New Jersey, Pennsylvania, Rhode Island and Vermont.

N.E. and N.E.2d. Northeastern Reporter (First and Second Series), which includes decisions from New York, Illinois, Indiana, Massachusetts and Ohio.

N.W. and N.W.2d. Northwestern Reporter (First and Second Series), which includes decisions from Iowa, Michigan, Minnesota, Nebraska, North Dakota, South Dakota and Wisconsin.

P. and P.2d. Pacific Reporter (First and Second Series), which includes decisions from Alaska, Arizona, California, Colorado, Hawaii, Idaho, Kansas, Montana, Nevada, New Mexico, Oklahoma, Oregon, Utah, Washington and Wyoming.

S.E. and S.E.2d. Southeastern Reporter (First and Second Series), which includes decisions from Georgia, North Carolina, South Carolina, Virginia and West Virginia.

So. and So.2d. Southern Reporter (First and Second Series), which includes decisions from Alabama, Florida, Louisiana and Mississippi.

S.W. and S.W.2d. Southwestern Reporter (First and Second Series), which includes decisions from Arkansas, Kentucky, Missouri, Tennessee and Texas.

All California appellate decisions are published in a separate volume, the California Reporter (Cal. Rptr.) and all decisions from New York appellate courts are published in a separate volume, New York Supplement (N.Y.S.). ■

Contractor's Screening Documents

Independent Contractor Questionnaire

Documentation Checklist

INDEPENDENT CONTRACTOR QUESTIONNAIRE

Name:_____

Fictitious business name (if any):_____

Business address:_____

Business phone and fax #:_____

Employer Identification Number or Social Security Number:_____

Form of business entity (check one):　　☐ Corporation　　☐ Partnership　　☐ Sole Proprietorship

1. Provide the name, address and dates of service of all companies for which you have performed services as an independent contractor for the past two years. But please do not provide any information you have a duty to keep confidential.

2. Have you ever hired employees? If yes, please complete the following:

   Name of company:_____

   Address:_____

   Title:_____

   Salary:_____ Dates of employment:_____

   Name of company:_____

   Address:_____

   Title:_____

   Salary:_____ Dates of employment:_____

   Name of company:_____

   Address:_____

   Title:_____

   Salary:_____ Dates of employment:_____

   Name of company:_____

   Address:_____

   Title:_____

   Salary:_____ Dates of employment:_____

3. Have you paid federal and state payroll taxes for your employees?　　☐ Yes　　☐ No

4. If you have hired employees, please provide the following:

   Name of workers' compensation insurance carrier:_____

   Workers' compensation policy number:_____

5. Do you hold a professional license? If so, please provide a copy.

6. Do you have a business license? If so, please provide a copy.

7. Describe the training you have received in your specialty:

   School attended:_____

   Dates of attendance:_____ Degrees received:_____

   School attended:_____

   Dates of attendance:_____ Degrees received:_____

School attended:_____

Dates of attendance:_____ Degrees received:_____

8. Do you advertise your services?   ☐ Yes   ☐ No

   If so, please provide a copy of these advertisements, including a Yellow Pages listing.

9. If you don't advertise, how do you market your services?

   _____

   _____

10. Do you have a White Pages business phone listing?   ☐ Yes   ☐ No   If so, please provide a copy.

11. Describe the business expenses you have paid in the past, including office or workplace rental, materials
    and equipment expenses, telephone and other expenses:_____

    _____

    _____

12. Describe the business expenses you pay now:_____

    _____

    _____

13. Describe the equipment and facilities you own:_____

    _____

    _____

14. Please describe the tools and materials you will use to perform the services in this job:

    _____

    _____

    _____

    How much do they cost?:_____

15. Please list your general liabilty insurance carrier:_____

    Policy number:_____

16. Please list your auto insurance carrier:_____

    Policy number:_____

17. Have you ever worked for us before? If so, please complete the following:

    Dates of employment:_____

    Services performed:_____

18. Do you have an independent contractor agreement? If so, please attach a copy.

19. Do you have your own business cards, stationery and invoice forms? If so, provide copies.

20. If you're a sole proprietor, have you paid self-employment taxes on your income and filed a Schedule C
    with your federal tax return?   ☐ Yes   ☐ No

    If so, will you provide copies of your tax returns for the past two years?   ☐ Yes   ☐ No

DOCUMENTATION CHECKLIST

Please provide the following documentation:

☐ copies of your business license and any professional licenses you have

☐ certificates showing that you have insurance, including general liability insurance and workers' compensation insurance if you have employees

☐ your business cards and stationery

☐ copies of any advertising you've done, such as a Yellow Pages listing

☐ a copy of your White Pages business phone listing, if there is one

☐ if you're operating under an assumed name, a copy of the fictitious business name statement

☐ a copy of your invoice form to be used for billing purposes

☐ a copy of any office lease and proof that you've paid the rent, such as copies of canceled rental checks

☐ the names and salaries of all assistants that you will use on the job

☐ the names and salaries of all assistants you have used on previous jobs for the past two years and proof that you paid them, such as copies of canceled checks or copies of payroll tax forms

☐ a list of all the equipment and materials you will use in performing the services and how much it costs; proof that you have paid for the equipment, such as copies of canceled checks, is very helpful

☐ the names and addresses of other clients or customers for whom you have performed services during the previous two years; but don't provide any information you have a duty to keep confidential

☐ if you're a sole proprietor and will agree, copies of your tax returns for the previous two years showing that you have filed a Schedule C, Profit or Loss From a Business.

2

Sample Agreements

Introduction to Sample Agreements

This Appendix contains the full text of six sample agreements, the specifics of which are discussed throughout this book.

Note that the agreements are also available on disk—and that additional clauses are available on disk so that you may best tailor your independent contractor agreement to meet your situation. (See Chapter 16.)

The following specific agreements are included here.

General Independent Contractor Agreement

You should be able to craft some form of this agreement to meet your needs if you hire any type of general independent contractor.

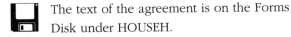 The text of a General Independent Contractor Agreement is in the Appendix and on the Forms Disk under GENAGREE.

Independent Contractor Agreement for Household Workers

Household workers—that is, people who perform services in and around your home such as gardeners, housekeepers, cooks and nannies—may or may not qualify as ICs. (See Chapter 11.) The agreement here is tailored to use with those workers who do qualify as ICs.

The text of the agreement is on the Forms Disk under HOUSEH.

Independent Contractor Agreement for Direct Seller

This agreement is for direct sellers such as traveling salespeople who are paid by commission only. (See Chapter 6, Section C.)

 The text of this agreement is on the Forms Disk under DIRSELL.

Independent Contractor Agreement for Real Estate Salesperson

This agreement is for real estate salespeople—called real estate agents in some states—who are paid by commission only. (See Chapter 6, Section C.)

 The text of this agreement is on the Forms Disk under REALEST.

Independent Contractor Agreement for Consultant

This agreement can be used for almost any type of independent consultant—that is, an IC you hire to give you expert professional advice.

 The text of this agreement is on the Forms Disk under CONSULT.

Independent Contractor Agreement for Work Made for Hire

This agreement is a work made for hire agreement. You can use this agreement only when you hire an IC to create or contribute to a work of authorship that falls within one of the following categories:

- a contribution to a collective work—a work created by more than one author, such as a newspaper, magazine, anthology or encyclopedia
- a part of an audiovisual work—for example, a motion picture screenplay
- a translation
- supplementary works such as forewords, afterwords, supplemental pictorial illustrations, maps, charts, editorial notes, bibliographies, appendixes and indexes
- a compilation—for example, an electronic database

- an instructional text
- a test
- answer material for a test, or
- an atlas.

Do not use this agreement for any work that does not fall within one of these categories.

 The text of this agreement is on the Forms Disk under FORHIRE.

GENERAL INDEPENDENT CONTRACTOR AGREEMENT

This Agreement is made between _____ (Client)

with a principal place of business at _____

and _____ (Contractor), with a

principal place of business at _____ .

This Agreement will become effective on _____, 19_____ and will end no later than

_____, 19_____.

Services to Be Performed

(Check and complete applicable provision.)

☐ Contractor agrees to perform the following services:

_____

_____

OR

☐ Contractor agrees to perform the services described in Exhibit A, which is attached to this Agreement.

_____

_____

Payment

(Check and complete applicable provision.)

☐ In consideration for the services to be performed by Contractor, Client agrees to pay Contractor

$_____ according to the terms set out below.

OR

☐ In consideration for the services to be performed by Contractor, Client agrees to pay Contractor at the rate of

$_____ per _____ according to the terms of payment set out below.

Additional Option

(Check and complete if applicable.)

☐ Unless otherwise agreed in writing, Client's maximum liability for all services performed during the term of

this Agreement shall not exceed $_____ .

Terms of Payment

(Check and complete applicable provision.)

☐ Upon completing Contractor's services under this Agreement, Contractor shall submit an invoice. Client shall

pay Contractor the compensation described within a reasonable time after receiving Contractor's invoice.

OR

☐ Contractor shall be paid $_____ upon signing this Agreement and the rest of the sum described

above when the Contractor completes services and submits an invoice.

OR

☐ Client shall pay Contractor according to the following schedule of payments

1. $_____ when an invoice is submitted and the following services are complete:

_____

2. $_____ when an invoice is submitted and the following services are complete:

_____

3. $_____ when an invoice is submitted and the following services are complete:

_____

OR

☐ Contractor shall submit an invoice to Client on the last day of each month for the work performed during that month. The invoice should include: an invoice number, the dates covered by the invoice, the hours expended and a summary of the work performed. Client shall pay Contractor's fee within a reasonable time after receiving the invoice.

Expenses

Contractor shall be responsible for all expenses incurred while performing services under this Agreement. This includes license fees, memberships and dues; automobile and other travel expenses; meals and entertainment; insurance premiums; and all salary, expenses and other compensation paid to employees or contract personnel the Contractor hires to complete the work under this Agreement.

Independent Contractor Status

Contractor is an independent contractor, not Client's employee. Contractor's employees or contract personnel are not Client's employees. Contractor and Client agree to the following rights consistent with an independent contractor relationship.

- Contractor has the right to perform services for others during the term of this Agreement.
- Contractor has the sole right to control and direct the means, manner and method by which the services required by this Agreement will be performed.
- Contractor has the right to perform the services required by this Agreement at any place, location or time.
- Contractor will furnish all equipment and materials used to provide the services required by this Agreement.
- Contractor has the right to hire assistants as subcontractors, or to use employees to provide the services required by this Agreement.
- The Contractor or Contractor's employees or contract personnel shall perform the services required by this Agreement; Client shall not hire, supervise or pay any assistants to help Contractor.
- Neither Contractor nor Contractor's employees or contract personnel shall receive any training from Client in the skills necessary to perform the services required by this Agreement.
- Client shall not require Contractor or Contractor's employees or contract personnel to devote full time to performing the services required by this Agreement.

Business Permits, Certificates and Licenses

Contractor has complied with all federal, state and local laws requiring business permits, certificates and licenses required to carry out the services to be performed under this Agreement.

State and Federal Taxes

Client will not:

- withhold FICA (Social Security and Medicare taxes) from Contractor's payments or make FICA payments on Contractor's behalf
- make state or federal unemployment compensation contributions on Contractor's behalf, or
- withhold state or federal income tax from Contractor's payments.

Contractor shall pay all taxes incurred while performing services under this Agreement—including all applicable income taxes and, if Contractor is not a corporation, self-employment (Social Security) taxes. Upon demand, Contractor shall provide Client with proof that such payments have been made.

Fringe Benefits

Contractor understands that neither Contractor nor Contractor's employees or contract personnel are eligible to participate in any employee pension, health, vacation pay, sick pay or other fringe benefit plan of Client.

Workers' Compensation

Client shall not obtain workers' compensation insurance on behalf of Contractor or Contractor's employees. If Contractor hires employees to perform any work under this Agreement, Contractor will cover them with workers' compensation insurance and provide Client with a certificate of workers' compensation insurance before the employees begin the work.

Additional Option

(Check if applicable.)

☐ If not operating as a corporation, Contractor shall obtain workers' compensation insurance coverage for Contractor. Contractor shall provide Client with proof that such coverage has been obtained before starting work.

Unemployment Compensation

Client shall make no state or federal unemployment compensation payments on behalf of Contractor or Contractor's employees or contract personnel. Contractor will not be entitled to these benefits in connection with work performed under this Agreement.

Insurance

Client shall not provide any insurance coverage of any kind for Contractor or Contractor's employees or contract personnel. Contractor agrees to maintain an insurance policy of at least $_____ to cover any negligent acts committed by Contractor or Contractor's employees or agents while performing services under this Agreement.

Contractor shall indemnify and hold Client harmless from any loss or liability arising from performing services under this Agreement.

Terminating the Agreement

(Check applicable provision.)

☐ With reasonable cause, either Client or Contractor may terminate this Agreement, effective immediately upon giving written notice.

Reasonable cause includes:

- a material violation of this Agreement, or
- any act exposing the other party to liability to others for personal injury or property damage.

OR

☐ Either party may terminate this Agreement any time by giving thirty days written notice to the other party of the intent to terminate.

Exclusive Agreement

This is the entire Agreement between Contractor and Client.

Severability

If any part of this Agreement is held unenforceable, the rest of the Agreement will continue in effect.

Applicable Law

This Agreement will be governed by the laws of the state of _____.

Notices

All notices and other communications in connection with this Agreement shall be in writing and shall be considered given as follows:

- when delivered personally to the recipient's address as stated on this Agreement
- three days after being deposited in the United States mail, with postage prepaid to the recipient's address as stated on this Agreement, or
- when sent by fax or telex to the last fax or telex number of the recipient known to the person giving notice. Notice is effective upon receipt provided that a duplicate copy of the notice is promptly given by first class mail, or the recipient delivers a written confirmation of receipt.

No Partnership

This Agreement does not create a partnership relationship. Contractor does not have authority to enter into contracts on Client's behalf.

Assignment

(Check applicable provision.)

☐ Either Contractor or Client may assign or subcontract any rights or obligations under this Agreement.

OR

☐ Contractor may not assign or subcontract any rights or obligations under this Agreement without Client's prior written approval.

Signatures

Client: _____
Name of Client

By: _____
Signature

_____
Typed or Printed Name

Title: _____

Date: _____

Contractor: _____
Name of Contractor

By: _____
Signature

_____
Typed or Printed Name

Title: _____

Taxpayer ID Number: _____

Date: _____

If Agreement Is Faxed:

Contractor and Client agree that this Agreement will be considered signed when the signature of a party is delivered by facsimile transmission. Signatures transmitted by facsimile shall have the same effect as original signatures.

INDEPENDENT CONTRACTOR AGREEMENT
FOR HOUSEHOLD WORKERS

This Agreement is made between _____ (Client) with a principal place of business at _____ and _____ (Contractor), with a principal place of business at _____.

This Agreement will become effective on _____, 19____ and will end no later than _____, 19____.

Services to be Performed

Contractor agrees to perform the following services.

a. Cleaning Interior

Contractor will clean the following rooms and areas:

_____

_____

_____

_____

b. Cleaning Exterior

Contractor will clean the following:

☐ Front porch or deck: _____

_____

_____

☐ Back porch or deck: _____

_____

_____

☐ Garage: _____

_____

_____

☐ Pool, hot tub or sauna: _____

_____

_____

☐ Other exterior areas: _____

_____

_____

_____

c. Gardening

Contractor will perform the following gardening services:

_____

_____

d. Other Responsibilities

☐ Cooking: _____

_____

_____

☐ Laundry: _____

_____

_____

☐ Ironing: _____

_____

_____

☐ Shopping and errands: _____

_____

_____

☐ Other: _____

_____

_____

_____

Payment

In consideration for the services to be performed by Contractor, Client agrees to pay Contractor at the rate of $_____ per [☐ hour, ☐ day, ☐ week, ☐ month] according to the terms of payment set forth below.

Terms of Payment

Upon completing Contractor's services under this Agreement, Contractor shall submit an invoice. Client shall pay Contractor the compensation described within a reasonable time after receiving Contractor's invoice.

Expenses

Contractor shall be responsible for all expenses incurred while performing services under this Agreement. This includes license fees, memberships and dues; automobile and other travel expenses; meals and entertainment; insurance premiums; and all salary, expenses and other compensation paid to employees or contract personnel the Contractor hires to complete the work under this Agreement.

Independent Contractor Status

Contractor is an independent contractor, not Client's employee. Contractor's employees or contract personnel are not Client's employees. Contractor and Client agree to the following rights consistent with an independent contractor relationship.

- Contractor has the right to perform services for others during the term of this Agreement.
- Contractor has the sole right to control and direct the means, manner and method by which the services required by this Agreement will be performed.
- Contractor has the right to perform the services required by this Agreement at any place, location or time.
- Contractor will furnish all equipment and materials used to provide the services required by this Agreement except for _____

  _____.

- Contractor has the right to hire assistants as subcontractors, or to use employees to provide the services required by this Agreement.
- The Contractor or Contractor's employees or contract personnel shall perform the services required by this Agreement; Client shall not hire, supervise or pay any assistants to help Contractor.
- Neither Contractor nor Contractor's employees or contract personnel shall receive any training from Client in the skills necessary to perform the services required by this Agreement.
- Client shall not require Contractor or Contractor's employees or contract personnel to devote full time to performing the services required by this Agreement.

Time and Place of Performance

Contractor shall perform the services at _____

_____ during reasonable hours on a schedule to be mutually agreed upon by Client and Contractor based upon Client's needs and Contractor's availability to perform such services.

Business Permits, Certificates and Licenses

Contractor has complied with all federal, state and local laws requiring business permits, certificates and licenses required to carry out the services to be performed under this Agreement.

State and Federal Taxes

Client will not:

- withhold FICA (Social Security and Medicare taxes) from Contractor's payments or make FICA payments on Contractor's behalf
- make state or federal unemployment compensation contributions on Contractor's behalf, or
- withhold state or federal income tax from Contractor's payments.

Contractor shall pay all taxes incurred while performing services under this Agreement—including all applicable income taxes and, if Contractor is not a corporation, self-employment (Social Security) taxes. Upon demand, Contractor shall provide Client with proof that such payments have been made.

Workers' Compensation

Client shall not obtain workers' compensation insurance on behalf of Contractor or Contractor's employees. If Contractor hires employees to perform any work under this Agreement, Contractor will cover them with workers' compensation insurance and provide Client with a certificate of workers' compensation insurance before the employees begin the work.

Unemployment Compensation

Client shall make no state or federal unemployment compensation payments on behalf of Contractor or Contractor's employees or contract personnel. Contractor will not be entitled to these benefits in connection with work performed under this Agreement.

Terminating the Agreement

(Check applicable provision.)

☐ With reasonable cause, either Client or Contractor may terminate this Agreement, effective immediately upon giving written notice.

Reasonable cause includes:

- a material violation of this Agreement, or
- any act exposing the other party to liability to others for personal injury or property damage.

OR

☐ Either party may terminate this Agreement any time by giving thirty days written notice to the other party of the intent to terminate.

Signatures

Client: _____
Name of Client

By: _____
Signature

_____
Typed or Printed Name

Title: _____

Date: _____

Contractor: _____
Name of Contractor

By: _____
Signature

_____
Typed or Printed Name

Title: _____

Taxpayer ID Number: _____

Date: _____

INDEPENDENT CONTRACTOR AGREEMENT
FOR DIRECT SELLER

This Agreement is made between _____ (Client)
with a principal place of business at _____
and _____ (Contractor), with a
principal place of business at _____.

   This Agreement will become effective on _____, 19____ and will end no later than
_____, 19____.

Services to be Performed

Contractor agrees to sell the following product or merchandise for owner: _____
_____

Contractor shall seek sales of the product in the homes of various individuals.

This work will be done by Contractor as an independent contractor, and not as an employee. Contractor shall have no obligation to perform any services other than the sale of the product described here.

Compensation

In consideration for the services to be performed by Contractor, Client agrees to pay Contractor a commission on completed sales as follows: _____
_____

   Contractor acknowledges that no other compensation is payable by Client, and that all of Contractor's compensation will depend on sales made by Contractor. None of Contractor's compensation shall be based on the number of hours worked by Contractor.

Expenses

Contractor shall be responsible for all expenses incurred while performing services under this Agreement. This includes license fees, memberships and dues; automobile and other travel expenses; meals and entertainment; insurance premiums; and all salary, expenses and other compensation paid to employees or contract personnel the Contractor hires to complete the work under this Agreement.

Independent Contractor Status

Contractor is an independent contractor, not Client's employee. Contractor's employees or contract personnel are not Client's employees. Contractor and Client agree to the following rights consistent with an independent contractor relationship.

- Contractor has the right to perform services for others during the term of this Agreement.
- Contractor has the sole right to control and direct the means, manner and method by which the services required by this Agreement will be performed.
- Subject to any restrictions on Contractor's sales territory contained in this Agreement, Contractor has the right to perform the services required by this Agreement at any location or time.
- Contractor will furnish all equipment and materials used to provide the services required by this Agreement.
- Contractor has the right to hire assistants as subcontractors, or to use employees to provide the services required by this Agreement, except that Client may supply Contractor with sales forms.
- The Contractor or Contractor's employees or contract personnel shall perform the services required by this Agreement; Client shall not hire, supervise or pay any assistants to help Contractor.

- Neither Contractor nor Contractor's employees or contract personnel shall receive any training from Client in the skills necessary to perform the services required by this Agreement.
- Client shall not require Contractor or Contractor's employees or contract personnel to devote full time to performing the services required by this Agreement.

Business Permits, Certificates and Licenses

Contractor has complied with all federal, state and local laws requiring business permits, certificates and licenses required to carry out the services to be performed under this Agreement.

State and Federal Taxes

Client will not:

- withhold FICA (Social Security and Medicare taxes) from Contractor's payments or make FICA payments on Contractor's behalf
- make state or federal unemployment compensation contributions on Contractor's behalf, or
- withhold state or federal income tax from Contractor's payments.

Contractor shall pay all taxes incurred while performing services under this Agreement—including all applicable income taxes and, if Contractor is not a corporation, self-employment (Social Security) taxes. Upon demand, Contractor shall provide Client with proof that such payments have been made.

Fringe Benefits

Contractor understands that neither Contractor nor Contractor's employees or contract personnel are eligible to participate in any employee pension, health, vacation pay, sick pay or other fringe benefit plan of Client.

Workers' Compensation

Client shall not obtain workers' compensation insurance on behalf of Contractor or Contractor's employees. If Contractor hires employees to perform any work under this Agreement, Contractor will cover them with workers' compensation insurance and provide Client with a certificate of workers' compensation insurance before the employees begin the work.

Optional Language

(Check if provision is applicable.)

☐ If not operating as a corporation, Contractor shall obtain workers' compensation insurance coverage for Contractor. Contractor shall provide Client with proof that such coverage has been obtained before starting work.

Unemployment Compensation

Client shall make no state or federal unemployment compensation payments on behalf of Contractor or Contractor's employees or contract personnel. Contractor will not be entitled to these benefits in connection with work performed under this Agreement.

Insurance

Client shall not provide any insurance coverage of any kind for Contractor or Contractor's employees or contract personnel. Contractor agrees to maintain an insurance policy of at least $_____ to cover any negligent acts committed by Contractor or Contractor's employees or agents while performing services under this Agreement.

Contractor warrants and represents that Contractor now carries automobile liability insurance for injuries to person and property. Contractor shall include Client's name as one of the named insureds under this policy and deliver a certificate of that policy.

Contractor shall indemnify and hold Client harmless from any loss or liability arising from performing services under this Agreement, including any claim for injuries or damages caused by Contractor while traveling in Contractor's automobile and performing services under this Agreement.

Confidentiality

Contractor will not disclose or use, either during or after the term of this Agreement, any proprietary or confidential information of Client without Client's prior written permission except to the extent necessary to perform services on Client's behalf.

Proprietary or confidential information includes:

- the written, printed, graphic or electronically recorded materials furnished by Client for Contractor to use
- business plans, customer lists, operating procedures, trade secrets, design formulas, know-how and processes, computer programs and inventories, discoveries and improvements of any kind, and
- information belonging to customers and suppliers of Client about whom Contractor gained knowledge as a result of Contractor's services to Client.

Contractor shall not be restricted in using any material which is publicly available, already in Contractor's possession or known to Contractor without restriction, or which is rightfully obtained by Contractor from sources other than Client.

Upon termination of Contractor's services to Client, or at Client's request, Contractor shall deliver to Client all materials in Contractor's possession relating to Client's business.

Terminating the Agreement

(Check applicable provision.)

☐ With reasonable cause, either Client or Contractor may terminate this Agreement, effective immediately upon giving written notice.

Reasonable cause includes:

- a material violation of this Agreement, or
- any act exposing the other party to liability to others for personal injury or property damage.

OR

☐ Either party may terminate this Agreement any time by giving thirty days written notice to the other party of the intent to terminate.

Exclusive Agreement

This is the entire Agreement between Contractor and Client.

Severability

If any part of this Agreement is held unenforceable, the rest of the Agreement will continue in effect.

Applicable Law

This Agreement will be governed by the laws of the state of _____.

Notices

All notices and other communications in connection with this Agreement shall be in writing and shall be considered given as follows:

- when delivered personally to the recipient's address as stated on this Agreement
- three days after being deposited in the United States mail, with postage prepaid to the recipient's address as stated on this Agreement, or
- when sent by fax or telex to the last fax or telex number of the recipient known to the person giving notice. Notice is effective upon receipt provided that a duplicate copy of the notice is promptly given by first class mail, or the recipient delivers a written confirmation of receipt.

No Partnership

This Agreement does not create a partnership relationship. Contractor does not have authority to enter into contracts on Client's behalf.

Assignment

(Check applicable provision.)

☐ Either Contractor or Client may assign or subcontract any rights or obligations under this Agreement.

OR

☐ Contractor may not assign or subcontract any rights or obligations under this Agreement without Client's prior written approval.

Signatures

Client: _____
Name of Client

By: _____
Signature

_____
Typed or Printed Name

Title: _____

Date: _____

Contractor: _____
Name of Contractor

By: _____
Signature

_____
Typed or Printed Name

Title: _____

Taxpayer ID Number: _____

Date: _____

If Agreement Is Faxed:

Contractor and Client agree that this Agreement will be considered signed when the signature of a party is delivered by facsimile transmission. Signatures transmitted by facsimile shall have the same effect as original signatures.

INDEPENDENT CONTRACTOR AGREEMENT
FOR REAL ESTATE SALESPERSON

This Agreement is made between _____ (Broker)

with a principal place of business at _____

and _____ (Salesperson),

with a principal place of business at _____.

This Agreement will become effective on _____, 19____ and will end no later than

_____, 19____.

Services to be Performed

Salesperson agrees to sell real estate for Broker as an independent contractor and not as an employee.

Compensation

In consideration for the services to be performed by Salesperson, Broker agrees to pay Salesperson a

commission on completed sales by Salesperson as follows: _____

_____

_____

Salesperson shall have no right to compensation based on the number of hours worked.

Expenses

Salesperson shall be responsible for all expenses incurred while performing services under this Agreement. This includes license fees, memberships and dues; automobile and other travel expenses; meals and entertainment; insurance premiums; and all salary, expenses and other compensation paid to employees or contract personnel the Salesperson hires to complete the work under this Agreement.

Broker's Sales Office

Broker agrees to maintain a central sales office and staff it with appropriate clerical personnel and forms. Salesperson agrees to use the forms supplied by Broker in accordance with Broker's policies. Salesperson also agrees to be present in Broker's office to handle inquiries concerning the purchase and sale of real estate according to a schedule prepared by Broker.

The schedule shall equitably divide the office time among all real estate salespersons selling for Broker and shall alternate the days and times assigned to each salesperson. No additional compensation shall be paid to Salesperson for Salesperson's presence in the office in accordance with the schedule.

Independent Contractor Status

Salesperson is an independent contractor, not Broker's employee. Salesperson's employees or contract personnel are not Broker's employees. Salesperson and Broker agree to the following rights consistent with an independent contractor relationship.

- Salesperson has the right to perform services for others during the term of this Agreement.
- Salesperson has the sole right to control and direct the means, manner and method by which the services required by this Agreement will be performed.
- Subject to any restrictions on Contractor's sales territory contained in this Agreement, Salesperson has the right to perform the services required by this Agreement at any location or time.

- Salesperson has the right to hire assistants as subcontractors, or to use employees to provide the services required by this Agreement.

Business Permits, Certificates and Licenses

Salesperson has complied with all federal, state and local laws requiring business permits, certificates and licenses required to carry out the services to be performed under this Agreement.

Salesperson represents and warrants that Salesperson is a licensed real estate salesperson in good standing, having been licensed by _____

on _____, 19_____.

State and Federal Taxes

Broker will not:

- withhold FICA (Social Security and Medicare taxes) from Salesperson's payments or make FICA payments on Salesperson's behalf
- make state or federal unemployment compensation contributions on Salesperson's behalf, or
- withhold state or federal income tax from Salesperson's payments.

Salesperson shall pay all taxes incurred while performing services under this Agreement—including all applicable income taxes and, if Salesperson is not a corporation, self-employment (Social Security) taxes. Upon demand, Salesperson shall provide Broker with proof that such payments have been made.

Fringe Benefits

Salesperson understands that neither Salesperson nor Salesperson's employees or contract personnel are eligible to participate in any employee pension, health, vacation pay, sick pay or other fringe benefit plan of Broker.

Workers' Compensation

Broker shall not obtain workers' compensation insurance on behalf of Salesperson or Salesperson's employees. If Salesperson hires employees to perform any work under this Agreement, Salesperson will cover them with workers' compensation insurance and provide Broker with a certificate of workers' compensation insurance before the employees begin the work.

Optional Language

(Check if provision is applicable.)

☐ If not operating as a corporation, Salesperson shall obtain workers' compensation insurance coverage for Salesperson. Salesperson shall provide Broker with proof that such coverage has been obtained before starting work.

Unemployment Compensation

Broker shall make no state or federal unemployment compensation payments on behalf of Salesperson or Salesperson's employees or contract personnel. Salesperson will not be entitled to these benefits in connection with work performed under this Agreement.

Insurance

Broker shall not provide any insurance coverage of any kind for Salesperson or Salesperson's employees or contract personnel. Salesperson agrees to maintain an insurance policy of at least $_____ to cover any negligent acts committed by Salesperson or Salesperson's employees or agents while performing services under this Agreement.

Salesperson shall indemnify and hold Broker harmless from any loss or liability arising from performing services under this Agreement.

This includes any claim for injuries or damages caused by Salesperson while traveling in Salesperson's automobile and performing sevices under this Agreement.

Terminating the Agreement

(Check applicable provision.)

☐ With reasonable cause, either Broker or Salesperson may terminate this Agreement, effective immediately upon giving written notice.

Reasonable cause includes:

- a material violation of this Agreement, or
- any act exposing the other party to liability to others for personal injury or property damage.

OR

☐ Either party may terminate this Agreement any time by giving thirty days written notice to the other party of the intent to terminate.

Exclusive Agreement

This is the entire Agreement between Salesperson and Broker.

Severability

If any part of this Agreement is held unenforceable, the rest of the Agreement will continue in effect.

Applicable Law

This Agreement will be governed by the laws of the state of _____.

Notices

All notices and other communications in connection with this Agreement shall be in writing and shall be considered given as follows:

- when delivered personally to the recipient's address as stated on this Agreement
- three days after being deposited in the United States mail, with postage prepaid to the recipient's address as stated on this Agreement, or
- when sent by fax or telex to the last fax or telex number of the recipient known to the person giving notice. Notice is effective upon receipt provided that a duplicate copy of the notice is promptly given by first class mail, or the recipient delivers a written confirmation of receipt.

No Partnership

This Agreement does not create a partnership relationship. Salesperson does not have authority to enter into contracts on Broker's behalf.

Assignment

(Check applicable provision.)

☐ Either Salesperson or Broker may assign or subcontract any rights or obligations under this Agreement.

OR

☐ Salesperson may not assign or subcontract any rights or obligations under this Agreement without Broker's prior written approval.

Signatures

Client: _____
Name of Broker

By: _____
Signature

_____
Typed or Printed Name

Title: _____

Date: _____

Contractor: _____
Name of Salesperson

By: _____
Signature

_____
Typed or Printed Name

Title: _____

Taxpayer ID Number: _____

Date: _____

If Agreement Is Faxed:

Contractor and Client agree that this Agreement will be considered signed when the signature of a party is delivered by facsimile transmission. Signatures transmitted by facsimile shall have the same effect as original signatures.

INDEPENDENT CONTRACTOR AGREEMENT
FOR CONSULTANT

This Agreement is made between _____ (Client)
with a principal place of business at _____
and _____ (Contractor), with a
principal place of business at _____.

This Agreement will become effective on _____, 19____ and will end no later than
_____, 19____.

Services to be Performed

Consultant agrees to perform the following consulting services on Client's behalf:

_____

_____

_____

_____

Payment

(Check and complete applicable provision.)

☐ In consideration for the services to be performed by Consultant, Client agrees to pay Consultant

$_____ according to the terms set out below.

OR

☐ In consideration for the services to be performed by Consultant, Client agrees to pay Consultant at the rate of

$_____ per _____ according to the terms of payment set out below.

Additional Option

(Check and complete if applicable.)

☐ Unless otherwise agreed in writing, Client's maximum liability for all services performed during the term of
this Agreement shall not exceed $_____.

Terms of Payment

(Check applicable provision.)

☐ Upon completing Consultant's services under this Agreement, Consultant shall submit an invoice. Client shall
pay Consultant the compensation described within a reasonable time after receiving Consultant's invoice.

OR

☐ Consultant shall be paid $_____ upon signing this Agreement and the rest of the sum described
above when the Consultant completes services and submits an invoice.

OR

☐ Client shall pay Consultant according to the following schedule of payments

1. $_____ when an invoice is submitted and the following services are complete:

_____

2. $_____ when an invoice is submitted and the following services are complete:

_____

3. $_____ when an invoice is submitted and the following services are complete:

_____

OR

☐ If paid hourly, Consultant shall submit an invoice to Client on the last day of each month for the work performed during that month. The invoice should include: an invoice number, the dates covered by the invoice, the hours expended and a summary of the work performed. Client shall pay Consultant's fee within a reasonable time after receiving the invoice.

Expenses

Consultant shall be responsible for all expenses incurred while performing services under this Agreement. This includes license fees, memberships and dues; automobile and other travel expenses; meals and entertainment; insurance premiums; and all salary, expenses and other compensation paid to employees or contract personnel the Consultant hires to complete the work under this Agreement.

Independent Contractor Status

Consultant is an independent contractor, not Client's employee. Consultant's employees or contract personnel are not Client's employees. Consultant and Client agree to the following rights consistent with an independent contractor relationship.

- Consultant has the right to perform services for others during the term of this Agreement.
- Consultant has the sole right to control and direct the means, manner and method by which the services required by this Agreement will be performed.
- Consultant has the right to perform the services required by this Agreement at any place, location or time.
- Consultant will furnish all equipment and materials used to provide the services required by this Agreement.
- Consultant has the right to hire assistants as subcontractors, or to use employees to provide the services required by this Agreement.
- The Consultant or Consultant's employees or contract personnel shall perform the services required by this Agreement; Client shall not hire, supervise or pay any assistants to help Consultant.
- Neither Consultant nor Consultant's employees or contract personnel shall receive any training from Client in the skills necessary to perform the services required by this Agreement.
- Client shall not require Consultant or Consultant's employees or contract personnel to devote full time to performing the services required by this Agreement.

Intellectual Property Ownership

Consultant assigns to Client all rights in all designs, creations, improvements, original works of authorship, formulas, processes, know-how, techniques, inventions and all other information or items created by Consultant during the term of this Agreement. The rights assigned include title and interest in all patent, copyright, trade secret, trademark and other proprietary rights.

Consultant shall help prepare any papers that Client considers necessary to secure any patents, copyrights, trademarks or other proprietary rights at no charge to Client. However, Client shall reimburse Consultant for reasonable out-of-pocket expenses incurred.

Consultant must obtain written assurances from Consultant's employees and contract personnel that they agree with this assignment.

Optional Addition

(Check if applicable.)

☐ Consultant agrees not to use any of the intellectual property mentioned above for the benefit of any other party without Client's prior written permission.

Confidentiality

Consultant will not disclose or use, either during or after the term of this Agreement, any proprietary or confidential information of Client without Client's prior written permission except to the extent necessary to perform services on Client's behalf.

Proprietary or confidential information includes:

- the written, printed, graphic or electronically recorded materials furnished by Client for Consultant to use
- business plans, customer lists, operating procedures, trade secrets, design formulas, know-how and processes, computer programs and inventories, discoveries and improvements of any kind, and
- information belonging to customers and suppliers of Client about whom Consultant gained knowledge as a result of Contractor's services to Client.

Consultant shall not be restricted in using any material which is publicly available, already in Consultant's possession or known to Consultant without restriction, or which is rightfully obtained by Consultant from sources other than Client.

Upon termination of Consultant's services to Client, or at Client's request, Consultant shall deliver to Client all materials in Consultant's possession relating to Client's business.

Business Permits, Certificates and Licenses

Consultant has complied with all federal, state and local laws requiring business permits, certificates and licenses required to carry out the services to be performed under this Agreement.

State and Federal Taxes

Client will not:

- withhold FICA (Social Security and Medicare taxes) from Consultant's payments or make FICA payments on Consultant's behalf
- make state or federal unemployment compensation contributions on Consultant's behalf, or
- withhold state or federal income tax from Consultant's payments.

Consultant shall pay all taxes incurred while performing services under this Agreement—including all applicable income taxes and, if Consultant is not a corporation, self-employment (Social Security) taxes. Upon demand, Consultant shall provide Client with proof that such payments have been made.

Fringe Benefits

Consultant understands that neither Consultant nor Consultant's employees or contract personnel are eligible to participate in any employee pension, health, vacation pay, sick pay or other fringe benefit plan of Client.

Workers' Compensation

Client shall not obtain workers' compensation insurance on behalf of Consultant or Consultant's employees. If Consultant hires employees to perform any work under this Agreement, Consultant will cover them with workers' compensation insurance and provide Client with a certificate of workers' compensation insurance before the employees begin the work.

Optional Language

(Check if provision is applicable.)

If not operating as a corporation, Consultant shall obtain workers' compensation insurance coverage for Consultant. Consultant shall provide Client with proof that such coverage has been obtained before starting work.

Unemployment Compensation

Client shall make no state or federal unemployment compensation payments on behalf of Consultant or Consultant's employees or contract personnel. Consultant will not be entitled to these benefits in connection with work performed under this Agreement.

Insurance

Client shall not provide any insurance coverage of any kind for Consultant or Consultant's employees or contract personnel. Consultant agrees to maintain an insurance policy of at least $_____ to cover any negligent acts committed by Consultant or Consultant's employees or agents while performing services under this Agreement.

Consultant shall indemnify and hold Client harmless from any loss or liability arising from performing services under this Agreement.

Terminating the Agreement

(Check applicable provision.)

☐ With reasonable cause, either Client or Consultant may terminate this Agreement, effective immediately upon giving written notice.

Reasonable cause includes:

- a material violation of this Agreement, or
- any act exposing the other party to liability to others for personal injury or property damage.

OR

☐ Either party may terminate this Agreement any time by giving thirty days written notice to the other party of the intent to terminate.

Exclusive Agreement

This is the entire Agreement between Consultant and Client.

Severability

If any part of this Agreement is held unenforceable, the rest of the Agreement will continue in effect.

Applicable Law

This Agreement will be governed by the laws of the state of _____.

Notices

All notices and other communications in connection with this Agreement shall be in writing and shall be considered given as follows:

- when delivered personally to the recipient's address as stated on this Agreement
- three days after being deposited in the United States mail, with postage prepaid to the recipient's address as stated on this Agreement, or

• when sent by fax or telex to the last fax or telex number of the recipient known to the person giving notice. Notice is effective upon receipt provided that a duplicate copy of the notice is promptly given by first class mail, or the recipient delivers a written confirmation of receipt.

No Partnership

This Agreement does not create a partnership relationship. Consultant does not have authority to enter into contracts on Client's behalf.

Assignment

(Check applicable provision.)

☐ Either Consultant or Client may assign or subcontract any rights or obligations under this Agreement.

OR

☐ Consultant may not assign or subcontract any rights or obligations under this Agreement without Client's prior written approval.

Signatures

Client: _____
Name of Client

By: _____
Signature

_____
Typed or Printed Name

Title: _____

Date: _____

Contractor: _____
Name of Contractor

By: _____
Signature

_____
Typed or Printed Name

Title: _____

Taxpayer ID Number: _____

Date: _____

If Agreement Is Faxed:

Contractor and Client agree that this Agreement will be considered signed when the signature of a party is delivered by facsimile transmission. Signatures transmitted by facsimile shall have the same effect as original signatures.

INDEPENDENT CONTRACTOR
AGREEMENT FOR WORK MADE FOR HIRE

This Agreement is made between _____ (Client)

with a principal place of business at _____

and _____ (Contractor), with a

principal place of business at _____.

This Agreement will become effective on _____, 19_____ and will end no later than

_____, 19_____.

Services to Be Performed

(Check and complete applicable provision.)

☐ Contractor agrees to perform the following services:

_____

_____

OR

☐ Contractor agrees to perform the services described in Exhibit A, which is attached to this Agreement.

Payment

(Check and complete applicable provision.)

☐ In consideration for the services to be performed by Contractor, Client agrees to pay Contractor

$_____ according to the terms set out below.

OR

☐ In consideration for the services to be performed by Contractor, Client agrees to pay Contractor at the rate of

$_____ per _____ according to the terms of payment set out below.

Additional Option

(Check and complete applicable provision.)

☐ Unless otherwise agreed in writing, Client's maximum liability for all services performed during the term of

this Agreement shall not exceed $_____.

Terms of Payment

(Check applicable provision.)

☐ Upon completing Contractor's services under this Agreement, Contractor shall submit an invoice. Client shall

pay Contractor the compensation described within a reasonable time after receiving Contractor's invoice.

OR

☐ Contractor shall be paid $_____ upon signing this Agreement and the rest of the sum described

above when the Contractor completes services and submits an invoice.

OR

☐ Client shall pay Contractor according to the following schedule of payments

1. $_____ when an invoice is submitted and the following services are complete:

_____

_____

2. $_____ when an invoice is submitted and the following services are complete:

_____

3. $_____ when an invoice is submitted and the following services are complete:

_____

_____

OR

☐ Contractor shall submit an invoice to Client on the last day of each month for the work performed during that month. The invoice should include: an invoice number, the dates covered by the invoice, the hours expended and a summary of the work performed. Client shall pay Contractor's fee within a reasonable time after receiving the invoice.

Expenses

Contractor shall be responsible for all expenses incurred while performing services under this Agreement. This includes license fees, memberships and dues; automobile and other travel expenses; meals and entertainment; insurance premiums; and all salary, expenses and other compensation paid to employees or contract personnel the Contractor hires to complete the work under this Agreement.

Independent Contractor Status

Contractor is an independent contractor, not Client's employee. Contractor's employees or contract personnel are not Client's employees. Contractor and Client agree to the following rights consistent with an independent contractor relationship.

- Contractor has the right to perform services for others during the term of this Agreement.
- Contractor has the sole right to control and direct the means, manner and method by which the services required by this Agreement will be performed.
- Contractor has the right to perform the services required by this Agreement at any place, location or time.
- Contractor will furnish all equipment and materials used to provide the services required by this Agreement.
- Contractor has the right to hire assistants as subcontractors, or to use employees to provide the services required by this Agreement.
- The Contractor or Contractor's employees or contract personnel shall perform the services required by this Agreement; Client shall not hire, supervise or pay any assistants to help Contractor.
- Neither Contractor nor Contractor's employees or contract personnel shall receive any training from Client in the skills necessary to perform the services required by this Agreement.
- Client shall not require Contractor or Contractor's employees or contract personnel to devote full time to performing the services required by this Agreement.

Intellectual Property Ownership

To the extent that the work performed by Contractor under this Agreement (Contractor's Work) includes any work of authorship entitled to protection under the copyright laws, the parties agree to the following provisions.

- Contractor's Work has been specially ordered and commissioned by Client as a contribution to a collective work, a supplementary work or other category of work eligible to be treated as a work made for hire under the United States Copyright Act.
- Contractor's Work shall be deemed a commissioned work and a work made for hire to the greatest extent permitted by law.

- Client shall be the sole author of Contractor's Work and any work embodying the Contractor's Work according to the United States Copyright Act.
- To the extent that Contractor's Work is not properly characterized as a work made for hire, Contractor grants to Client all right, title and interest in Contractor's Work, including all copyright rights, in perpetuity and throughout the world.
- Contractor shall help prepare any papers Client considers necessary to secure any copyrights, patents, trademarks or intellectual property rights at no charge to Client. However, Client shall reimburse Contractor for reasonable out-of-pocket expenses incurred.
- Contractor agrees to require any employees or contract personnel Contractor uses to perform services under this Agreement to assign in writing to Contractor all copyright and other intellectual property rights they may have in their work product. Contractor shall provide Client with a signed copy of each such assignment.

Optional Addition

(Check if applicable.)

☐ Contractor agrees not to use any of the intellectual property mentioned above for the benefit of any other party without Client's prior written permission.

Confidentiality

Contractor will not disclose or use, either during or after the term of this Agreement, any proprietary or confidential information of Client without Client's prior written permission except to the extent necessary to perform services on Client's behalf.

Proprietary or confidential information includes:

- the written, printed, graphic or electronically recorded materials furnished by Client for Contractor to use
- business plans, customer lists, operating procedures, trade secrets, design formulas, know-how and processes, computer programs and inventories, discoveries and improvements of any kind, and
- information belonging to customers and suppliers of Client about whom Contractor gained knowledge as a result of Contractor's services to Client.

Contractor shall not be restricted in using any material which is publicly available, already in Contractor's possession or known to Contractor without restriction, or which is rightfully obtained by Contractor from sources other than Client.

Upon termination of Contractor's services to Client, or at Client's request, Contractor shall deliver to Client all materials in Contractor's possession relating to Client's business.

State and Federal Taxes

Client will not:

- withhold FICA (Social Security and Medicare taxes) from Contractor's payments or make FICA payments on Contractor's behalf
- make state or federal unemployment compensation contributions on Contractor's behalf, or
- withhold state or federal income tax from Contractor's payments.

Contractor shall pay all taxes incurred while performing services under this Agreement—including all applicable income taxes and, if Contractor is not a corporation, self-employment (Social Security) taxes. Upon demand, Contractor shall provide Client with proof that such payments have been made.

Fringe Benefits

Contractor understands that neither Contractor nor Contractor's employees or contract personnel are eligible to participate in any employee pension, health, vacation pay, sick pay or other fringe benefit plan of Client.

Workers' Compensation

Client shall not obtain workers' compensation insurance on behalf of Contractor or Contractor's employees. If Contractor hires employees to perform any work under this Agreement, Contractor will cover them with workers' compensation insurance and provide Client with a certificate of workers' compensation insurance before the employees begin the work.

Optional Additional

(Check if provision is applicable.)

☐ If not operating as a corporation, Contractor shall obtain workers' compensation insurance coverage for Contractor. Contractor shall provide Client with proof that such coverage has been obtained before starting work.

Unemployment Compensation

Client shall make no state or federal unemployment compensation payments on behalf of Contractor or Contractor's employees or contract personnel. Contractor will not be entitled to these benefits in connection with work performed under this Agreement.

Insurance

Client shall not provide any insurance coverage of any kind for Contractor or Contractor's employees or contract personnel. Contractor agrees to maintain an insurance policy of at least $_____ to cover any negligent acts committed by Contractor or Contractor's employees or agents while performing services under this Agreement.

Contractor shall indemnify and hold Client harmless from any loss or liability arising from performing services under this Agreement.

Terminating the Agreement

(Check applicable provision.)

☐ With reasonable cause, either Client or Contractor may terminate this Agreement, effective immediately upon giving written notice.

Reasonable cause includes:

- a material violation of this Agreement, or
- any act exposing the other party to liability to others for personal injury or property damage.

OR

☐ Either party may terminate this Agreement any time by giving thirty days written notice to the other party of the intent to terminate.

Exclusive Agreement

This is the entire Agreement between Contractor and Client.

Severability

If any part of this Agreement is held unenforceable, the rest of the Agreement will continue in effect.

Applicable Law

This Agreement will be governed by the laws of the state of _____.

Notices

All notices and other communications in connection with this Agreement shall be in writing and shall be considered given as follows:

- when delivered personally to the recipient's address as stated on this Agreement
- three days after being deposited in the United States mail, with postage prepaid to the recipient's address as stated on this Agreement, or
- when sent by fax or telex to the last fax or telex number of the recipient known to the person giving notice. Notice is effective upon receipt provided that a duplicate copy of the notice is promptly given by first class mail, or the recipient delivers a written confirmation of receipt.

No Partnership

This Agreement does not create a partnership relationship. Contractor does not have authority to enter into contracts on Client's behalf.

Assignment

(Check applicable provision.)

☐ Either Contractor or Client may assign or subcontract any rights or obligations under this Agreement.

OR

☐ Contractor may not assign or subcontract any rights or obligations under this Agreement without Client's prior written approval.

Signatures

Client: _____
Name of Client

By: _____
Signature

_____
Typed or Printed Name

Title: _____

Date: _____

Contractor: _____
Name of Contractor

By: _____
Signature

_____
Typed or Printed Name

Title: _____

Taxpayer ID Number: _____

Date: _____

If Agreement Is Faxed:

Contractor and Client agree that this Agreement will be considered signed when the signature of a party is delivered by facsimile transmission. Signatures transmitted by facsimile shall have the same effect as original signatures.

3

Blank IRS Forms

Form **843**

(Rev. January 1994)

Department of the Treasury
Internal Revenue Service

Claim for Refund and Request for Abatement

▶ **See separate instructions.**

OMB No. 1545-0024
Expires 1-31-97

Use Form 843 only if your claim involves one of the taxes shown on line 3a or a refund or abatement of interest, penalties, or additions to tax on line 4a.

Note: *Do not use Form 843 if your claim is for—*
- *An overpayment of income taxes;*
- *A refund of fuel taxes; or*
- *An overpayment of excise taxes reported on Form 720, 730, or 2290.*

Please type or print

Name of claimant	Your social security number
Address (number, street, and room or suite no.)	Spouse's social security number
City or town, state, and ZIP code	Employer identification number
Name and address shown on return if different from above	Daytime telephone number ( )

1 Period—prepare a separate Form 843 for each tax period

From _____, 19____, to _____, 19____

2 Amount to be refunded or abated

$

3a Type of tax, penalty, or addition to tax:

☐ Employment ☐ Estate ☐ Gift ☐ Excise (other than excise taxes reported on Form 720, 730, or 2290)

☐ Penalty IRC section ▶ _____

b Type of return filed (see instructions):

☐ 706 ☐ 709 ☐ 940 ☐ 941 ☐ 990-PF ☐ 4720 ☐ Other (specify) _____

4a Request for abatement or refund of:

☐ Interest caused by IRS errors and delays (under Rev. Proc. 87-42—see instructions).

☐ A penalty or addition to tax as a result of erroneous advice from the IRS.

b Dates of payment ▶

5 **Explanations and additional claims.** Explain why you believe this claim should be allowed, and show computation of tax refund or abatement of interest, penalty, or addition to tax.

Signature. If you are filing Form 843 to request a refund or abatement relating to a joint return, both you and your spouse must sign the claim. Claims filed by corporations must be signed by a corporate officer authorized to sign, and the signature must be accompanied by the officer's title.

Under penalties of perjury, I declare that I have examined this claim, including accompanying schedules and statements, and, to the best of my knowledge and belief, it is true, correct, and complete.	Director's Stamp (Date received)
Signature (Title, if applicable. Claims by corporations must be signed by an officer.) Date	
Signature Date	

For Paperwork Reduction Act Notice, see separate instructions.

Cat. No. 10180R

Form **843** (Rev. 1-94)

*U.S. Government Printing Office: 1995 — 387-095/00365

| Form **4669** (Rev. January 1993) | Department of the Treasury — Internal Revenue Service
Statement of Payments Received |

| 1. Name and Address of Payee | 2. Social Security Number |

| 3. Name and Address of Payor | 4. Calendar Year |
| | 5. Amount of Payments (Including Commissions, Bonuses, Prizes, etc.) on Which Income Tax and Social Security Tax Were Not Withheld
$ |

The above Payments on which there was no withholding of federal income or social security tax, were reported on my tax return described below. The taxes due on that return have been paid in full.

| 6. Name and Address Shown on Return | 7. Spouse's Social Security Number if a Joint Return was Filed |

| 8. Return Form Number | 9. Service Center Where Filed |

10. The Payments Shown in Item 5, Above, Are Reported On:

   a. Line, _____ , Page _____ , of my return

   b. Schedule _____ of my return. If reported on Schedule C, F, or SE, Self-Employment Tax of

      $ _____ was paid.

Under penalties of perjury, I declare that to the best of my knowledge and belief the above information is true, correct, and complete.

| 11. Signature of Payee | 12. Date |

For Privacy Act Notice, see back of form   Catalog Number 41877Z   Form **4669** (Rev. 1-93)

Privacy Act Notice

Under the Privacy Act of 1974 we must tell you:

■ Our legal right to ask for the information and whether the law says you must give it.

■ What major purposes we have in asking for it, and how it will be used.

■ What could happen if we do not receive it.

The law covers:

■ Tax returns and any papers filed with them.

■ Any questions we need to ask you so we can:

>   Complete, correct, or process your return.
>   Figure your tax.
>   Collect tax, interest, or penalties.

Our legal right to ask for information is Internal Revenue Code sections 6001, 6011, and 6012(a), and their regulations. They say that you must file a return or statement with us for any tax you are liable for. Code section 6109 and its regulations say that you must show your social security number on what you file. This is so we know who you are, and can process your return and papers.

You must fill in all parts of the tax form that apply to you. But you do not have to check boxes for the Presidential Election Campaign Fund.

We ask for tax return information to carry out the Internal Revenue laws of the United States. We need it to figure and collect the right amount of tax.

We may give the information to the Department of Justice and to other Federal agencies, as provided by law. We may also give it to cities, states, the District of Columbia, and U.S. commonwealths or possessions to carry out their tax laws. And we may give it to foreign governments because of tax treaties they have with the United States.

If you do not file a return, do not provide the information we ask for, or provide fradulent information, the law provides that you may be charged penalties and, in certain cases, you may be subject to criminal prosecution. We may also have to disallow the exemptions, exclusions, credits, deductions, or adjustments shown on the tax return. This could make the tax higher or delay any refund. Interest may also be charged.

Please keep this notice with your records. It may help you if we ask you for other information.

If you have questions about the rules for filing and giving information, please call or visit any Internal Revenue Service office.

This is the only notice we must give you to explain the Privacy Act. However, we may give you other notices if we have to examine your return or collect any tax, interest, or penalties.

GPO : 1993 O – 338–003

Form **4670** (Rev. 12-93)	Department of the Treasury — Internal Revenue Service **Request for Relief from Payment of Income Tax Withholding**

Name and address of payor	Payor identification number	Return form number
	Tax period covered by Examination From: To:	

As provided by Internal Revenue Code section 3402(d), explained on the back of this form, please relieve me from the payment of income tax required to be withheld from payments covered by the attached Forms 4669, Statement of Payments Received, listed below.

Year	Number of Statements
_____	_____
_____	_____
_____	_____
_____	_____
_____	_____
Total statements attached ⟶	_____

I certify that either (1) the statements were signed in my presence, or (2) to the best of my knowledge and belief the signatures on the statements are valid and legal.

Signatures

	Date
	Date
By	Title	Date

Cat. No. 23290O

(Over, please)

Form **4670** (Rev. 12-93)

Instructions for Payor

Section 3402(d) of the Internal Revenue Code provides that you can be relieved of payment of income tax not withheld from a payee, provided you can show that the payee has reported the payments and paid the tax. You should obtain a separate Form 4669, Statement of Payments Received, from each payee for each year relief is requested. However, you are still liable for any penalty or addition to the tax that applies to your failure to deduct and withhold. After you get all Statements of Payments Received, please summarize them by year on the front of this form, and send them with this form to the Internal Revenue Service Center address shown below for the district in which your principal place of business, office, or agency is located.

Florida, Georgia, South Carolina	Atlanta, GA 39901
New Jersey, New York City and counties of Nassau, Rockland, Suffolk, and Westchester	Holtsville, NY 00501
Illinois, Iowa, Missouri, Minnesota, Wisconsin	Kansas City, MO 64999
Delaware, District of Columbia, Maryland, Pennsylvania, Virginia	Philadelphia, PA 19255
Connecticut, Maine, Massachusetts, New Hampshire, New York *(all other counties)*, Rhode Island, Vermont	Andover, MA 05501
Indiana, Kentucky, Michigan, Ohio, West Virginia	Cincinnati, OH 45999
Kansas, New Mexico, Oklahoma, Texas	Austin, TX 73301
Alaska, Arizona, California *(counties of Alpine, Amador, Butte, Calaveras, Colusa, Contra Costa, Del Norte, El Dorado, Glenn, Humboldt, Lake, Lassen, Marin, Mendocino, Modoc, Napa, Nevada, Placer, Plumas, Sacramento, San Joaquin, Shasta, Sierra, Siskiyou, Solano, Sonoma, Sutter, Tehama, Trinity, Yolo, and Yuba)*, Colorado, Idaho, Montana, Nebraska, Nevada, North Dakota, Oregon, South Dakota, Utah, Washington, Wyoming	Ogden, UT 84201
California *(all other counties)*, Hawaii	Fresno, CA 93888
Alabama, Arkansas, Louisiana, Mississippi, North Carolina, Tennessee	Memphis, TN 37501

If you have no legal residence or principal place of business in any state, file with the Internal Revenue Service Center, Philadelphia, PA 19255

Important: It is to your advantage to file this form and the required attachments at the earliest possible date, to avoid collection action.

*U.S. GPO: 1994-301-643/92200

Form **4670** (Rev. 12-93)

Form **SS-8**

(Rev. July 1993)

Department of the Treasury
Internal Revenue Service

Determination of Employee Work Status
for Purposes of Federal Employment Taxes
and Income Tax Withholding

OMB No. 1545-0004
Expires 7-31-96

Paperwork Reduction Act Notice

We ask for the information on this form to carry out the Internal Revenue laws of the United States. You are required to give us this information. We need it to ensure that you are complying with these laws and to allow us to figure and collect the right amount of tax.

The time needed to complete and file this form will vary depending on individual circumstances. The estimated average time is: **recordkeeping, 34 hr., 55 min., learning about the law or the form,** 6 min. and **preparing and sending the form to IRS,** 40 min. If you have comments concerning the accuracy of these time estimates or suggestions for making this form more simple, we would be happy to hear from you. You can write to both the **Internal Revenue Service,** Attention: Reports Clearance Officer, T:FP, Washington, DC 20224; and the **Office of Management and Budget,** Paperwork Reduction Project (1545-0004), Washington, DC 20503. **DO NOT** send the tax form to either of these offices. Instead, see **General Information** for where to file.

Purpose

Employers and workers file Form SS-8 to get a determination as to whether a worker is an employee for purposes of Federal employment taxes and income tax withholding.

General Information

This form should be completed carefully. If the firm is completing the form, it should be completed for **ONE** individual who is representative of the class of workers whose status is in question. If a written determination is desired for more than one class of workers, a separate Form SS-8 should be completed for one worker from each class whose status is typical of that class. A written determination for any worker will apply to other workers of the same class if the facts are not materially different from those of the worker whose status was ruled upon.

Please return Form SS-8 to the Internal Revenue Service office that provided the form. If the Internal Revenue Service did not ask you to complete this form but you wish a determination on whether a worker is an employee, file Form SS-8 with your District Director.

Caution: Form SS-8 is not a claim for refund of social security and Medicare taxes or Federal income tax withholding. Also, a determination that an individual is an employee does not necessarily reduce any current or prior tax liability. A worker must file his or her income tax return even if a determination has not been made by the due date of the return.

Name of firm (or person) for whom the worker performed services	Name of worker
Address of firm (include street address, apt. or suite no., city, state, and ZIP code)	Address of worker (include street address, apt. or suite no., city, state, and ZIP code)

Trade name

Telephone number (include area code)
( )

Worker's social security number
– –

Telephone number (include area code)
( )

Firm's taxpayer identification number
–

Check type of firm for which the work relationship is in question:
☐ **Individual** ☐ **Partnership** ☐ **Corporation** ☐ **Other** (specify) ▶

Important Information Needed to Process Your Request

This form is being completed by: ☐ Firm ☐ Worker

If this form is being completed by the worker, the IRS **must** have your permission to disclose your name to the firm.

Do you object to disclosing your name and the information on this form to the firm? . . . . ☐ **Yes** ☐ **No**
If you answer "Yes," the IRS cannot act on your request. **DO NOT complete the rest of this form unless the IRS asks for it.**

Under section 6110 of the Internal Revenue Code, the information on this form and related file documents will be open to the public if any ruling or determination is made. However, names, addresses, and taxpayer identification numbers must be removed before the information can be made public.

Is there any other information you want removed? . . . . ☐ **Yes** ☐ **No**
If you check "Yes," we cannot process your request unless you submit a copy of this form and copies of all supporting documents showing, in brackets, the information you want removed. Attach a separate statement telling which specific exemption of section 6110(c) applies to each bracketed part.

This form is designed to cover many work activities, so some of the questions may not apply to you. ***You must answer ALL items or mark them "Unknown" or "Does not apply."*** *If you need more space, attach another sheet.*

Total number of workers in this class. (Attach names and addresses. If more than 10 workers, attach only 10.) ▶ _____

This information is about services performed by the worker from _____ to _____
(month, day, year)   (month, day, year)

Is the worker still performing services for the firm? . . . . ☐ **Yes** ☐ **No**

If "No," what was the date of termination? ▶ _____
(month, day, year)

Cat. No. 16106T

Form **SS-8** (Rev. 7-93)

1a Describe the firm's business ....

b Describe the work done by the worker ....

....

2a If the work is done under a written agreement between the firm and the worker, attach a copy.

b If the agreement is not in writing, describe the terms and conditions of the work arrangement ....

....

c If the actual working arrangement differs in any way from the agreement, explain the differences and why they occur ....

....

....

3a Is the worker given training by the firm? . . . . ☐ **Yes** ☐ **No**
   If "Yes": What kind? ....
   How often? ....

b Is the worker given instructions in the way the work is to be done (exclusive of actual training in 3a)? . ☐ **Yes** ☐ **No**
   If "Yes," give specific examples. ....

c Attach samples of any written instructions or procedures.

d Does the firm have the right to change the methods used by the worker or direct that person on how to
   do the work? . . . . ☐ **Yes** ☐ **No**
   Explain your answer ....

....

e Does the operation of the firm's business require that the worker be supervised or controlled in the
   performance of the service? . . . . ☐ **Yes** ☐ **No**
   Explain your answer ....

....

4a The firm engages the worker:
   ☐ To perform and complete a particular job only
   ☐ To work at a job for an indefinite period of time
   ☐ Other (explain) ....

b Is the worker required to follow a routine or a schedule established by the firm? . . . . ☐ **Yes** ☐ **No**
   If "Yes," what is the routine or schedule? ....

....

....

c Does the worker report to the firm or its representative?. ☐ **Yes** ☐ **No**
   If "Yes": How often? ....
   For what purpose? ....
   In what manner (in person, in writing, by telephone, etc.)? ....
   Attach copies of report forms used in reporting to the firm.

d Does the worker furnish a time record to the firm?. . . . . ☐ **Yes** ☐ **No**
   If "Yes," attach copies of time records.

5a State the kind and value of tools, equipment, supplies, and materials furnished by:
   The firm ....

....

   The worker ....

....

b What expenses are incurred by the worker in the performance of services for the firm? ....

....

c Does the firm reimburse the worker for any expenses? . . . . ☐ **Yes** ☐ **No**
   If "Yes," specify the reimbursed expenses ....

....

6a Will the worker perform the services personally? . . . . ☐ **Yes** ☐ **No**

b Does the worker have helpers? . . . . ☐ **Yes** ☐ **No**
   If "Yes": Who hires the helpers?   ☐ Firm ☐ Worker
   If hired by the worker, is the firm's approval necessary? . . . . ☐ **Yes** ☐ **No**
   Who pays the helpers?   ☐ Firm ☐ Worker
   Are social security and Medicare taxes and Federal income tax withheld from the helpers' wages? . . ☐ **Yes** ☐ **No**
   If "Yes": Who reports and pays these taxes? ☐ Firm ☐ Worker
   Who reports the helpers' incomes to the Internal Revenue Service? ☐ Firm ☐ Worker
   If the worker pays the helpers, does the firm repay the worker? . . . . ☐ **Yes** ☐ **No**
   What services do the helpers perform?

7   At what location are the services performed? ☐ Firm's ☐ Worker's ☐ Other (specify) ....

8a   Type of pay worker receives:

     ☐ Salary   ☐ Commission ☐ Hourly wage   ☐ Piecework ☐ Lump sum   ☐ Other (specify) ....

   b   Does the firm guarantee a minimum amount of pay to the worker? . . . . ☐ **Yes**   ☐ **No**

   c   Does the firm allow the worker a drawing account or advances against pay? . . . . ☐ **Yes**   ☐ **No**

     If "Yes": Is the worker paid such advances on a regular basis? . . . . ☐ **Yes**   ☐ **No**

   d   How does the worker repay such advances? ....

9a   Is the worker eligible for a pension, bonus, paid vacations, sick pay, etc.? . . . . ☐ **Yes**   ☐ **No**

     If "Yes," specify ....

   b   Does the firm carry workmen's compensation insurance on the worker? . . . . ☐ **Yes**   ☐ **No**

   c   Does the firm deduct social security and Medicare taxes from amounts paid the worker? . . . . . ☐ **Yes**   ☐ **No**

   d   Does the firm deduct Federal income taxes from amounts paid the worker? . . . . ☐ **Yes**   ☐ **No**

   e   How does the firm report the worker's income to the Internal Revenue Service?

     ☐ Form W-2 ☐ Form 1099-MISC   ☐ Does not report ☐ Other (specify) ....

     Attach a copy.

   f   Does the firm bond the worker? . . . . ☐ **Yes**   ☐ **No**

10a   Approximately how many hours a day does the worker perform services for the firm? ....

     Does the firm set hours of work for the worker? . . . . ☐ **Yes**   ☐ **No**

     If "Yes," what are the worker's set hours? _____ am/pm to _____ am/pm (Circle whether am or pm)

   b   Does the worker perform similar services for others? . . . . ☐ **Yes**   ☐ **No**   ☐ **Unknown**

     If "Yes": Are these services performed on a daily basis for other firms? . . . . ☐ **Yes**   ☐ **No**   ☐ **Unknown**

     Percentage of time spent in performing these services for:

     This firm .... % Other firms .... % ☐ **Unknown**

     Does the firm have priority on the worker's time? . . . . ☐ **Yes**   ☐ **No**

     If "No," explain ....

   c   Is the worker prohibited from competing with the firm either while performing services or during any later

     period? . . . . ☐ **Yes**   ☐ **No**

11a   Can the firm discharge the worker at any time without incurring a liability? . . . . ☐ **Yes**   ☐ **No**

     If "No," explain ....

   b   Can the worker terminate the services at any time without incurring a liability? . . . . ☐ **Yes**   ☐ **No**

     If "No," explain ....

12a   Does the worker perform services for the firm under:

     ☐ The firm's business name   ☐ The worker's own business name ☐ Other (specify) ....

   b   Does the worker advertise or maintain a business listing in the telephone directory, a trade

     journal, etc.? . . . . ☐ **Yes**   ☐ **No**   ☐ **Unknown**

     If "Yes," specify ....

   c   Does the worker represent himself or herself to the public as being in business to perform

     the same or similar services? . . . . ☐ **Yes**   ☐ **No**   ☐ **Unknown**

     If "Yes," how? ....

   d   Does the worker have his or her own shop or office? . . . . ☐ **Yes**   ☐ **No**   ☐ **Unknown**

     If "Yes," where? ....

   e   Does the firm represent the worker as an employee of the firm to its customers? . . . . ☐ **Yes**   ☐ **No**

     If "No," how is the worker represented? ....

   f   How did the firm learn of the worker's services? ....

13   Is a license necessary for the work? . . . . ☐ **Yes**   ☐ **No**   ☐ **Unknown**

     If "Yes," what kind of license is required? ....

     By whom is it issued? ....

     By whom is the license fee paid? ....

14   Does the worker have a financial investment in a business related to the services performed? ☐ **Yes**   ☐ **No**   ☐ **Unknown**

     If "Yes," specify and give amounts of the investment ....

15   Can the worker incur a loss in the performance of the service for the firm? . . . . ☐ **Yes**   ☐ **No**

     If "Yes," how? ....

16a   Has any other government agency ruled on the status of the firm's workers? . . . . ☐ **Yes**   ☐ **No**

     If "Yes," attach a copy of the ruling.

   b   Is the same issue being considered by any IRS office in connection with the audit of the worker's tax

     return or the firm's tax return, or has it recently been considered? . . . . ☐ **Yes**   ☐ **No**

     If "Yes," for which year(s)?

17 Does the worker assemble or process a product at home or away from the firm's place of business? ☐ **Yes** ☐ **No**
If "Yes":

Who furnishes materials or goods used by the worker? ☐ Firm ☐ Worker
Is the worker furnished a pattern or given instructions to follow in making the product? . . . . . ☐ **Yes** ☐ **No**
Is the worker required to return the finished product to the firm or to someone designated by the firm? . ☐ **Yes** ☐ **No**

Answer items 18a through n only if the worker is a salesperson or provides a service directly to customers.

18a Are leads to prospective customers furnished by the firm? . . . . ☐ **Yes** ☐ **No** ☐ **Does not apply**
  b Is the worker required to pursue or report on leads? . . . . ☐ **Yes** ☐ **No** ☐ **Does not apply**
  c Is the worker required to adhere to prices, terms, and conditions of sale established by the firm? . . ☐ **Yes** ☐ **No**
  d Are orders submitted to and subject to approval by the firm? . . . . ☐ **Yes** ☐ **No**
  e Is the worker expected to attend sales meetings? . . . . ☐ **Yes** ☐ **No**
If "Yes": Is the worker subject to any kind of penalty for failing to attend? . . . . ☐ **Yes** ☐ **No**
  f Does the firm assign a specific territory to the worker? . . . . ☐ **Yes** ☐ **No** ☐ **Does not apply**
  g Who does the customer pay? ☐ Firm ☐ Worker
If worker, does the worker remit the total amount to the firm? . . . . ☐ **Yes** ☐ **No**
  h Does the worker sell a consumer product in a home or establishment other than a permanent retail
establishment? . . . . ☐ **Yes** ☐ **No**
  i List the products and/or services distributed by the worker, such as meat, vegetables, fruit, bakery products, beverages (other than milk), or laundry or dry cleaning services. If more than one type of product and/or service is distributed, specify the principal one. ....
  j Did the firm or another person assign the route or territory and a list of customers to the worker? . . ☐ **Yes** ☐ **No**
If "Yes," enter the name and job title of the person who made the assignment. ....
....
  k Did the worker pay the firm or person for the privilege of serving customers on the route or in the territory? ☐ **Yes** ☐ **No**
If "Yes," how much did the worker pay (not including any amount paid for a truck or racks, etc.)? $ ....
What factors were considered in determining the value of the route or territory? ....
  l How are new customers obtained by the worker? Explain fully, showing whether the new customers called the firm for service, were solicited by the worker, or both. ....
  m Does the worker sell life insurance? . . . . ☐ **Yes** ☐ **No**
If "Yes":
Is the selling of life insurance or annuity contracts for the firm the worker's entire business activity? . . ☐ **Yes** ☐ **No**
If "No," list the other business activities and the amount of time spent on them ....
Does the worker sell other types of insurance for the firm? . . . . ☐ **Yes** ☐ **No**
If "Yes," state the percentage of the worker's total working time spent in selling other types of insurance .... %
At the time the contract was entered into between the firm and the worker, was it their intention that the worker sell life insurance for the firm: ☐ on a full-time basis ☐ on a part-time basis
State the manner in which the intention was expressed. ....
  n Is the worker a traveling or city salesperson? . . . . ☐ **Yes** ☐ **No**
If "Yes": From whom does worker principally solicit orders for the firm? ....
If the worker solicits orders from wholesalers, retailers, contractors, or operators of hotels, restaurants, or other similar establishments, specify the percentage of the worker's time spent in this solicitation. .... %
Is the merchandise purchased by the customers for resale or for use in their business operations? If used by the customers in their business operations, describe the merchandise and state whether it is equipment installed on their premises or a consumable supply. ....
....

---

19 Attach a detailed explanation of any other reason why you believe the worker is an independent contractor or is an employee of the firm.

Under penalties of perjury, I declare that I have examined this request, including accompanying documents, and to the best of my knowledge and belief, the facts presented are true, correct, and complete.

Signature ▶   Title ▶   Date ▶

If this form is used by the firm in requesting a written determination, the form must be signed by an officer or member of the firm.
If this form is used by the worker in requesting a written determination, the form must be signed by the worker. If the worker wants a written determination about services performed for two or more firms, a separate form must be completed and signed for each firm.
Additional copies of this form may be obtained from any Internal Revenue Service office or by calling 1-800-TAX-FORM (1-800-829-3676).

Form **W-9**
(Rev. March 1994)
Department of the Treasury
Internal Revenue Service

Request for Taxpayer
Identification Number and Certification

Give form to the requester. Do NOT send to the IRS.

Please print or type

Name (If joint names, list first and circle the name of the person or entity whose number you enter in Part I below. **See instructions on page 2 if your name has changed.**)

Business name (Sole proprietors see instructions on page 2.)

Please check appropriate box: ☐ Individual/Sole proprietor ☐ Corporation ☐ Partnership ☐ Other ▶ _____

Address (number, street, and apt. or suite no.)

Requester's name and address (optional)

City, state, and ZIP code

Part I	**Taxpayer Identification Number (TIN)**

Enter your TIN in the appropriate box. For individuals, this is your social security number (SSN). For sole proprietors, see the instructions on page 2. For other entities, it is your employer identification number (EIN). If you do not have a number, see **How To Get a TIN** below.

Note: *If the account is in more than one name, see the chart on page 2 for guidelines on whose number to enter.*

Social security number
☐☐☐ | ☐☐ | ☐☐☐☐

OR

Employer identification number
☐☐ | ☐☐☐☐☐☐☐

List account number(s) here (optional)

Part II	**For Payees Exempt From Backup Withholding** (See **Part II** instructions on page 2)

▶

Part III	**Certification**

Under penalties of perjury, I certify that:

1. The number shown on this form is my correct taxpayer identification number (or I am waiting for a number to be issued to me), **and**

2. I am not subject to backup withholding because: **(a)** I am exempt from backup withholding, or **(b)** I have not been notified by the Internal Revenue Service that I am subject to backup withholding as a result of a failure to report all interest or dividends, or **(c)** the IRS has notified me that I am no longer subject to backup withholding.

Certification Instructions.—You must cross out item **2** above if you have been notified by the IRS that you are currently subject to backup withholding because of underreporting interest or dividends on your tax return. For real estate transactions, item **2** does not apply. For mortgage interest paid, the acquisition or abandonment of secured property, cancellation of debt, contributions to an individual retirement arrangement (IRA), and generally payments other than interest and dividends, you are not required to sign the Certification, but you must provide your correct TIN. (Also see **Part III instructions** on page 2.)

Sign Here | Signature ▶   Date ▶

Section references are to the Internal Revenue Code.

Purpose of Form.—A person who is required to file an information return with the IRS must get your correct TIN to report income paid to you, real estate transactions, mortgage interest you paid, the acquisition or abandonment of secured property, cancellation of debt, or contributions you made to an IRA. Use Form W-9 to give your correct TIN to the requester (the person requesting your TIN) and, when applicable, (1) to certify the TIN you are giving is correct (or you are waiting for a number to be issued), (2) to certify you are not subject to backup withholding, or (3) to claim exemption from backup withholding if you are an exempt payee. Giving your correct TIN and making the appropriate certifications will prevent certain payments from being subject to backup withholding.

Note: *If a requester gives you a form other than a W-9 to request your TIN, you must use the requester's form if it is substantially similar to this Form W-9.*

What Is Backup Withholding?—Persons making certain payments to you must withhold and pay to the IRS 31% of such payments under certain conditions. This is called "backup withholding." Payments that could be subject to backup withholding include interest, dividends, broker and barter exchange transactions, rents, royalties, nonemployee pay, and certain payments from fishing boat operators. Real estate transactions are not subject to backup withholding.

If you give the requester your correct TIN, make the proper certifications, and report all your taxable interest and dividends on your tax return, your payments will not be subject to backup withholding. Payments you receive will be subject to backup withholding if:

1. You do not furnish your TIN to the requester, or

2. The IRS tells the requester that you furnished an incorrect TIN, or

3. The IRS tells you that you are subject to backup withholding because you did not report all your interest and dividends on your tax return (for reportable interest and dividends only), or

4. You do not certify to the requester that you are not subject to backup withholding under 3 above (for reportable interest and dividend accounts opened after 1983 only), or

5. You do not certify your TIN. See the Part III instructions for exceptions.

Certain payees and payments are exempt from backup withholding and information reporting. See the Part II instructions and the separate **Instructions for the Requester of Form W-9.**

How To Get a TIN.—If you do not have a TIN, apply for one immediately. To apply, get **Form SS-5,** Application for a Social Security Number Card (for individuals), from your local office of the Social Security Administration, or **Form SS-4,** Application for Employer Identification Number (for businesses and all other entities), from your local IRS office.

If you do not have a TIN, write "Applied For" in the space for the TIN in Part I, sign and date the form, and give it to the requester. Generally, you will then have 60 days to get a TIN and give it to the requester. If the requester does not receive your TIN within 60 days, backup withholding, if applicable, will begin and continue until you furnish your TIN.

Note: *Writing "Applied For" on the form means that you have already applied for a TIN **OR** that you intend to apply for one soon.*

As soon as you receive your TIN, complete another Form W-9, include your TIN, sign and date the form, and give it to the requester.

Penalties

Failure To Furnish TIN.—If you fail to furnish your correct TIN to a requester, you are subject to a penalty of $50 for each such failure unless your failure is due to reasonable cause and not to willful neglect.

Civil Penalty for False Information With Respect to Withholding.—If you make a false statement with no reasonable basis that results in no backup withholding, you are subject to a $500 penalty.

Criminal Penalty for Falsifying Information.— Willfully falsifying certifications or affirmations may subject you to criminal penalties including fines and/or imprisonment.

Misuse of TINs.—If the requester discloses or uses TINs in violation of Federal law, the requester may be subject to civil and criminal penalties.

Specific Instructions

Name.—If you are an individual, you must generally enter the name shown on your social security card. However, if you have changed your last name, for instance, due to marriage, without informing the Social Security Administration of the name change, please enter your first name, the last name shown on your social security card, and your new last name.

Sole Proprietor.—You must enter your **individual** name. (Enter either your SSN or EIN in Part I.) You may also enter your business name or "doing business as" name on the business name line. Enter your name as shown on your social security card and business name as it was used to apply for your EIN on Form SS-4.

Part I—Taxpayer Identification Number (TIN)

You must enter your TIN in the appropriate box. If you are a sole proprietor, you may enter your SSN or EIN. Also see the chart on this page for further clarification of name and TIN combinations. If you do not have a TIN, follow the instructions under **How To Get a TIN** on page 1.

Part II—For Payees Exempt From Backup Withholding

Individuals (including sole proprietors) are **not** exempt from backup withholding. Corporations are exempt from backup withholding for certain payments, such as interest and dividends. For a complete list of exempt payees, see the separate Instructions for the Requester of Form W-9.

If you are exempt from backup withholding, you should still complete this form to avoid possible erroneous backup withholding. Enter your correct TIN in Part I, write "Exempt" in Part II, and sign and date the form. If you are a nonresident alien or a foreign entity not subject to backup withholding, give the requester a completed **Form W-8,** Certificate of Foreign Status.

Part III—Certification

For a joint account, only the person whose TIN is shown in Part I should sign.

1. Interest, Dividend, and Barter Exchange Accounts Opened Before 1984 and Broker Accounts Considered Active During 1983. You must give your correct TIN, but you do not have to sign the certification.

2. Interest, Dividend, Broker, and Barter Exchange Accounts Opened After 1983 and Broker Accounts Considered Inactive During 1983. You must sign the certification or backup withholding will apply. If you are subject to backup withholding and you are merely providing your correct TIN to the requester, you must cross out item **2** in the certification before signing the form.

3. Real Estate Transactions. You must sign the certification. You may cross out item **2** of the certification.

4. Other Payments. You must give your correct TIN, but you do not have to sign the certification unless you have been notified of an incorrect TIN. Other payments include payments made in the course of the requester's trade or business for rents, royalties, goods (other than bills for merchandise), medical and health care services, payments to a nonemployee for services (including attorney and accounting fees), and payments to certain fishing boat crew members.

5. Mortgage Interest Paid by You, Acquisition or Abandonment of Secured Property, Cancellation of Debt, or IRA Contributions. You must give your correct TIN, but you do not have to sign the certification.

Privacy Act Notice

Section 6109 requires you to give your correct TIN to persons who must file information returns with the IRS to report interest, dividends, and certain other income paid to you, mortgage interest you paid, the acquisition or abandonment of secured property, cancellation of debt, or contributions you made to an IRA. The IRS uses the numbers for identification purposes and to help verify the accuracy of your tax return. You must provide your

TIN whether or not you are required to file a tax return. Payers must generally withhold 31% of taxable interest, dividend, and certain other payments to a payee who does not give a TIN to a payer. Certain penalties may also apply.

What Name and Number To Give the Requester

For this type of account:	Give name and SSN of:
1. Individual	The individual
2. Two or more individuals (joint account)	The actual owner of the account or, if combined funds, the first individual on the account [1]
3. Custodian account of a minor (Uniform Gift to Minors Act)	The minor [2]
4. a. The usual revocable savings trust (grantor is also trustee)	The grantor-trustee [1]
b. So-called trust account that is not a legal or valid trust under state law	The actual owner [1]
5. Sole proprietorship	The owner [3]

For this type of account:	Give name and EIN of:
6. Sole proprietorship	The owner [3]
7. A valid trust, estate, or pension trust	Legal entity [4]
8. Corporate	The corporation
9. Association, club, religious, charitable, educational, or other tax-exempt organization	The organization
10. Partnership	The partnership
11. A broker or registered nominee	The broker or nominee
12. Account with the Department of Agriculture in the name of a public entity (such as a state or local government, school district, or prison) that receives agricultural program payments	The public entity

[1] List first and circle the name of the person whose number you furnish.

[2] Circle the minor's name and furnish the minor's SSN.

[3] You must show your individual name, but you may also enter your business or "doing business as" name. You may use either your SSN or EIN.

[4] List first and circle the name of the legal trust, estate, or pension trust. (Do not furnish the TIN of the personal representative or trustee unless the legal entity itself is not designated in the account title.)

Note: *If no name is circled when more than one name is listed, the number will be considered to be that of the first name listed.*

⸫ U.S. GOVERNMENT PRINTING OFFICE: 1994 345-126

Index

CATALOG

...more from Nolo Press

Book with disk

CALL 800-992-6656 OR USE THE ORDER FORM IN THE BACK OF THE BOOK

	EDITION	PRICE	CODE
True Odds: How Risk Affects Your Everyday Life	1st	$19.95	TROD
What Do You Mean It's Not Covered?	1st	$19.95	COVER

ESTATE PLANNING & PROBATE

	EDITION	PRICE	CODE
How to Probate an Estate (California Edition)	8th	$34.95	PAE
Make Your Own Living Trust	2nd	$19.95	LITR
Nolo's Simple Will Book	2nd	$17.95	SWIL
Plan Your Estate	3rd	$24.95	NEST
The Quick and Legal Will Book	1st	$15.95	QUIC
Nolo's Law Form Kit: Wills	1st	$14.95	KWL

FAMILY MATTERS

	EDITION	PRICE	CODE
A Legal Guide for Lesbian and Gay Couples	8th	$24.95	LG
Child Custody: Building Agreements That Work	1st	$24.95	CUST
Divorce & Money: How to Make the Best Financial Decisions During Divorce	2nd	$21.95	DIMO
How to Adopt Your Stepchild in California	4th	$22.95	ADOP
How to Do Your Own Divorce in California	21st	$21.95	CDIV
How to Do Your Own Divorce in Texas	6th	$19.95	TDIV
How to Raise or Lower Child Support in California	3rd	$18.95	CHLD
Nolo's Pocket Guide to Family Law	4th	$14.95	FLD
Practical Divorce Solutions	1st	$14.95	PDS
The Guardianship Book (California Edition)	2nd	$24.95	GB
The Living Together Kit	7th	$24.95	LTK

GOING TO COURT

	EDITION	PRICE	CODE
Collect Your Court Judgment (California Edition	2nd	$19.95	JUDG
Everybody's Guide to Municipal Court (California Edition)	1st	$29.95	MUNI
Everybody's Guide to Small Claims Court (California Edition)	12th	$18.95	CSCC
Everybody's Guide to Small Claims Court (National Edition)	6th	$18.95	NSCC
Fight Your Ticket ... and Win! (California Edition)	6th	$19.95	FYT
How to Change Your Name (California Edition)	6th	$24.95	NAME
Represent Yourself in Court: How to Prepare & Try a Winning Case	1st	$29.95	RYC
The Criminal Records Book (California Edition)	5th	$21.95	CRIM

HOMEOWNERS, LANDLORDS & TENANTS

	EDITION	PRICE	CODE
Dog Law	2nd	$12.95	DOG
⌨ Every Landlord's Legal Guide (National Edition)	1st	$29.95	ELLI
For Sale by Owner (California Edition)	2nd	$24.95	FSBO
Homestead Your House (California Edition)	8th	$9.95	HOME
How to Buy a House in California	3rd	$24.95	BHCA
Neighbor Law: Fences, Trees, Boundaries & Noise	2nd	$16.95	NEI
Safe Homes, Safe Neighborhoods: Stopping Crime Where You Live	1st	$14.95	SAFE
Tenants' Rights (California Edition)	12th	$18.95	CTEN
The Deeds Book (California Edition)	3rd	$16.95	DEED
The Landlord's Law Book, Vol. 1: Rights & Responsibilities (California Edition)	5th	$34.95	LBRT
The Landlord's Law Book, Vol. 2: Evictions (California Edition)	5th	$34.95	LBEV

HUMOR

	EDITION	PRICE	CODE
29 Reasons Not to Go to Law School	1st	$9.95	29R
Poetic Justice	1st	$9.95	PJ

IMMIGRATION

	EDITION	PRICE	CODE
How to Become a United States Citizen	5th	$14.95	CIT

⌨ Book with disk

CALL 800-992-6656 OR USE THE ORDER FORM IN THE BACK OF THE BOOK

	EDITION	PRICE	CODE
How to Get a Green Card: Legal Ways to Stay in the U.S.A.	2nd	$24.95	GRN
U.S. Immigration Made Easy	5th	$39.95	IMEZ

MONEY MATTERS

	EDITION	PRICE	CODE
Building Your Nest Egg With Your 401(k)	1st	$16.95	EGG
Chapter 13 Bankruptcy: Repay Your Debts	1st	$29.95	CH13
How to File for Bankruptcy	5th	$25.95	HFB
Money Troubles: Legal Strategies to Cope With Your Debts	3rd	$18.95	MT
Nolo's Law Form Kit: Personal Bankruptcy	1st	$14.95	KBNK
Nolo's Law Form Kit: Rebuild Your Credit	1st	$14.95	KCRD
Simple Contracts for Personal Use	2nd	$16.95	CONT
Smart Ways to Save Money During and After Divorce	1st	$14.95	SAVMO
Stand Up to the IRS	2nd	$21.95	SIRS

PATENTS AND COPYRIGHTS

	EDITION	PRICE	CODE
Copyright Your Software	1st	$39.95	CYS
Patent, Copyright & Trademark: A Desk Reference to Intellectual Property Law	1st	$24.95	PCTM
Patent It Yourself	4th	$39.95	PAT
▣ Software Development: A Legal Guide (Book with disk—PC)	1st	$44.95	SFT
The Copyright Handbook: How to Protect and Use Written Works	2nd	$24.95	COHA
The Inventor's Notebook	1st	$19.95	INOT

RESEARCH & REFERENCE

	EDITION	PRICE	CODE
Law on the Net	1st	$39.95	LAWN
Legal Research: How to Find & Understand the Law	4th	$19.95	LRES
Legal Research Made Easy (Video)	1st	$89.95	LRME

SENIORS

	EDITION	PRICE	CODE
Beat the Nursing Home Trap: A Consumer's Guide	2nd	$18.95	ELD
Social Security, Medicare & Pensions	6th	$19.95	SOA
The Conservatorship Book (California Edition)	2nd	$29.95	CNSV

SOFTWARE

	EDITION	PRICE	CODE
California Incorporator 2.0—DOS	2.0	$47.97	INCI2
Living Trust Maker 2.0—Macintosh	2.0	$47.97	LTM2
Living Trust Maker 2.0—Windows	2.0	$47.97	LTWI2
Small Business Legal Pro—Macintosh	2.0	$39.95	SBM2
Small Business Legal Pro—Windows	2.0	$39.95	SBW2
Nolo's Partnership Maker 1.0—DOS	1.0	$47.97	PAGI1
Nolo's Personal RecordKeeper 3.0—Macintosh	3.0	$29.97	FRM3
Patent It Yourself 1.0—Windows	1.0	$149.97	PYW1
WillMaker 6.0—Macintosh	6.0	$41.97	WM6
WillMaker 6.0—Windows	6.0	$41.97	WIW6

SPECIAL UPGRADE OFFER

Get 25% off the latest edition of your Nolo book

It's important to have the most current legal information. Because laws and legal procedures change often, we update our books and kits regularly. To help keep you up-to-date we are extending this special upgrade offer. Cut out and mail the title portion of the cover of your old Nolo book and we'll give you 25% off the retail price of the NEW EDITION or latest kit when you purchase directly from us. For more information call us at 1-800-992-6656. This offer is to individuals only.

▣ Book with disk

ORDER FORM

Code	Quantity	Title	Unit price	Total

Subtotal

California residents add Sales Tax

Basic Shipping (*$5 for 1 item; $6 for 2-3 items, $7 for 4 or more*)

UPS RUSH delivery $7–any size order*

TOTAL

Name

Address

(UPS to street address, Priority Mail to P.O. boxes) * Delivered in 3 business days from receipt of order. S.F. Bay area use regular shipping.

FOR FASTER SERVICE, USE YOUR CREDIT CARD AND OUR TOLL-FREE NUMBERS

Order 24 hours a day 1-800-992-6656

Fax your order 1-800-645-0895

e-mail NoloInfo@nolopress.com

General Information 1-510-549-1976

Customer Service 1-800-728-3555, Mon.-Sat. 9am-5pm, PST

METHOD OF PAYMENT

☐ Check enclosed

☐ VISA ☐ MasterCard ☐ Discover Card ☐ American Express

Account #   Expiration Date

Authorizing Signature

Daytime Phone

Prices subject to change.

Visit our store

If you live in the Bay Area, be sure to visit the Nolo Press Bookstore on the corner of 9th and Parker Streets in West Berkeley. You'll find our complete line of books and software, all at a discount. We also have t-shirts, posters and a selection of business and legal self-help books from other publishers. Open every day.

NOLO PRESS 950 PARKER ST., BERKELEY, CA 94710